Practical English

Practical English

Carol A. Pemberton

Normandale Community College

SCOTT, FORESMAN AND COMPANY

Glenview, Illinois   Boston   London

Library of Congress Cataloging-in-Publication Data

Pemberton, Carol A. (Carol Ann), 1939–
    Practical English.

    Includes index.
    1. English language—Grammar—1950–
2. English language—Rhetoric.   I. Title.
PE1112.P43   1989   428.2   88-11479
ISBN 0–673–39824–2

1 2 3 4 5 6 7 8 9 10—MVN—95 94 93 92 91 90 89

Printed in the United States of America

Text Credits

Page 119: "Pity the pronoun snobs, There's no help for they" by Suzanne
Britt Jordan, *Star Tribune*, October 2, 1981. Reprinted with permission
from the *Star Tribune*, Minneapolis–St. Paul.

Page 302: "Weed Control Guide for 1987" by Dr. Michael Owen, Cooperative
Extension Service, Iowa State University. Reprinted by permission.

Pages 352–353: "Lucky It Wasn't an Umlaut" by Sandra Hoyt, *Twin Cities*,
November, 1987. Reprinted by permission.

Page 357: "The Road Not Taken" by Robert Frost. Copyright 1916 by Holt,
Rinehart and Winston, Inc. and renewed 1944 by Robert Frost. Reprinted
from *The Poetry of Robert Frost* edited by Edward Connery Lathem, by
permission of Henry Holt and Company, Inc.

Preface

Practical English grew out of a manuscript written in 1978 for college freshmen. Since that year I have taught from many revisions of the manuscript, continuously testing and refining the material with hundreds of students.

This book presents grammar and sentence structure as a coherent body of knowledge and applies that knowledge to day-to-day writing in school and on the job. The writing assignments range from accounts of personal experience to business letters, memos, and short reports. I want students to integrate their grammar and sentence skills into their writing in college and on the job.

The study of grammar and sentence structure moves in an orderly progression, unit by unit. Topics covered include the following:

- Understanding basic sentence patterns and avoiding fragments and run-ons
- Selecting pronouns and verbs correctly and ensuring subject/verb agreement
- Mastering phrases and clauses and using them for subordination
- Refining wording, avoiding pitfalls with modifiers, and developing variety and parallelism in sentences
- Editing for improved punctuation, capitalization, and spelling

Writing assignments also move in an orderly progression, from the casual and simple to the more structured and complex:

- Writing sentences about personal experiences
- Building well-focused paragraphs
- Revising and creating memos, short letters
- Putting several paragraphs together in narratives, letters, and short reports
- Creating a job-application letter and other routine correspondence

- Writing letters and short reports designed to solve "real world" problems as identified by the students

Students are encouraged to write on topics they select, preferably topics related to their lives as students, workers or prospective workers in a particular discipline, and citizens of their communities. Writing and editing skills are stressed as students work on examples drawn from many occupations.

Students are given an opportunity to review their skills and monitor their own progress through unit practice tests and a practice final examination. Answers are provided at the back of the book.

During my years of working with *Practical English* I have seen students develop respect for the language and its conventions. Given a better understanding of how English works, they develop confidence in their handling of the language. Moreover, they can apply their knowledge of grammar and sentence structure to many kinds of writing. It is my hope that users of this book will have equally satisfying results.

ACKNOWLEDGMENTS

For years, while my manuscript consisted of imperfectly typed, loose pages, Normandale students good naturedly endured both imperfection and inconvenience. I am grateful for their patience, but even more for their constructive suggestions. My students helped me see my manuscript from the most important perspective of all: that of struggling but determined learners. Many of my students also permitted me to share their writing in this book. Some of that writing appears exactly as written; some of it has been modified slightly but retains its original shape.

Students whose work appears in this book are as follows: Dan Arms, Jane Barclay, Mary Bell, Molly Birney, Craig Ciecmierowski, Pete Daly, George Flach, Julia Harvey, Sue Hoese, Tana Karels, Mike Kleber, Joe Klug, Leslie Kusisto, Brian Lake, Kyle Lewis, Mitzi Mabry, Dennis Malecha, Rich Marlier, Pat McKinley, Deb Mooney, Alexis Peterson, Darbie Rasmussen, Todd Rodewald, Dan Rossow, Terri Lee Rutt, Lynn Schauer, Jeff Snethen, Pat Sutton, Kari Tersteeg, Karen Thompson, Mike Tracy, Mark Vermilyea, Michael Virnig, Mike Wagner, and Suzanne Yant.

I am also grateful to English teachers who read the manuscript and made valuable suggestions; many of these suggestions have been incorporated into the text. In particular I wish to thank Paul Ady, Assumption College; Barbara Carson, University of Georgia; Linda Coblentz, University of Houston; Jan Delasara, Metropolitan State College; Muriel Harris, Purdue University; Eric Hibbison, J. Sargeant Reynolds Community College; Cecilia Macheski, LaGuardia Community College; Jeanette Morgan, University of Houston; Randy Popken, Tarleton

State University; Audrey Roth, Miami Dade Community College; Eileen Schwartz, Purdue University; Judith Stanford, Rivier College; and Betty Stolarek, University of Illinois.

Without the skilled guidance of the Scott, Foresman/Little, Brown staff, this work could not have been completed. I am especially grateful to my editor, Joe Opiela, for his support and leadership in developing this book.

Finally, I am indebted to gifted teachers whose classroom skill and commitment to scholarship inspired my life's work. Two teachers in particular influenced my career: Bonny Wick Hammer and Ruth Crockett Colwell. This book is dedicated to them in gratitude for the high standards they exemplified and encouraged.

Introduction: To the Student

The goal of this book can be stated simply: to improve your writing. You know the advantages of good writing in school and on the job: better grades, better jobs, better chance for advancement, and, in general, more success throughout your life.

Your past experience with writing is the basis upon which you will develop your skills in this class. Here you will review grammar and sentence structure, then put that knowledge into practice in your writing. The connections between studying grammar and sentence structure and doing actual writing will be clear in every chapter of *Practical English.*

Writing well—or even acceptably—requires knowledge, care, and practice. To write well we need a basic understanding of our language. Of course, good grammar and sentence structure are not *everything* we need. They are *some* of the things we need, and they are necessary if we are to write acceptably—or to write well.

What this book will do for you. You can expect two benefits from using this book. **First, you will learn how English works so that you can use the language to your advantage.** You will acquire a practical understanding of grammar, usage, sentence structure, punctuation, capitalization, and spelling. If you are already strong in some of these areas, you will grow stronger; if you need help in some of these areas, you will get that help.

Learning grammar and sentence structure is similar to the complicated process an auto mechanic goes through in taking an engine apart and then putting it back together. You will take the engine of language apart, examining each piece as you go. You will find that some pieces cause lots of trouble, while others seldom cause any trouble. Then you will rebuild the engine of language, piece by piece, seeing how pieces fit together and where problems arise. Neither you nor the mechanic can take shortcuts because shortcuts don't work. There is no substitute for rolling up your sleeves and digging in.

Second, you will learn to use better grammar and sentence structures in the kinds of writing required of you day after day. You will practice putting your ideas together in many different situations, including business letters, memos, essays, stories, and short reports. While practicing your English skills, you will also be gaining insights into some of the demands of college and on-the-job writing.

Writing *is* demanding because it requires knowledge, diligence, and attention to detail. If you master grammar and sentence skills, you will be well on the way to producing good writing in school and on the job.

What this book will not do for you. This book will not help you overcome your inhibitions about first drafts; it will not tell you how to get words on paper initially. It is presumed that you *will* put words on paper as a matter of necessity, if not desire.

This book does not provide detailed analysis of business forms, report forms, or other specialized documents. Here you will learn only enough of the basic guidelines of standard business correspondence and short reports to serve your immediate needs. For example, you will learn a standard business-letter form that would serve personal needs, such as job-application letters. More detailed information about business correspondence and report forms can be found in many other sources.

In short, this book will not tell you everything you need to know about writing in college and in your career. Instead, assignments are limited to shorter forms typical of the kinds used in school and on many jobs. Nonetheless, when you need to write research papers, essays, abstracts, proposals, literary reviews, and technical reports, you can rely on the basic principles presented in this book.

How to use this book. This book is meant to be easy to understand and pleasant to use. To help you master the concepts, this book keeps you actively involved. Within each chapter you will practice skills as they are introduced. At the end of each chapter you will get more practice with exercises that are interesting and varied. Unit practice tests and a final examination give you an opportunity to review what you have learned.

Use the book as a text and as a workbook. Underline, fill in examples of your own, and write in the margins. It is important that you read the chapters carefully, answering questions as you go, and that you complete the exercises as well as you can. Answers to some of the exercises and to all the unit practice tests are in the back of the book so that you can check yourself.

As you know, textbooks work no magic; they are only tools for learning. The heart of any writing course is your writing. It is hoped that this book will serve as an able guide as you develop your writing skills through practice.

Contents

Practical English

RECOGNIZING SENTENCE PATTERNS

OBJECTIVES

Grammar and Sentence Structure

To review the parts of speech

To understand subjects, verbs, objects, and complements

To avoid fragments and run-ons

To handle compound units

Writing

To write individual sentences on personal experience

To write freely, then revise individual sentences

1

Understanding the Basics

Considering How Words Work

You can begin to understand English by comparing words to players on a team. When you watch a football game, you keep track of eleven players per team, twenty-two in all. When you watch a baseball game, you keep track of nine players per team, eighteen in all. When you watch a basketball game, you keep track of five players per team, ten in all.

If you can follow complex games with many players, you can learn to follow the ins and outs of English as well. In English we find only eight players comparable to players on a team. These eight players are called the *parts of speech.* You may know their names already:

noun	adjective	adverb	conjunction
pronoun	verb	preposition	interjection

Each part of speech has its own special role to play in English, just as each player on a team has a role to play. To understand English, we must first know what all the roles are. Then we must recognize these roles regardless of what a particular word looks like. This second step is difficult because words switch roles depending on the context—that is, the situation in which the word is used. Here, for example, in the first sentence, the word *play* is a noun; in the second, it is a verb:

The *play* began when the curtain went up.
Children *play* games at birthday parties.

Thus, the word *play* serves as one part of speech in one context and as a different part of speech in another context. Thousands of words change from one part of speech to another, depending on the context.

You will not be confused by these changes if you follow these two steps:

1. Know the eight parts of speech so well that you recognize them regardless of which words are involved.
2. Judge a word by what it does, not by how it looks.

Does the word *play* look like a verb or a noun in the sentences above? The best answer is that it doesn't matter what the word looks like. We can discover which part of speech is used when we see how a particular word is used.

Reviewing the Parts of Speech

Noun.   A noun names a person, place, or thing. That thing may be tangible—like a table, chair, or desk—or it can be intangible—like any of these:

> love, envy, trust, fear (emotions)
> ambition, loyalty, enthusiasm (qualities)
> typing, swimming, dancing (skills, activities)
> democracy, privacy, poverty (abstractions)

In English, plural nouns usually end in s or *es:*

> baseball→baseballs   coach→coaches

Some common words change form internally to form the plural:

> man→men   foot→feet

In a few cases, the word changes more drastically:

> child→children   mouse→mice

In a few other cases, nouns stay the same whether they are singular or plural:

> deer   reindeer   sheep

Proper nouns require capital letters because they name specific persons, places, or things:

> Carol Pemberton   _____ (your name)
> Miami-Dade Community College   Missouri River
> Empire State Building   Western Shopping Center

Common nouns do not require capital letters. Common nouns name persons, places, or things generally:

> girls   days   cities   orchestras   teams   senators

PRACTICE 1

Add three common nouns and corresponding proper nouns to this list.

Common Nouns	Proper Nouns
1. *team*	*Dallas Cowboys*
2.	
3.	
4.	

Nouns are critical players in our language. We use them in almost every statement we make, beginning with our earliest words. What was the first word you spoke? The chances are good that it was a noun, perhaps *Mama.* As an infant, you began to name persons, places, and things, and you have used nouns constantly ever since.

Pronoun.   A pronoun is a noun substitute. It refers to a noun already mentioned or understood in the context. Like nouns, some pronouns change form to indicate singular or plural: *I* becomes *we.* Others do not change form: the word *you* can be singular or plural. Like some nouns, some pronouns indicate gender (*he, she*), but others do not (*it, anybody, who, whom, someone, one*).

Pronouns cause problems because they change form depending on how they are used. Notice the changes here:

We turned *our* attention to the football fans near *us.*

The words *we, our,* and *us* refer to the same people, but no one pronoun fits in all three positions in that sentence. The three positions require three different pronoun *cases:*

Nominative case for subjects (*we* in the example above)
Possessive case for words that show possession (*our* in the example above)
Objective case for words that are objects (*us* in the example above)

Pronouns also change form depending on what is called *person:*

First person: The person or persons speaking or writing:

I, me, my, we, us, our

Second person: The person or persons spoken or written to:

you, your, yours

Third person: The person or persons, objects, or ideas spoken about:

he, she, they, them, everyone, it

The following is a summary of common pronouns. Most of these are called **personal pronouns** because they refer to persons:

Singular Pronouns

Person	Nominative Case	Possessive Case	Objective Case
First	I	my, mine	me
Second	you	your, yours	you
Third	he, she, it	his, hers	him, her
	one, who	its, whose	it, whom

Plural Pronouns

Person	Nominative Case	Possessive Case	Objective Case
First	we	our, ours	us
Second	you	your, yours	you
Third	they	their, theirs	them

PRACTICE 2

Underline the pronouns in these sentences.

Example: We were winning our final game when he fell.

1. He sprained his ankle in the final minute of our last game.

2. We knew that he and his team had played their best.

3. The coach ran past us on his way to the injured player.

Adjective. An adjective modifies a noun or a pronoun; in other words, it changes the meaning of a noun or a pronoun. It may describe or limit, enrich or refine, or add to the meaning. Adjectives answer the following questions about nouns or pronouns: Whose? Which one or ones? What kind or kinds? How many?

The words *a, an,* and *the* are special adjectives, sometimes called **articles.** They do not describe, but they serve as pointers, calling attention to other words. Generally, we use the word *a* to point to words that begin with a consonant sound and the word *an* to point to words that begin with a vowel or a vowel sound:

an evening	an hour	an impromptu speech
a morning	a history book	a rehearsed speech

PRACTICE 3

Use a *or* an *to point to these words.*

_____ honest man   _____ long day   _____ British accent

_____ obvious answer   _____ heavy schedule   _____ attractive offer

---

In the following examples, the adjectives are italicized:

the *two large upstairs* bedrooms in the *red brick* house
the *chocolate birthday* cake on *our kitchen* table

Adjectives usually precede the words they modify, as they do in these examples.

Some of the adjectives in the examples above can be nouns in other contexts (*brick, chocolate, birthday,* and *kitchen*). The possessive word *our* is a pronoun as well as an adjective, but because we are concerned mainly with how words are used, we consider this pronoun (and other possessive words) an adjective because it works like an adjective.

PRACTICE 4

Underline the adjectives in these sentences.

1. The World Series game took students' minds off their English assignments on that Saturday afternoon.

2. Our team did win the first two games, but then we lost four consecutive heart-breaking games.

3. Faithful baseball fans cheered for every player, even after they had lost all hope for their team's victory.

Verb. A verb expresses action or state of being. It also indicates time (past, present, or future) through a property called *tense.*

When we think of verbs, we normally think of **action** words, such as *walk, run, jump, drive, swim,* and *ski.* Some action words refer to mental or emotional actions, such as *study, think, daydream, hope, plan,* and *love.*

The second kind of verb expresses **state of being**—that is, existence itself. These verbs are known by various names and descriptions: state-of-being verbs, being verbs, linking verbs, and verbs expressing existence. The most common examples of these verbs are the forms of the word *be*. You could think of these verbs as part of one family, the *be* family:

| is | are | was | were | am | been |

PRACTICE 5 ———————————————————

Underline the verbs in these sentences.

1. The World Series is an autumn event.

2. We enjoy the games every year.

3. This year we cheered for our local team.

4. Our team was in the World Series twenty years ago, and again this year, the team played in the series.

PRACTICE 6 ———————————————————

List the action verbs you found in the four sentences in Practice 5.

—————————————————————————————————

List the be *verbs you found in those four sentences.*

—————————————————————————————————

—————————————————————————————————

The *be* verbs are among the most commonly used verbs in the language, partly because they do double duty:

- When used as the only verbs in sentences, these verbs are called **linking verbs** because they link essential parts of sentences. Although members of the *be* family are not the only possible linking verbs, they are the most common ones.
- When used with other verbs (often action verbs), the *be* verbs are helpers.

Consider the difference between these two sentences:

> Joan *is* intelligent.
> Joan *is dancing.*

In the first sentence, the only verb is the word *is*. There is no action in that sentence. Rather, the sentence expresses an idea about Joan's state of being—namely, that she is intelligent. In the other sentence, the verb *is* helps express an action—namely, that Joan is dancing. Because the main verb in the sentence is *dancing,* the verb *is* serves only as a helper.

To find the main verb in the sentence, follow this simple step: find the last verb in the group of verbs and remember that it is the main one; all other verbs are helpers.

Here is a list of verbs that often work as helpers:

can	have	has	could	should	would	will	shall
might	must	do	did	may			
is	are	was	were	am	been		

(Note the *be* family here again.)

PRACTICE 7

Underline all the verbs in these sentences. Circle the main verbs.

Example: The guests have (enjoyed) the music and the food at this

party.

1. By 11 P.M., Joan will have been dancing for three hours.

2. Band members are playing three sets before their break.

3. We had played tennis twice on Saturday before the rain.

4. Vince was serving just before the thunderstorm.

To understand the structure of sentences, we need to keep two distinctions in mind: main verbs versus helping verbs, and action verbs versus linking verbs.

PRACTICE 8

In the four sentences in Practice 7, you circled action verbs as the main verbs. In the four sentences below, follow the same directions, but notice that here the main verbs are not always action verbs.

1. After 11:30 P.M., only the band members will be there.

2. Joan and David will be leaving the dance around 11 P.M.

3. Vince and I have been playing tennis regularly for three years.

4. Before that, we were only spectators at tennis matches.

Adverb. An adverb modifies a verb, adjective, or other adverb. Adverbs answer these questions: When? Where? How? How much? How well? Why? To what extent? Under what circumstances?

Four clues help us identify adverbs; however, the first two clues are the most reliable:

1. Find a word that fits the definition above.
2. Find a word that tells when, where, how, how much, how well, why, to what extent, or under what circumstances.
3. Find a word that can be moved in the sentence without changing the meaning. This trait is more likely to be found with adverbs than with other parts of speech.
4. Find a word with an *ly* ending. Such a word is often (but not always) an adverb. Furthermore, many adverbs do not have *ly* endings, such as *not, never, very, too, here,* and *there.*

Adverbs can be used between parts of a verb unit, or they can be closely connected to verbs in other ways. In the sentences below, the verbs are italicized and the adverbs are circled. Consider the placement of the adverbs in relationship to the verbs.

We *will* (not) *play* tennis this Saturday.

In the summer, we (usually) *can find* time for a quick game after work.

Tennis pros *are playing* (constantly) for practice.

The word *not* is unique because it can be part of a contraction; for example, *is not* can be shortened to *isn't* and *could not* can be shortened to *couldn't.*

No matter where it is, the word *not* is an adverb, even when it is the *n't* part of a contraction, as in *couldn't, shouldn't,* and *won't.*

PRACTICE 9 _____

Underline the adverbs in these sentences.

Example: We <u>generally</u> play football through the fall season.

1. Matt usually plays in the starting line-up.

2. Friday's game ran far into overtime.

3. The tie was finally broken in our team's favor.

4. Sports fans aren't often left in such suspense over the outcome of a game.

As stated earlier, unlike other parts of speech, adverbs can often be moved without damaging the meaning of a sentence. Which *ly* word in this sentence is an adverb?

The lonely man stood quietly by the door.

Even if the answer is obvious, try changing the word order. If the word *lonely* is moved to other places in the sentence, we get strange results. If the word *quietly* is moved to other places, we get the same meaning:

> Quietly the lonely man stood by the door.
> The lonely man stood by the door quietly.

For further proof that the word *quietly* is an adverb in this sentence, test it against the clues above. What does it modify? Does it explain when, where, or how? Because adverbs can be hard to recognize, we need to consider all the possible clues. Then we can identify adverbs (or other words) by how they work, not how they look.

Preposition. By definition, a preposition shows relationships between the words that follow it and the words that precede it. This definition makes little sense until we examine the kinds of relationships that can be shown by prepositions.

Picture a lamp and a table. Their relationship can be expressed by prepositions, such as the italicized words here:

> The lamp is *on* the table.
> The lamp is *beside* the table.
> The lamp is *behind* the table.
> The lamp is *above* the table.
> The lamp is *near* the table.

The words *on, beside, behind, above, near* are all typical prepositions. Notice that they are short words, containing one or two syllables. Here is a partial list of typical prepositions:

in	under	during	into	near
on	over	after	upon	above
for	down	behind	from	about
of	beneath	up	with	except
by	beside	around	beyond	toward
to	before	along	against	until

With a little practice, prepositions—though numerous—are easy to recognize.

Prepositions begin units called ***prepositional phrases.*** This is the pattern of a prepositional phrase:

preposition + object = prepositional phrase

In the examples concerning the lamp and the table, we saw the following prepositional phrases:

on the table	beside the table	behind the table
above the table	near the table	

In each case, the phrase begins with a preposition and ends with the answer to the question "What?" For example, the question "Near what?" could be answered with "Near the table." The word *table* is the object of the preposition *near*.

Sometimes the question is not "What?" but "Whom?" For instance, the lamp might not be near the table, but rather near me. Then the object of the word *near* would be *me*.

PRACTICE 10

Create prepositional phrases by giving each of these prepositions an object or objects.

Examples: for *the party* _____   with *our friends and relatives*

near _____   among _____

by _____   beside _____

over _____   about _____

before _____   until _____

A prepositional phrase can contain adjectives modifying the object, making the phrase longer. Consider again the lamp and the table:

The lamp is near the dining room table.

The preposition *near* has the same object as before, namely, *table*. The question "Near what?" has the same answer: near the table. The only difference is that now adjectives tell us which table, and those adjectives make the phrase longer. We can put modifiers into this revised version of the pattern above:

preposition + modifiers + object = prepositional phrase

With or without modifiers, the basic structure is the same: the phrase begins with a preposition and ends with its object, and that object is a noun or a pronoun.

PRACTICE 11

Underline the prepositional phrases in these sentences.

Example: All of us write for our teachers in college classes.

1. Success in college depends to a large extent on writing ability.

2. For many students, college requires writing in class and during study hours.

3. Students in college prepare for writing and for speaking on many topics in various courses.

4. Assignments may include the writing of a paper in each class during each term.

Prepositional phrases work just like single-word adjectives and adverbs, modifying another part of the sentence. For instance, look at the two italicized prepositional phrases in this sentence:

Under the newspaper, I found the keys *to my office.*

One phrase, *under the newspaper,* acts as an adverb, telling where the keys were found; the other phrase, *to my office,* acts as an adjective, identifying which keys were found.

PRACTICE 12

Underline the prepositional phrases in these sentences. Then draw arrows to the words being modified, as shown in the example above.

1. The large key on the round ring opens the door to my house.

2. The quarterback from our team played Sunday at the all-star game.

3. Students in college must write on many topics.

4. Heavy rains during recent weeks swelled rivers over their banks.

Although prepositional phrases are numerous and commonplace, they are only modifiers. They add extra information, but we can set them aside when looking for vital parts of sentences. No subjects, no verbs, no objects of verbs, no subject complements can be found in prepositional phrases.

Conjunction. Conjunctions are joiners that connect words or groups of words. We are concerned mainly with the following *coordinating conjunctions:*

> for   and   nor   but   or   yet   so

(The acronym FANBOYS is helpful in remembering these seven words.)

Although some of these words are also used as other parts of speech, as conjunctions they are particularly important. As conjunctions, they can join equals: a word to a word, a phrase to a phrase, a sentence to a sentence. The fact that they can join sentences proves their strength; any one of these seven words can be used with a comma (by itself, a weak mark) to join complete sentences correctly.

In the following examples, notice that a comma plus a conjunction joins two separate, independent ideas, each of which could be a complete sentence by itself:

> We ran hard, *and* we got home in ten minutes.
> We ran single file, *for* the path was narrow.
> We run often, *yet* the distance seems long.

If the same conjunctions are used to join a word to a word or a phrase to a phrase, no comma is needed. Look at these examples carefully, noticing how they differ from the examples above:

> We jog *or* run frequently.
> The exercise *and* fresh air are wholesome for us.
> The effort is time-consuming *but* worthwhile.

PRACTICE 13

Underline the conjunctions in these sentences and add commas when the conjunctions join complete thoughts.

Example: We organized the party, <u>and</u> we sent out the invitations.

1. I watched the tennis game and learned more about serving.

2. Janet ran for class president and she won easily.

3. Paul wrote his paper before noon but typed it later.

4. The fire alarm rang in our dorm so we went outside.

Interjection. Interjections show strong, dramatic, or sudden feeling. They have no grammatical significance. Usually set off with commas or exclamation marks, they stand apart from our sentences. Common interjections are words like *oh, well, gee, aw, gosh, wow,* and *darn.* Sometimes two or more words form interjections, as in *good heavens* and *oh well.*

> *Oh,* I think interjections are easy.
> *Good heavens!* Watch out for that jogger.

Points to Use

- Capitalize proper nouns but not common nouns. For example, capitalize the name of your high school (East High School) but not the words *high school* when used in a general sense.
- Use adjectives and adverbs to modify when you are sure they are necessary. It is generally better to find nouns and verbs that convey your meaning.

- Pay attention to verbs because they are central to any statement. The verb part must be complete, sometimes with helpers. A verb form ending with *ing*, for example, requires a helper if it is to do the work of a verb in a sentence.
- Sometimes sentences can be reworded to use action verbs rather than linking verbs. This usually results in stronger and more concise sentences.
- Watch for sentences that contain many words that look like verbs but are not used as verbs. Perhaps some of those words can be dropped if the right action verb is used. (Exercise 4 below illustrates this point.)
- Remember that pronouns have various forms. Using the right form requires special attention and practice.
- Use a comma plus a coordinating conjunction to join complete thoughts.

Points to Remember

- The eight parts of speech are noun, pronoun, verb, adjective, adverb, preposition, conjunction, and interjection.
- Determine the part of speech of a word by seeing how the word is used in context.
- Nouns name persons, places, or things.
- Pronouns are noun substitutes. They change form depending on how they are used.
- Adjectives change the meaning of nouns and pronouns. They tell us which ones, what kinds, whose, and how many.
- Verbs express action or state of being. Verbs expressing states of being are called being or linking verbs. The most common linking verbs are forms of *be: is, are, was, were, am,* and *been.*
- The last verb in a group of verbs is the main verb. Other verbs are called helpers. Look at the last verb in a group to see whether action or state of being is indicated.
- Adverbs change the meaning of verbs, adjectives, and other adverbs. They tell when, where, how, how much, how well, why, under what circumstances, and to what extent. They often end with *ly,* and they often can be moved within a sentence.
- Prepositions show relationships between words. They are followed by objects (nouns or pronouns) to form prepositional phrases.
- Conjunctions join individual words, or they join groups of words including independent ideas (sentences).
- These seven coordinating conjunctions can be used with commas to join sentences: *for, and, nor, but, or, yet, so.*
- Interjections express emotion. They stand apart from sentences, separated from other words by commas or exclamation points.

EXERCISE 1. Identifying Parts of Speech

Indicate how the italicized words are used in the sentences below. Most of the eight parts of speech are represented in these sentences. Check your answers with those at the back of the book.

Examples: __*adj*__ The natives performed a *rain* dance for us.

__*noun*__ Soon afterward, *rain* began to fall.

_____ 1. He has the *right* to remain silent.

_____ 2. The suspect had a small tatoo on his *right* hand.

_____ 3. A *barking* dog will annoy the neighbors.

_____ 4. That dog is *barking* all the time.

_____ 5. The *party* is scheduled for Saturday night.

_____ 6. The *party* platform pleases many voters.

_____ 7. It was a good party, *for* many of my friends were there.

_____ 8. Weekends are good times *for* parties.

_____ 9. The school band played a spirited *march*.

_____ 10. *Marching* bands maintain a brisk tempo.

_____ 11. *Marching* in the school band was exciting.

_____ 12. The canoe hit the *rapids* unexpectedly.

_____ 13. Jean's fern grew *rapidly* in the shady corner.

_____ 14. Such *rapid* growth surprised Jean.

_____ 15. *Fasting*, an old practice, has religious significance in many cultures.

_____ 16. The devout monk *fasted* five days each month.

_____ 17. Attached with rubber cement, the photograph stuck *fast* to the paper.

_____ 18. Always keep your *checks* in a safe place.

_____ 19. *Check* to be sure they are properly printed.

_____ 20. You will find my umbrella *near* the door.

_____ 21. You are naturally concerned with the welfare of your *near* relatives.

_____ 22. The exercise is *nearly* done.

_____ 23. Coats are less expensive during the *off* season.

_____ 24. Don, please take your books *off* the table.

_____ 25. "You may like something on sale," *one* of the salesladies said as I walked past.

_____ 26. I did find *one* sweater that I liked.

_____ 27. The game was tied with no hits and no *runs.*

_____ 28. The jogger made her usual *run* around the lake.

_____ 29. The runner was proud of her *running.*

_____ 30. "I can *run* fast," the child proclaimed.

_____ 31. "On your mark! Get set! *Go!*" are the words we waited to hear.

_____ 32. If you must pass through the alley at night, *go* warily.

_____ 33. The umpire declared that the player committed a *foul.*

_____ 34. That *foul* ball went outside the foul lines of the infield.

_____ 35. The batter hit the ball *more* directly, and it went straight toward second base.

_____ 36. That player made three *more* runs during the game.

EXERCISE 2. Writing Sentences

Select a common word, such as saw, walk, labor, dance, fold, friend, color, camp, *or another of your choice. Write two sentences using that word (or a slight variation of the word) but as different parts of speech. Create six pairs of sentences.*

Underline your key words and indicate their parts of speech in the margin.

Example: *The force of the wind blew the door shut.* noun

I could not force the door open again. verb

1. _____

_____

2. _____

_____

3. _____

_____

4. _____

_____

5. _____

_____

6. _____

_____

EXERCISE 3. *Finding Prepositional Phrases*

Underline the prepositional phrases in the following sentences. On the lines, indicate how many phrases you find in each sentence. (You will find from two to five.) Check your answers with those at the back of the book.

Example: ___4___ Students build confidence in college by meeting

new challenges from day to day.

_____ 1. A forty-two-year-old freshman at our school was nervous before

her first exam.

_____ 2. For older students, taking exams is difficult after many years

away from school.

_____ 3. Beneath their calm appearances, these students hide a lot of anxiety about tests.

_____ 4. The forty-two-year-old freshman lay awake worrying until 3 A.M. on the night before her first college exam.

_____ 5. The exam consisted of fifty items, and the students were limited to thirty minutes for the exam.

_____ 6. Most of the students finished their work in twenty minutes, handed their papers to the teacher, and left the room with sighs of relief.

_____ 7. The older freshman used the entire thirty minutes, turned in her paper with hesitation, and left the room with a rather dazed look on her face.

_____ 8. The teacher looked at the papers during her office hours and found some of them unusual for one reason or another.

_____ 9. At the beginning of the next class meeting, the teacher announced the exam results to a tense and eager class of students.

_____ 10. "Many of you students apparently worked too fast," were the first words the class heard from that teacher.

_____ 11. "Next time you should use all of the given time and check all of your answers."

_____ 12. Many students had made quick, careless errors, and in their haste, they had not checked their answers for accuracy.

_____ 13. The older student wondered about catching her careless errors, but she felt that she had used all of the allotted time to her best advantage.

_____ 14. On the top of her paper, the student found a better grade than she had expected.

15. Along with that grade, she found a note commending her for the completeness of her answers.

EXERCISE 4. *Revising Sentences*

Improve the sentences below. Rewrite them so that they use stronger verbs. Change the wording as much as you like, but preserve the meaning. Here are some general guidelines to help you improve your writing.

- When possible, use fewer words rather than more, but use exact words.
- Use action verbs rather than linking verbs as the main verbs in sentences.
- Be careful how you use words that look like verbs. Do your sentences contain many such words? If so, try to eliminate some of them or replace them with stronger verbs.

These generalizations are easier to apply than to read about. For example, contrast these versions of a sentence used in this chapter:

> Prepositions are the beginning points of units called prepositional phrases.
> Prepositions begin units called prepositional phrases.
> Prepositions begin prepositional phrases.

Consider how you as a reader respond to the length, tone, rhythm, and impact of these different versions. In class, your teacher will discuss these three sentences with you. Together you will consider such questions as: Which words are verb forms? Do the sentences all mean the same thing? Is one version better than another? If so, what makes it better?

Example: The squirrel was trying to climb the tree quickly.

The squirrel scampered up the tree.

The squirrel darted up the tree.

1. The train was late in arriving.

_____

2. Brandon became worried about being exhausted.

_____

3. Marilyn was working on trying to jog.

_____

4. The children were thinking about going out to play.

_____

5. The bread was slow in rising on that cool morning.

_____

6. Animals are eager to seek shelter during snowstorms.

_____

7. Pat was ready to begin selling her used furniture.

_____

8. Pat was uncertain about setting her asking price.

_____

9. I was unclear about the considerations important in selecting a college.

_____

10. Try to work to get your revising to move along faster.

_____

EXERCISE 5.   Writing Sentences on a Given Topic

Write ten sentences describing an achievement that makes you feel proud of yourself. The sentences will show your teacher how you put words together to form your thoughts. At the same time, they will help your teacher get acquainted with you. You may use an achievement in sports, drama, music, a hobby, employment, or any other area of your choice.

An Achievement That Makes Me Proud

1. _____

2. _____

3. _____

4. _____

5. _____

6. _____

7. _____

8. _____

9. _____

10. _____

Now look at your ten sentences. You will probably find most of the features listed below in your sentences. Fill in the list, indicating the sentences in which these features appear. Then underline the items in the sentences.

Item	Location (sentence number)
Prepositional phrase	_____
Action verb with a helping verb	_____
Linking verb	_____
Adverb	_____
Adjective	_____
Pronoun used as a subject	_____
Proper noun	_____
Possessive pronoun used as an adjective	_____
Coordinating conjunction	_____

EXERCISE 6.   Analyzing Student Sentences

The examples below were written by college freshmen in response to Exercise 5. In these examples, find verbs, prepositional phrases, conjunctions, and other elements as directed by your teacher.

Example 1

One achievement that makes me proud came about four years ago. It was a very difficult time for me, and this is the first time I have ever written anything about it. My dad had bypass surgery, and he left me in charge of my mom and sister. I took care of the yard and made sure the cars were running well. This happened in the summer, so I had to give up a lot of free time. That year I didn't try out for football either. After my dad's surgery, things were going well until one night he had a major setback, and this is when the family really pulled together. After that night, things went along well. When school started, we had to talk about summer in class, but I got through it without problems. The summer might not seem like an achievement to other people, but this part of my life is the biggest thing that has affected me and made me proud.

Example 2

Getting my mom to accept my dog, Penny, was an achievement that makes me proud. My mom had forbidden any animals in the house, including dogs. She thought dogs were too hairy, and she said we would soon lose interest in them. I wanted one so much that I began searching through the newspaper on my own. A black lab puppy was my first choice, but instead, I had to settle for a golden retriever. I persuaded my brother to pick up the puppy with me when we were asked to get milk. The puppy we wanted was already taken, so we chose the lazy one in the corner. When we came home, my mom was expecting milk in the bag, but instead she found a puppy. She threw a fit and told us to take it back. But gradually she fell in love with the puppy and now wouldn't give her up for a million dollars.

Example 3

Last spring, I joined the Navy. The Navy offered a lot for my future. I took full advantage of all my opportunities. I worked very hard and many long hours and usually was exhausted at the end of the day. I was running constantly, but that hard work paid off. I was chosen the honor recruit of our company. I then went on to compete against all the honor recruits in our training division for the Navy League Honor Recruit. The outcome was wonderful, and I was elected for that honor. I received a big blue and yellow ribbon. The greatest feeling of all was seeing the pride in my parents' eyes.

2

Recognizing the Sentence

Finding Subjects, Action Verbs, and Objects

Generally we use word groups to make statements. There are some exceptions, of course: the word *hello* expresses meaning by itself. Although in context individual words can convey meaning, ordinarily we need to use combinations of words to express ourselves. Word combinations that express complete thoughts are sentences. To be a sentence, a unit must have at least these two parts:

subject + verb (predicate)

The ***subject***—a noun or a pronoun—names the person(s), place(s), or thing(s) about which a statement is being made. The subject can be either a single word or a group of words. The subject of a sentence is like the subject of a good photograph. It stands out as the focal point and commands attention, as do the italicized subjects here:

> *Michael Owens* ran the marathon in record time.
> *Swimming* strengthened his leg muscles.

A sentence can have a ***compound subject***—that is, a subject made up of two or more separate, equally important, individual subjects, as shown in the following sentences:

> *Michael* and *Peter* have run in marathons many times.
> *Peter* and *Michael* have run in marathons many times.

Each of these sentences has a compound subject, a subject made up of two individual subjects about whom a statement is made. No matter how many individual subjects are involved, they can usually appear in any order. When the subject *I* is used, however, it always comes last:

> *Michael*, *Peter*, and *I* have run in marathons many times.
> *Peter*, *Michael*, and *I* have run in marathons many times.

Verbs give subjects their meaning. (In this book, the word *verb* is used, but the words *predicate* or *simple predicate* are also appropriate.) The subjects in the sentences above would have little meaning without the verbs.

The verb in a sentence can be either one word or a combination of words (a main verb plus helpers). Adverbs can be placed between the individual words. The verb part of the sentence can also be *compound*, just as the subject can be. A compound verb expresses two or more actions or states of being about the subject.

In the following sentences, two separate actions or states of being are expressed about the subjects (the subjects are underlined once, the verbs twice):

Jim has run in several marathons and has won twice.

Paula was present at the marathon last year but can not attend this year.

Pam will watch the entire race but will not stay for the victory party afterward.

Compound subjects and compound verbs can be used in the same sentence, as in this example:

The sidewalks and side streets were crowded with spectators during the race and littered with debris after the race.

PRACTICE 1

Underline the subjects once and the verbs twice.

Example: Joan and Mark competed in the marathon last year but may not participate this year.

1. Jim and Paul have entered many local races and have won several trophies.

2. Pam and Laura will watch the contest from the sidelines but will not attend the party afterward.

3. After the race, the winners will probably rest for a few hours and then celebrate with their friends.

4. Spectators and reporters also may relax for a few hours after the event.

Although subjects and verbs often are fairly obvious, the following steps can help us find them:

- Eliminate all nonessentials: adverbs, adjectives, and prepositional phrases. Then you can more easily see which of the remaining words serve as subjects and verbs.
- Ask yourself who is doing what. Often the subject is the doer, and the verb tells what is being done.
- Rely on normal word order—namely, subject + verb + completing element (if any). Turn questions into statements, or restate the idea in your own words, and the subject and verb may emerge.

Has Larry entered the race this year?

Larry has entered the race this year.

PRACTICE 2

In the sentences below, cross out the nonessentials (adjectives, adverbs, and prepositional phrases). Then underline the subjects once and the verbs twice.

Example: ~~Experienced marathon~~ runners prefer ~~cool~~ days ~~for marathons~~. They ~~also~~ enjoy ~~the~~ cheering ~~of the crowds~~ and ~~the encouraging~~ words ~~of well-wishers~~.

1. Many runners have entered marathons across the country during the past few years.

2. Three neighbors in my apartment complex ran in last year's local marathon.

3. Matt's supervisor at work nearly won that race but fell behind in the last two miles.

4. Around the west side of the lake, the jogging paths wind in a zigzag pattern, then turn into a straight line on the northwest corner.

SENTENCE PATTERNS WITH ACTION VERBS

Three sentence patterns are possible with action verbs. We can think of them as formulas:

Subject + action verb: S + AV
Subject + action verb + direct object: S + AV + DO
Subject + action verb + indirect object + direct object:
S + AV + IO + DO

Pattern 1: Subject + Action Verb (S + AV). A sentence with the S + AV pattern can be a short sentence, but it does not need to be. If modifiers are used, they add length. Note the different lengths of the following sentences, both of which use the S + AV pattern:

<u>Michael Owens</u> <u><u>won</u></u>.

Well-conditioned by long years of strenuous training, <u>Michael Owens</u>, a twenty-year-old college student, <u><u>won</u></u> with a thirty-second margin over his nearest competitor in the race.

Pattern 2: Subject + Action Verb + Direct Object (S + AV + DO). The S + AV + DO pattern adds a new element, called the *direct object*. The direct object receives the action of the verb. We can find the direct object by asking these questions: "What?" or "Whom?" after the action verb. For example, after the action verbs in the following sentences, ask the question "What?" The answers are enclosed in the rectangles.

DO

The <u>photographer</u> <u><u>took</u></u> |pictures| of the winner.

(Took what? pictures)

DO   DO

The <u>newspaper</u> <u><u>printed</u></u> |pictures| and a |story| about the race.

(Printed what? pictures and story)

The next example shows that a sentence can have more than one verb, each with a direct object. The basic pattern stays the same, but we have this variation:

S + AV + DO + AV + DO

DO   DO

<u>Michael</u> <u><u>ran</u></u> the |race| and <u><u>won</u></u> the |prize.|

(Ran what? race   Won what? prize)

Some verbs indicate possession, such as *have*, *has*, and *possess*. These verbs can also take direct objects.

PRACTICE 3

Underline the subjects once and the verbs twice. Enclose the direct objects in rectangles, as shown in the examples above.

1. The spectators enjoyed the day and now have happy memories of the marathon.

2. Shopkeepers along the route sold refreshments to the crowd of spectators and made good profits throughout the day.

3. The winner of the race has a tall, shiny trophy for his victory.

4. He also possesses happy memories and pride in his achievement.

Pattern 3: Subject + Action Verb + Indirect Object + Direct Object (S + AV + IO + DO). The S + AV + IO + DO pattern is used less often than either of other action-verb patterns. When it is used, all four parts of this pattern must appear in exactly the order shown. Thus, the least common action-verb pattern is also the most rigid.

An *indirect object* tells us to whom or for whom something is done. Usually the verb involved in this pattern expresses the idea of giving or offering something to someone. The indirect object is a recipient. In the following sentences, the indirect object is circled. Notice the meaning of the verbs and the rigid order of the items in this sentence pattern:

IO   DO

The marathon <u>judges</u> <u>gave</u> (Michael) his prize.

(Gave what? prize   Gave to whom? Michael)

IO   DO

The <u>sportscaster</u> <u>offered</u> (him) a chance for a television interview.

(Offered what? chance   Offered to whom? him)

By contrast, consider the structure in these sentences:

DO

The marathon <u>judges</u> <u>gave</u> the prize to Michael.

DO

The <u>sportscaster</u> <u>offered</u> the chance for a television interview to him.

In these last two sentences, we find no indirect objects. The recipients are named, but they are in prepositional phrases. Furthermore, the order of the items does not fit the S + AV + IO + DO pattern. When we have an indirect object, it can be in only one place—between the action verb and the direct object.

Underline the subjects once and the verbs twice. Put rectangles around the direct objects and circles around the indirect objects, as shown in the examples above.

1. After the race, the trainers brought the runners water and fresh clothing.

2. An editor from the leading runners' magazine offered three marathoners opportunities to write their stories.

3. Later, the editor sent his boss a letter about the offers.

4. But Michael had previously given another magazine the rights to his story.

Finding Linking Verbs and Complements

Because they play a special role in our language, linking verbs deserve special attention. Although there are few of them, they are highly important and much used. Here are the most common of these verbs:

    is   are   was   were   am   been   be

As discussed earlier, these verbs express the concept of state of being—that is, of existence. When we consider how they are used, however, we can see that the term *linking* is also appropriate.

The term *linking* makes more sense when we see these verbs at work. Notice how they look in some sample sentences:

Your children are strong and healthy.

Marie's garden was beautiful last summer.

Those roses are hybrid plants.

These sentences express no action, but rather the condition (state of being) or the existence of the roses or the garden or the children. Thus, linking verbs have the following characteristics:

• They convey no action.
• They express existence or state of being.

Note: The very same verbs, the *be* verbs, are not always used as linking verbs; sometimes they work as helpers, often with action verbs.

In the sample sentences above, the *be* verbs act alone as the entire verb within each of the sentences. They are linking verbs because they link the subject of the sentence to the subject complement, the part of the sentence that follows the verb.

At other times, the *be* verbs are helpers that are used with other verbs. As noted in Chapter 1, the last verb in a group of verbs is the main verb; all other verbs in the group are helpers. Contrast these two sentences:

The white <u>rose</u> <u><u>is growing</u></u> faster than the red one.   (AV)

The red <u>rose</u> <u><u>will be</u></u> beautiful during August.   (LV)

In the first sentence, the word *is* works as a helper with the main verb *growing*, an action verb. In the second sentence, the word *will* is the helper with the main verb *be*, a linking verb. The first sentence expresses an action, the growing of the rose; the second sentence expresses only a condition of existence—namely, what the rose will be.

PRACTICE 5

Underline the subjects once and the verbs twice. Label the main verbs AV or LV, as shown in the examples above.

1. The crowd of spectators is cheering the winner.

2. Recognition, prize money, and trophies are typical awards for winners.

3. In the midst of winter, fresh flowers are cheerful reminders of spring.

4. Athletes will be training for spring sports in a few weeks.

Certain verbs—particularly verbs pertaining to the senses—can be action or linking verbs, depending on how they are used:

look	feel	taste	smell	appear
remain	seem	stay	grow	prove

In the following sentences, the sense verbs act as linking verbs:

The <u>rose</u> <u><u>smells</u></u> sweet.

The <u>marigolds</u> <u><u>look</u></u> handsome along the patio fence.

The gladiola <u>blossoms</u> <u><u>feel</u></u> velvet-like to the touch.

Flower <u>nectar</u> <u><u>tastes</u></u> sweet to the bees.

To determine whether a sense verb is acting as a linking verb, substitute a form of the word *be* for that verb. If the substitution provides approximately the same meaning, the sense verb is acting as a linking verb. In the four sentences above, the substitutions would produce sensible statements:

The <u>rose</u> <u><u>is</u></u> sweet.

The <u>marigolds</u> <u><u>are</u></u> handsome along the patio fence.

The gladiola <u>blossoms</u> <u><u>were</u></u> velvet-like to the touch.

Flower <u>nectar</u> <u><u>was</u></u> sweet to the bees.

(Tenses were changed in the last two sentences to show that various forms of the verb *be* would work as substitutes.)

PRACTICE 6

Underline the subjects once and the verbs twice. Write a form of be *above the verbs in these sentences. Then write the letter L after the sentences in which the verb is a linking verb.*

Examples: The <u>winner</u> <u><u>touches</u></u> *is (was)* the finish line with joy and relief.

<u>He</u> <u><u>feels</u></u> *was* his aching muscles.

<u>He</u> also <u><u>feels</u></u> *was* happy. L

1. He looks for his friends in the crowd of spectators.

2. We smell the fragrant roses around the patio in the summer.

3. The gardener feels the firm cabbage heads before cutting them.

4. By early August, most of the vegetables look ripe.

5. The family tasted the fresh vegetable soup at lunch.

Substituting a form of the word *be* for an action verb destroys the intended meaning and often creates nonsense. Thus, it is an easy way to distinguish between linking and action verbs.

SUBJECT + LINKING VERB + SUBJECT COMPLEMENT (S + LV + SC)

After a linking verb, we need another element to finish the meaning of the sentence. Without another element, a subject and a linking verb leave us wondering:

The flower <u>garden</u> <u><u>is</u></u> _____?_____.

My favorite <u>flowers</u> <u><u>are</u></u> _____?_____.

We proceed with our ideas automatically, finishing the meaning:

The flower <u>garden</u> <u>is</u> beautiful.

My favorite <u>flowers</u> <u>are</u> the yellow roses.

The element that completes the meaning is the **subject complement**. The word *complement* means that which completes; the word *subject* is appropriate because the complement refers to the subject of the sentence, either describing or renaming it. In this book, the term *subject complement* includes both the adjective and the noun (or pronoun) completers.

A subject complement that describes the subject is an adjective, such as the word *beautiful* here:

SC
The flower <u>garden</u> <u>is</u> (beautiful.)

The term **predicate adjective** can also be used for this kind of subject complement, calling attention to the special placement of the adjective. Here the adjective does not precede the noun, as is normally the case.

A subject complement that renames the subject is a noun or a pronoun, such as the word *roses* in this sentence:

SC
My favorite <u>flowers</u> <u>are</u> the yellow (roses.)

The term **predicate noun** or **predicate nominative** is sometimes used for this kind of subject complement because the noun or pronoun after the linking verb refers to the subject.

PRACTICE 7

Underline the subjects once and the verbs twice in the following sentences. All the verbs in these sentences are linking verbs. Circle the subject complements, as shown in the examples above.

1. Strong winds and heavy rain may be hard on the flowers.

2. Slow, steady rain over several hours will be good for all the plants.

3. Farmers and gardeners across the region are fearful of thunderstorms with hail.

4. The grass in that pasture is sweet-smelling red clover.

In normal word order, sentences follow this pattern:

subject + verb + (object or complement)

Objects and complements are found in the same part of the sentence, but they are easier to tell apart if we follow these two steps:

- Examine the verb. Subject complements follow linking verbs. Direct objects follow action verbs.
- Examine the subject. Subject complements refer to the subject, either describing or renaming it. Direct objects have no connection with the subject; they cannot be confused with it.

Examine the subject complements and objects in the following sentences and consider their relationship to the subject *flowers:*

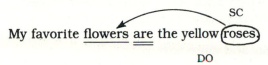

SC

My favorite <u>flowers</u> <u>are</u> the yellow (roses)

DO

My favorite <u>flowers</u> <u>filled</u> the vase on the table.

The arrow can help you visualize the connection between the subject complement and the subject; the subject complement *roses* renames the subject *flowers.* In the second sentence, there is no connecting arrow because the direct object *vase* does not rename the subject *flowers.*

PRACTICE 8

Underline the subjects once and the verbs twice in the following sentences. Draw arrows from subject complements to subjects. Put rectangles around the direct objects.

DO

Examples: The <u>wind</u> <u>blew</u> the lawn chair across the patio.

SC

The <u>wind</u> with that rainstorm <u>was</u> powerful.

1. The broken chair will require a carpenter's skill and patience.

2. The children's swing set on the east side of the yard is old but sturdy.

3. The evergreens look stately along our neighbor's fence.

4. On our long driveway, the neighborhood children run races and play

   basketball.

Points to Use

- Locate subjects and verbs in your sentences. If you are watching for them, you will be checking to be sure that they are both present, and they will be more likely to agree (a matter to be discussed in detail in Chapter 6).
- Be aware of all parts of compound subjects and compound verbs. As a general rule, keep parts of compound subjects together.
- Watch the subject/verb relationship in sentences, using that relationship as a guide for standard word order and as an aid to punctuation. Ordinarily, do not separate the subject from the verb with punctuation.
- Use standard word order (subject, verb, object or complement) unless there is good reason to depart from it. This word order fits readers' expectations and makes communication with readers easier and more natural.

Points to Remember

- A sentence is a word group that expresses a complete thought. A sentence must have at least a subject and a verb.
- The subject of a sentence is the person, place, or thing about which (or whom) a statement is made. Subjects are nouns or pronouns.
- The verb (or predicate) is the word or group of words that makes an assertion about the subject. Verbs express action or state of being.
- Both subjects and verbs can be compounds. The term *compound* means having two or more separate, independent parts.
- One common sentence pattern is subject plus action verb, abbreviated to this formula: S + AV.
- Another common sentence pattern is subject plus action verb plus direct object, abbreviated to this formula: S + AV + DO.
- The direct object receives the action of the verb and answers the questions "What?" or "Whom?" after the verb.
- A third sentence pattern consists of subject plus action verb plus indirect object plus direct object, abbreviated to this formula: S + AV + IO + DO.
- The indirect object tells to whom or for whom something is done.
- Linking verbs are called *state of being verbs* because they express being or existence. The most common linking verbs are *is, are, was, were, am, been,* and *be.*

- When forms of the word *be* act alone in a sentence, doing the work of a verb, they are linking verbs. When used with other verbs, they are helping verbs.
- Some verbs can be either action or linking verbs. Many such verbs refer to the senses, such as *look, smell, taste,* and *feel.*
- To find out whether a verb is an action or a linking verb, substitute a form of *be* and see if the meaning remains essentially the same. If it does, the verb is a linking verb.
- Linking verbs typically are followed by subject complements, creating this pattern: S + LV + SC.
- A subject complement describes or renames the subject. If it describes the subject, it is an adjective; if it renames or identifies the subject, it is a noun or pronoun.
- Unlike the direct object, the subject complement is directly related to the subject, describing or renaming it.

EXERCISE 1. Finding Subjects, Action Verbs, and Objects

A. *Draw a line through the adverbs, adjectives, and prepositional phrases.*
B. *Underline the subjects once and the verbs twice.*
C. *Circle the indirect objects, and draw rectangles around the direct objects. Check your answers with those at the back of the book.*

Examples: Students ~~in English classes~~ want ~~quick~~ [improvement] ~~in their writing~~.

Progress comes ~~slowly~~ and ~~steadily for most of us in most writing classes~~.

1. Students can make immediate improvements in their writing.

2. You can improve your writing with practice and care.

3. You should underline titles of books, magazines, newspapers, and movies.

4. Careful writers underline or italicize those titles.

5. You can also improve your spelling with attention to troublesome expressions like *a lot.*

6. Careful writers always use two words for *a lot.*

7. Every sentence must contain at least a subject and a verb.

8. Separate parts of a two-part compound subject usually are not separated with a comma.

9. English students struggle over erratic spelling.

10. Root words give us clues about meanings.

11. The connection between the words *sign* and *signature* gives us a clue about spelling.

12. Silent letters in words can be important parts of root words, like the silent *g* in *sign.*

13. The silent ending *b* in *bomb* is important in the derivative words *bombardier* and *bombardment.*

14. The typical college student has reading assignments of a million words for each term.

15. To the surprise of very few people, good readers earn higher grades in most of their classes.

16. The human brain can process about 500 words per minute.

17. Some people read only about 200 words per minute.

18. A slow reading pace allows too much lag or empty time for the brain.

19. During the lag time, the brain runs ahead of the printed page, or the brain works on other ideas.

20. Good readers develop good reading habits and avoid bad habits, such as pausing on big words, moving the lips, pronouncing words mentally, and looking back frequently.

21. Speed reading is sometimes called "free fall" reading.

22. In free-fall reading, the reader's eyes glance down the page quickly and catch only the main points.

23. Newspapers are ideal material for the free-fall style of reading.

24. A steady pace of about 500 words per minute is excellent for most college textbook material.

25. Reading experts use the term *rhythmic perusal* for a steady pace of about 500 words per minute.

26. Students often talk about vocabulary development.

27. Vocabulary drills bore most people, and they do little good.

28. For building vocabulary, experts recommend reading more.

EXERCISE 2. *Finding Subjects, Verbs, Objects, and Complements*

A. *Draw a line through the adverbs, adjectives, and prepositional phrases.*
B. *Underline the subjects once and the verbs twice.*
C. *If you find indirect objects, circle them, and draw rectangles around direct objects.*
D. *If you find subject complements, write them on the line.*
E. *Check your answers with those at the back of the book.*

Examples: _____ There in the corner of the room stands my favorite easy chair beside a reading lamp.

quick Teenagers are particularly quick with their homework on nights before important games.

_____ Indirect objects usually follow certain common action verbs.

_____ 1. Long words need not intimidate readers.

_____ 2. A big word like *hippopotamus* often has just one meaning.

_____ 3. By contrast, a small word like *run* can have many different meanings.

_____ 4. You can bank on the bank by the river bank.

_____ 5. In sentence 4, the word *bank* has two different roles and three different meanings.

_____ 6. A typical person may know 200,000 words.

_____ 7. In spite of his or her acquaintance with 200,000 words, that person may read only at the tenth-grade level.

_____ 8. Modern daily newspapers provide today's readers much valuable current information.

_____ 9. Representatives of England and the United States signed a treaty on Christmas Eve, 1814.

_____ 10. That treaty ended the War of 1812.

_____ 11. Today, international news arrives in our homes within seconds through the media.

_____ 12. In 1814, news of the peace treaty arrived in the United States after days of delay.

_____ 13. The war had been very unpopular in New England.

_____ 14. Some leaders in New England were advocates of secession from the federal union.

_____ 15. Congress debated the treaty and ratified it by unanimous approval on February 16, 1815.

_____ 16. Secessionist talk ceased in a moment with the arrival of peace.

_____ 17. In Boston, musicians and orators hastily staged festive public celebrations.

_____ 18. Out of the momentum and public enthusiasm for those musical performances came a new music organization.

_____ 19. That organization was the Boston Handel and Haydn Society.

_____ 20. The name of the group reflects the popularity of two eighteenth-century composers.

_____ 21. The long and distinguished history of that organization is the topic of several good books.

_____ 22. The publication of successful music books gave the society a solid financial base.

_____ 23. One editor of money-making books for the society was the Boston musician Lowell Mason.

_____ 24. You can think of sentences with objects and complements.

_____ 25. For example, the governor offered the prisoner a pardon.

_____ 26. The prisoner didn't hesitate for long.

_____ 27. He sent the governor a note of thanks.

_____ 28. Your own examples are more memorable than examples in a textbook.

EXERCISE 3. _Finding Subjects, Verbs, Objects, and Complements_

A. _Draw a line through the adverbs, adjectives, and prepositional phrases._
B. _Underline the subjects once and the verbs twice._
C. _If you find direct objects, draw rectangles around them._
D. _If you find subject complements, connect them to the subjects with arrows._
E. _Check your answers with those at the back of the book._

Examples:

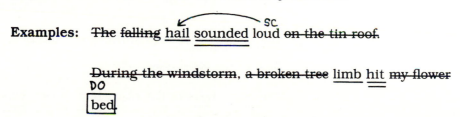

1. The tallest flowers were gladiolas and zinnias.

2. Judges at the flower show praised the gladiolas.

3. Floral arrangements must include greenery with the flowers.

4. Good arrangements look attractive in any setting.

5. All the moisture has been removed from pressed flowers.

6. Pressed flowers are thin and fragile to the touch.

7. The lilies appear in mid-June after long dormancy.

8. Lilies seem miraculous in their sudden appearance.

9. Daffodils and tulips delight gardeners with a burst of color early in the spring.

10. Spring flowers stay fresh for days in a vase of water.

11. Lilacs in a long hedge separate our houses.

12. They smell fragrant during May and early June.

13. The prize winners in this year's flower show will be Marie's roses and Karen's mums.

14. At the fair, leading floral designers display their most beautiful arrangements.

15. Those arrangements look beautiful all week.

EXERCISE 4. *Identifying Sentence Patterns*

Match these patterns with the sentences below and then check your answers with those at the back of the book:

a. S + AV c. S + AV + IO + DO
b. S + AV + DO d. S + LV + SC

Examples: ___d___ Donna and Carl were enthusiastic about their part in the local marathon.

___b___ The organizers of the event had eagerly promoted it in the media.

_____ 1. Many joggers are serious about their running.

_____ 2. Strenuous running can give beginners some unexpected aches and pains.

_____ 3. Running looks easy to a bystander.

_____ 4. Trained runners dream of marathon running.

_____ 5. A magazine for joggers and runners provides detailed information about the Boston marathon.

_____ 6. Runners travel from all parts of the country to the famous Boston marathon.

_____ 7. The marathon is a race of 26 miles, 385 yards.

_____ 8. The marathon commemorates the feat of a Greek runner in the fifth century B.C.

_____ 9. That runner carried news of victory from Marathon to Athens, Greece.

_____ 10. At Marathon, the Greeks defeated the Persians.

_____ 11. Modern runners participate in marathons for other reasons.

_____ 12. The record time for a Boston marathon is approximately two hours, eight minutes.

_____ 13. Running gives athletes and amateurs much pleasure.

_____ 14. Beginners should start with gentle warm-ups and short distances.

_____ 15. Experienced joggers gladly help beginners and answer their questions.

EXERCISE 5. *Writing Sentences*

On a separate piece of paper, write ten sentences on the topic indicated below or on another topic assigned by your teacher. Next, see if you can improve the way you expressed your ideas. If your teacher so indicates, bring your sentences to class for peer evaluation and discussion. Individually or with others, evaluate your sentences on the basis of information covered in this and the previous chapter.

When you are satisfied that you have expressed yourself as well as you can, examine your sentences to be sure they are all complete. Then write your finished sentences in the space below.

A Turning Point in My Life: My Feelings and Reactions

1. _____

   _____

2. _____

   _____

3. _____

   _____

4. _____

   _____

5. _____

   _____

6. _____

   _____

7. _____

   _____

8. _____

   _____

9. _____

   _____

10. _____

   _____

Now recheck your sentences to be sure they are all complete and worded as well as they can be. Find the sentence patterns in your sentences and write them in the left margin. Underline subjects once and verbs twice, and label the other parts of your sentences.

EXERCISE 6. Writing Sentences

On a separate piece of paper, write ten sentences in response to the question below. Add exact details, but stick to the position and topic expressed in your first sentence.

> **Question:** What have you seen recently that was vivid or unusual? Consider all possibilities, from television ads to new cars in a dealer's showroom to the mist over a lake to a political cartoon or anything else.

Write your sentences in paragraph form but number them as shown in Exercise 7 below. Follow manuscript form as described in Appendix B, page 403.

EXERCISE 7. Examining Student Sentences

The sentences in Examples 1, 2, and 3 below were written by students in response to the question in Exercise 6. Read them for class discussion. Consider the following points, among others:

1. *Are the sentences complete and correct? Do the compound sentences join related thoughts?*
2. *Which linking verbs could be replaced with action verbs?*
3. *Do all the sentences pertain to the central idea expressed in the first sentence? If not, which sentences do not?*
4. *Have the writers supported their main ideas with clear, exact details? Which details stand out in your mind as striking and vivid?*

Example 1

[1]Women's fashions today are very diversified. [2]I went shopping last week, and I found that there is something for every woman's tastes. [3]There are skirts below the knee, above the knee, and skirts up to the top of the thigh. [4]I found full gathered hems and narrow tapered hems on dresses. [5]Women can wear either boxy, loose-fitting blazers or very tailored, double-breasted blazers. [6]I saw pants that are baggy around the waist and tapered at the ankle. [7]The fashion in jeans is dark blue in color or a white washed-out look called a chemical wash. [8]Soft, feminine colors like peach, pink, or mint green are all in fashion, and bright, bold colors like red, turquoise, and purple are also in fashion. [9]In accessories, the fashion is everything from hats and gloves to scarves and belts. [10]Today I can wear whatever I like; everything is in fashion.

Example 2

[1]Recently, a television commercial caught my eye because it is so clever, just good humor in its purest form. [2]I am still trying to figure out what I like best about it. [3]The commercial is about a grown man, who, while eating his crunchy cereal, is spotted by a very hungry squirrel. [4]We first see this squirrel drooling outside on the window sill. [5]He is pleading, begging this man with his eyes, for just one tiny morsel of his cereal. [6]But this man will not share. [7]In desperation, the squirrel breaks into the house and looks for a way to get close to the cereal without being seen. [8]He even pretends to be a bookend to escape the man's quick eye. [9]End of the story? [10]We'll never know for sure, but one thing is certain; the squirrel will not give up until he has had at least one bite of that crunchy cereal.

Example 3

[1]The sight most memorable to me was seeing Kent Hrbek of the Minnesota Twins hit a grand slam in game six of the 1987 World Series. [2]His facial expression and the ready-to-burst movement of his arms showed the excitement and the thrill and pleasure running through his mind and body. [3]Any Twins fan could see that when Kent stepped on home plate, he wanted to win, and he wanted the rest of the players to feel the same tremor of excitement. [4]Nobody but Kent Hrbek can imagine what it felt like to watch that ball soar, then just keep going until it hit the bleachers beyond the wall of the baseball park. [5]I had a feeling some of the fans felt that the Twins weren't going to win, heading into game six against the Cardinals, a really fine ball club. [6]But after Hrbek hit his grand slam, the faces of the fans lit up. [7]A new attitude seemed to come over the crowd and the team. [8]Without that grand slam, the Twins might not have had the confidence to win the series.

3

Avoiding Fragments and Run-ons

Recognizing Varied Sentence Patterns

The four sentence patterns discussed in Chapter 2 provide the underlying structure for the sentences we use all our lives. (As a reminder, those patterns are S + AV, S + AV + DO, S + AV + IO + DO, and S + LV + SC.) Subjects, verbs, objects, and complements are like components of a stereo or computer system: although the components are few in number, the output from those components can be infinite, depending on the user's needs and inclinations.

Building upon a few sentence elements and patterns, we put words together in an infinite array. Most obviously, we build sentences that are greatly varied in length and complexity of thought. Less obviously, we use many structural variations.

We may vary *normal word order.* This is the standard pattern:

subject + verb + completing element, if any (object or complement)

Three exceptions vary the standard sentence pattern.

Exception 1. Questions often begin with a helping verb. To find the underlying sentence pattern, we turn these questions into statements:

Will Jennifer need the computer this morning?

DO
Jennifer will need the computer this morning.   (S + AV + DO)

Did Kevin finish his work on the inventory last night?

DO
Kevin did finish his work on the inventory last night.

(S + AV + DO)

Is he being careful with the billings?

SC
He is being careful with the billings.   (S + LV + SC)

PRACTICE 1

Rewrite the following questions to form statements. Then underline the subjects once and the verbs twice. Label any direct objects, indirect objects, and subject complements. In the margin, indicate the sentence pattern used, as shown in the examples above.

1. Has Charles used the new computer program for inventory control?

   _____

2. Will Jennifer be ready for lunch at 11:30?

   _____

3. Are training classes planned for users of the new system?

   _____

4. Did the company offer employees training classes last year?

   _____

   _____

Some questions begin with adverbs, such as *how, when, why,* or *where.* When turning such questions into statements, we drop or ignore the introductory words to find the sentence patterns.

When will the training classes begin?

The training classes will begin.   (S + AV)

How can employees enroll for those classes?

Employees can enroll for those classes.   (S + AV)

PRACTICE 2

Rewrite the following questions to form statements. Then underline the subjects once and the verbs twice. In the margin, indicate the sentence pattern used, as shown in the examples above.

1. Why do employees need training classes again this year?

   _____

2. How are Jennifer and Kevin spending this long weekend?

_____

3. When will you be ready for your next vacation?

_____

4. When does your manager allow you vacation time?

_____

Exception 2. The subject, typically found at the beginning of the sentence, is delayed if other words precede it. Sometimes groups of words precede the subject. Prepositional phrases are typical examples, but other word groups can also begin sentences.

In these examples, the subjects are underlined once and the verbs twice. Notice that the subjects are delayed by other words at the start of the sentences.

> In the last week of the month, there is extra paperwork in
>
> our office.

> There go the monthly billings into today's mail.

> Here comes the mail with more inquiries and orders.

Note: Because the words *here* and *there* are adverbs, they cannot be subjects; they must not be confused with subjects, even when they begin sentences.

Word groups that precede the subject-verb part of the sentence generally are set off with commas, signaling to readers that the main part of the sentence will follow. For example, notice here that the subjects and verbs are delayed by word groups at the very beginning of the sentences:

> By the middle of April, this office is flooded with inquiries
>
> about tax returns.

> In spite of warnings from both experts and nonexperts, many
>
> taxpayers wait until the last minute before completing
>
> their returns.

> With the pressure of the April 15 deadline, some taxpayers
>
> become impatient with the long lines of people in our wait-
>
> ing room.

Draw a line through words that delay the subjects in these sentences.
Underline the subjects once and the verbs twice.

1. After the morning coffee break, there will be a meeting with the supervisor.

2. Amazingly, here in this office, supervisors rarely call meetings.

3. On the calendar outside the reception area, there are reminders of dead-lines.

4. Here beside my desk calendar lies the note from my supervisor's assistant.

Exception 3. Statements that are commands or make requests start with a verb, usually an action verb. The subject is not stated, but it is understood to be *you*, the person addressed. The word order is typical in that the subject, in effect, precedes the verb, but in this case the subject is like a ghost, present but unseen:

Shut the door, please.

(You) shut the door, please.

Stop!

(You) stop!

When we analyze these sentences, we enclose the understood subject in parentheses, as shown in the examples.

PRACTICE 4

Create three sentences, using the understood subject you. You do not need to write the subject; it will be present automatically.

Example: Follow the directions on the label.

1. _____

2. _____

3. _____

Another variation on the four standard sentence patterns is the *compound sentence:* a sentence that consists of two or more separate, independent thoughts. Each thought contains a complete idea; each thought follows one of the standard patterns or a variation on that pattern. The parts of the compound sentence are joined either by a comma plus a conjunction or by a semicolon.

Although each independent thought could stand alone as an individual sentence, the ideas are combined into a compound sentence because they are closely related in thought. Sometimes being related in thought means that the second idea follows naturally, almost automatically from the first:

> Peggy writes her papers with a word processor, and she prints them on a laser printer.

Sometimes being related in thought means that the second idea sets up a qualification, exception, or contrast to the first idea:

> Pam writes satisfactory papers with the typewriter, but she works harder, spends two or three times as long, and has only so-so results.
> Leo uses the word processor constantly, but he turns to a typewriter for filling in the blanks on his tax return.
> Sally prefers the typewriter for short memos, yet she relies on the computer system for the monthly statements.

Sometimes being related in thought means that a cause-effect relationship is implied:

> Pam handles the typewriter keyboard well, so she could quickly learn basic word processing.

When two ideas are related in thought, a compound sentence is appropriate and effective because, by its very structure, it pulls the two ideas together.

Note that a comma is used when two independent thoughts are joined, but no comma is used between parts of a compound subject or a compound verb.

PRACTICE 5

*Are the sentences in these examples related in thought? If so, put an ×	 in the margin beside them.*

> **Example:** ___X___ Ted bought a microcomputer last month. He has already found several ways to use it for his sales reports.

_____ 1. Portable computers may weigh only fifteen to twenty pounds. They can be taken on airplanes like carry-on luggage.

_____ 2. A small screen folds down to make the portable machine compact. Peter won a box of floppy disks at the grand opening of a new computer store.

_____ 3. One frequently used key on the word processor is labeled "*delete.*" Another useful key is labeled "*insert.*"

_____ 4. Peggy writes letters and memos almost every day. She writes reports and proposals almost every month.

When thoughts are unrelated, putting them together into a compound sentence makes no sense. For instance, if you joined the statements in the second sentence above with a comma plus the word *and*, the combination would be jarring. Here is a less extreme example, but even here, the ideas do not relate closely enough to be joined in a compound sentence:

> *Poor:*   My papers are thoroughly revised on the word processor, and I bought this system three years ago.
>
> *Better:*   My papers are thoroughly revised on the word processor. I bought this system three years ago.
>
>   *or*
>
> My papers are thoroughly revised on the word processor that I bought three years ago.
>
>   *or*
>
> My papers are thoroughly revised on my three-year-old word processor.

When ideas belong together in compound sentences, join them either with a comma plus a coordinating conjunction (FANBOYS: *for, and, nor, but, or, yet, so*) or with a semicolon.

The semicolon can be used either alone or with such transitional words as *however, moreover, consequently, in addition, therefore, furthermore, in fact,* and *nevertheless.* Transitional words ease the reader into the second statement; they are not required for the joining of the separate statements. Here, for comparison, are versions of the same compound sentences, with and without transitional words:

> Many authorities have advocated word processing as an aid to writers; many writers have discovered the advantages of word processors.
>
> Many authorities have advocated word processing as an aid to writers; furthermore, many writers have discovered the advantages of word processors.

> Writers work long hours over a piece of writing, adding, subtracting, rearranging their words; they need a system that makes adding, subtracting, and rearranging easy.
>
> Writers work long hours over a piece of writing, adding, subtracting, rearranging their words; therefore, they need a system that makes adding, subtracting, and rearranging easy.

Join these sentences with a comma plus a coordinating conjunction or a semicolon. Add transitional words with the semicolons if you like.

1. Compound subjects are not separated with commas. Compound sentences are separated with commas plus conjunctions or with semicolons.

2. Compound subjects and compound verbs can be used within a single independent thought. Compound sentences involve two or more independent thoughts.

3. Pam typed a new copy of her history report. She could turn in a clean, revised copy.

4. Pam's report described the treaty ending the Spanish-American War. Pam's paper showed the significance of that treaty.

Writing and Joining Complete Sentences

Examined individually, sentences fall into one of the patterns or variations described in this book so far. It would seem, then, that sentences could be managed quite easily, yet that is not the case.

Two serious problems can arise: sentence fragments and run-ons. These problems are opposites in that fragments are less than sentences and run-ons are more than individual sentences.

A *fragment* is a word group that does not express a complete thought. The fragment (often designated as *frag*) may be lacking a subject or a verb or both subject and verb. The fragment may have a subject and a verb yet fail to express an independent idea; the fragment may only lead up to an idea:

Frag: If the plants are withering.
Frag: When I looked closely at the leaves.

These word groups depend on the rest of the sentence for their meaning.

Sentence: If the plants are withering, I must discover the reason.
Sentence: When I looked closely at the leaves, I found insects.

Fragments sometimes occur because a verb ending with *ing* is used alone as the verb in a sentence.

Frag: Aphids nesting on the underside of the leaves.
Frag: The leaves turning brown and curling tight.

A verb ending with *ing* must have a helping verb with it; otherwise it cannot work as the verb part of the sentence. Adding helping verbs to the examples above converts the fragments into sentences. Note that one helping verb can provide enough help for two (or more) main verbs, as in the second sentence below:

> *Sentence:* Aphids are nesting on the underside of the leaves.
> *Sentence:* The leaves are turning brown and curling tight.

As these examples show, the difference between a fragment and a sentence can appear to be slight—perhaps involving only a single word—yet the difference in effect is tremendous.

PRACTICE 7

Change these fragments into sentences by adding helping verbs to the ing *verb forms. Write between the lines.*

1. The organic gardeners not using chemicals.

2. Birds holding down insect populations in our yard.

3. This spring the birds not keeping up with the aphids on the dogwood.

4. The garden center specialists advising limited use of chemicals.

Run-ons are two or more complete sentences that have been joined incorrectly. The comma splice (comma fault) is joined with a comma alone; the run-together (fused) sentence has no punctuation between the two or more independent thoughts.

The comma splice (often designated as CS) looks like this:

> *CS:* The chemical was diluted with water, then it was sprayed on the dogwood.
> *CS:* That chemical is systemic, it enters the plant's system.
> *CS:* Some insecticides remain on the surface, however, the aphid infestation required systemic treatment.

To repair comma splices, use one of these methods:

- Create separate sentences with a period at the end of the first independent thought and a capital letter at the start of the next.
- Create compound sentences with a comma plus a coordinating conjunction or a semicolon between the separate thoughts.

Compare these versions with the comma splice sentences above:

> *Correct:* The chemical was diluted with water; then it was sprayed on the dogwood.

Correct:	That chemical is systemic, so it enters the plant's system.
Correct:	Some insecticides remain on the surface; however, the aphid infestation required systemic treatment.

PRACTICE 8

Repair these comma splice sentences. Write your corrections between the lines.

1. Dogwood is a hearty plant, it can withstand fairly extreme temperatures.

2. Rhododendron is also hearty, it is more limited to moderate climates.

3. Rachel Carson warned of excessive use of chemicals, her book *Silent Spring* described their dangers.

4. Carson was a biologist, she was concerned with people as well as plants and animals.

Run-together (fused) sentences are confusing to readers because there is no visual signal marking the division between thoughts. These sentences may have punctuation elsewhere, but at the critical point between the independent thoughts, there is no mark, as in these examples:

Fused:	Besides the aphids on the dogwood, I found mites on the evergreens this discovery led to more spraying.
Fused:	Most summers I use no insecticides on the shrubbery, flowers, or trees this year was an exception.

To repair fused sentences, use the same methods as for comma splices:

- Create separate sentences with a period at the end of the first independent thought and a capital letter at the start of the next.
- Create compound sentences with a comma plus a coordinating conjunction or a semicolon between the separate thoughts.

PRACTICE 9

Repair these fused sentences. Write your corrections between the lines.

1. Besides the aphids on the dogwood, I found mites on the evergreens this discovery led to more spraying.

2. Most summers I use no insecticides on the shrubbery, flowers, or trees this year was an exception.

3. After the spraying, the dogwood recovered quickly the evergreens took longer but gradually improved as well.

4. Gardeners should apply chemicals on clear, calm days they should be positioned with any slight breeze carrying fumes away from them.

Points to Use

- Use normal word order unless you have good reason to do otherwise. Normal word order fits readers' expectations and makes communication with readers easier and more natural.
- Arrange ideas in normal word order to find sentence patterns and to be sure that all the essential parts of the sentence are present.
- Use compound sentences to connect related thoughts. Use separate sentences to convey separate, unrelated, or distantly related thoughts.
- Join parts of compound sentences with a comma plus a coordinating conjunction (FANBOYS) or with a semicolon. Use the semicolon either alone or with transitional words.
- Avoid fragments by testing word groups to be sure that they are sentences. Remember that both subjects and verbs are required in sentences; complete thoughts are also required.
- Make sure that *ing* verb forms have helping verbs if they are doing the work of the verb in the sentence. Without helping verbs, the *ing* forms can create fragments.
- Avoid comma splices (comma faults) by creating separate sentences. When independent thoughts are closely related, create compound sentences.
- Avoid run-together (fused) sentences by using the proper punctuation between independent thoughts.

Points to Remember

- Although complete sentences require both subjects and verbs, the subjects do not always precede the verbs. Many variations of sentence patterns and word order are possible.
- The normal word order in English is subject + verb + complet-

ing elements (if any). Exceptions occur when sentences ask questions or begin with adverbs or other introductory words or word groups.

- Questions often begin with helping verbs or with such adverbs as *how, why,* or *when.* Turning questions into statements makes the sentence pattern clear.
- Subjects are sometimes delayed by the use of introductory phrases, such as prepositional phrases, or single adverbs, such as *here* and *there.*
- A sentence that makes a request or gives a command typically starts with the action verb. The subject is understood to be the word *you,* but the subject is not written or spoken.
- A compound sentence consists of two or more separate, independent thoughts. Although these thoughts are related, they are structurally separate, with their own subjects and verbs.
- Unless separate ideas are logically related, they should not be combined into compound sentences.
- A compound subject is joined with a comma plus a conjunction or with a semicolon. The semicolon can be used either alone or with transitional words, such as *however, therefore,* and *in addition,* among others.
- A sentence fragment is a group of words that lacks one or more of the requirements for a sentence.
- A verb that ends with *ing* requires a helping verb if it is to serve as the verb part of a sentence.
- Run-on sentences consist of two or more separate sentences that run together. They contain separate, independent statements that have not been joined correctly.
- Run-on sentences fall into two categories: comma splices (comma faults) or run-together (fused) sentences.
- The comma splice (or comma fault) means that two or more separate sentences have been joined with only a comma. The comma is too weak by itself to connect sentences, but it can be used with a coordinating conjunction.
- The run-together or fused sentence has no punctuation between the end of the first complete thought and the start of the second, though there may be punctuation within the individual statements.

EXERCISE 1. Reviewing Parts of Speech, Parts of Sentences, and Sentence Patterns

Answer each question in the space provided. Each group of questions refers to the sentence above it. Check your answers with those at the back of the book.

The wise old man advised his sons but never gave them orders.

1. Name an adjective in the sentence, disregarding the word *the*. _____

2. What is the subject? _____

3. What is the verb? _____

4. Do we have action or linking verbs? _____

5. Name an adverb in the sentence. _____

6. What is the sentence pattern? _____

Over the ridge rode Stuart's cavalry with their banners and bugles.

7. Name one prepositional phrase in the sentence. _____

8. Name another prepositional phrase. _____

9. What is the subject? _____

10. What is the verb? _____

11. What is the sentence pattern? _____

Wow! You can't really be serious!

12. What part of speech is the word *wow?* _____

13. What part of speech is the word *you?* _____

14. What part of speech is the word *really?* _____

15. What is the subject? _____

16. What is the verb? _____

17. What is the sentence pattern? _____

Do they know the full truth of the matter?

18. What is the subject? _____

19. What is the verb? _____

20. What is the sentence pattern? _____

21. How is the word *matter* used? _____

22. How is the word *full* used? _____

There in the middle of the flower garden stands a small birdhouse.

23. Name one prepositional phrase. _____

24. Name another prepositional phrase. _____

25. How is the word *there* used? _____

26. Name the subject and verb. _____

27. What part of speech is the word *flower* in this example? _____

EXERCISE 2.   *Identifying and Revising Fragments*

A. *Find the complete sentences. Underline the subjects once and the verbs twice. Check your answers with those at the back of the book.*

B. *Add words to the fragments to make them into sentences. Then underline the subjects once and the verbs twice in those sentences.*

1. Swimming, a popular activity for people of all ages.

   _____

2. By learning to swim when you are very young.

   _____

3. Mary, who learned to swim when she was four years old.

   _____

4. The swimming coach changed my diving techniques.

   _____

5. Doing the backstroke, practicing the side stroke, and relaxing with the front crawl for half an hour.

   _____

6. The back stroke is hard, but beginners can handle it with practice.

   _____

7. Beginning his swimming lessons just before age seven.

   _____

8. Move your arms and kick your feet faster.

   _____

9. Of all the sports in the public schools of this city.

   _____

10. Goals like swimming faster, swimming farther, and swimming more gracefully.

    _____

11. The municipal pool from the 1930s WPA project.

    _____

12. Many excellent public works still standing from the 1930s projects.

    _____

13. Parks and recreation areas set aside for generations to come.

    _____

14. Good swimmers must follow safety rules and common sense, and beginners must be even more careful.

    _____

15. Alone or with one or two other people, swimming at night in a remote bay, turning a swimming party into a scary adventure.

EXERCISE 3. *Revising Fragments in Context*

In the passage below, change the fragments into complete sentences.

The phone rang at 3:27 that Sunday afternoon, September 28, 1986. All of a sudden, two policemen sprang to their feet and ran for the squad car. A nervous dispatcher holding the phone and jotting down details, glancing out the window. Saw the officers speed away. He had to reach the paramedics. Not an easy task in a small rural community. Getting help to the house fast, remembering how alarmed the caller had sounded on the phone.

An 83-year-old man had been found in his house. Feared dead. A man who lived alone and seemed to be in good health. Even that very morning had gone out for a walk and had talked to his neighbors. He had seemed all right then, but later in the day neighbors who phoned him got no response. One neighbor had a key to his house. Worrying about the lack of response, about 3:20, decided to go into the house. Her husband walked across the street with her. No particular reason. But soon glad he was along.

Once inside the front door, they called the man's name. No response. They had wondered if he had fallen and could not get to his phone. If so, he would have answered when they walked in and called his name. Silence, eerie silence. Calling again, but getting no answer, became uneasy and started looking around. They had not gone far. When there he was. Lying on his bed, looking totally peaceful. Fully dressed, lying on a bed neatly made early that morning. He had pulled an extra blanket over him as if he had wanted a quick nap.

The neighbor touched his shoulder. No question in her mind. "George! Call the police!" she cried. He was halfway to the phone already. Right there, on the wall in the kitchen, only a few feet from the bedroom. He looked up a moment. The kitchen clock read 3:27. He dialed fast. Glancing around, he saw an important name and phone number written on a pad near the phone. The man's doctor. A name and number useful to the police dispatcher.

At 3:32 the police arrived. The doctor and the paramedics were there within minutes. But there was no rush. The doctor confirmed what had been feared. Death, probably by a heart attack. No sign of struggle, and no sign of foul play. The police calmed the neighbors, called the funeral director, then began to notify relatives. What relatives? The man's wife, an invalid in a nursing home in that town. Their one child, a daughter, living in another state. Her phone number had to be around the house somewhere. But where?

It was a beautiful autumn day. But not for shocked friends and neighbors. Not for the man's wife or daughter. Not for the police in that small town, yet they knew their job, and they did it professionally.

EXERCISE 4. *Handling Punctuation in Compound Units*

A. *If a comma should be added before the italicized conjunction, write a plus sign (+) on the line and add the comma.*
B. *If no comma is needed, write a zero (0) on the line.*
C. *Check your answers with those at the back of the book.*

Examples: ___+___ Dave likes duck hunting, *and* he also likes deer hunting.

___O___ Paul goes deer hunting *but* seldom gets a deer.

_____ 1. Venison steak is delicious *but* venison sausage is even better.

_____ 2. Deer hunting season opens soon *so* class attendance may drop off for the next few weeks.

_____ 3. Few hunters bother to write home *or* take the time to call home during their brief hunting trips.

_____ 4. Hunters often have wonderful stories to tell *and* love to share them with interested friends and family.

_____ 5. One young man, going deer hunting for the first time with his father and older brother, was a bit hesitant about the experience *but* his family encouraged him.

_____ 6. At his father's direction, he crept through the woods quietly *and* watched for signs of movement ahead.

_____ 7. Soon he thought he glimpsed a large figure move through the grass ahead *yet* he was too far away to be sure.

_____ 8. Stealthily he approached the area *for* he wanted to prove his hunting abilities.

_____ 9. The large creature was still there upon his approach *so* the young hunter raised his gun and steadied it.

_____ 10. Suddenly a firm hand grasped the young man's arm *and* brought the gun down swiftly, pointing it to the ground.

_____ 11. "Don't shoot that animal, son," said the father "*or* some farmer will be upset with you for shooting his cow."

_____ 12. The cow paid no attention *and* went on grazing.

EXERCISE 5. *Evaluating and Revising Compound Sentences*

A. *Read the sentences below and decide whether the conjunction links related or unrelated ideas.*
B. *If the ideas are related, revise the sentences to make the connections clear.*
C. *If the ideas are not related, make them stand apart in separate sentences.*

Example: We have received your order, but we cannot fill the order, for we manufacture the product, and we do not sell it retail.

We have received your order. However, we cannot fill it because we are manufacturers, not retailers.

1. I saw the postman deliver a package to my neighbor's house, but he was late that afternoon.

_____

_____

_____

2. The horse threw its rider to the ground almost at once, so the rodeo was exciting from its first moments.

_____

_____

_____

3. The pet shop ran a sale on cockatoos last week, and my grandmother had a parrot once.

_____

_____

_____

4. The best kind of soap to use has a cocoa butter base, or you can pamper your skin with special cleansers produced by cosmetic companies.

_____

_____

_____

5. Workers moved the crane across the intersection to the construction site before rush hour today, and I was late to work two days last week.

_____

_____

_____

6. Galileo made important discoveries as a mathematician and astronomer, and he was born in Italy.

_____

_____

_____

7. Narcissus blossoms are among the first flowers to appear in the spring, and the narcissus plant is related to the daffodil and jonquil plants.

_____

_____

_____

8. In Greek mythology, Narcissus was a young man who admired his own image in a pool of water, so he was transformed into the flower named "narcissus."

_____

_____

_____

9. The Tennessee River flows through eastern Tennessee, northern Alabama, western Tennessee, and western Kentucky, and our neighbors lived here in Tennessee, but then they moved to Arkansas.

_____

_____

_____

10. I was happy to see you at the football game last Saturday, so call me after work, and we can go to next week's game, or I will call you sometime, and we can make other plans.

_____

_____

_____

11. The word *cubbyhole* is familiar, but it uses the root word *cubby* that is obsolete, and both words mean a small compartment or room.

_____

_____

_____

12. Broccoli, Brussels sprouts, and cauliflower are members of the cabbage family, and Brussels sprouts grow on the side of a thick stem.

_____

_____

_____

13. Cauliflower is named for its compact, whitish flower, and that flower is the edible part.

_____

_____

_____

14. The word *cauliflower* can be traced to Italian root words, and they mean "flowered cabbage."

_____

_____

_____

15. Peanuts are grown in semitropical regions, but few people realize that the edible part ripens underground.

_____

_____

_____

EXERCISE 6. *Repairing Fragments and Run-ons*

A. *In the following passage, revise the fragments to create complete sentences.*
B. *Repair run-ons either by using a comma plus a coordinating conjunction or a semicolon or by creating separate sentences.*
C. *Write your revisions between the lines.*

Biographers write interesting accounts of James Brown. A self-made man in the Horatio Alger tradition. Brown lived in Boston in the early nineteenth century. As a young man, he worked as a printer's apprentice, in that way, he learned the mechanics of book publishing. Later he clerked in a book store. Ideal opportunity for learning the strategies of book selling. Still later Brown joined another bookseller/book publisher as a partner, and with that partner, he built a thriving firm.

Brown worked long and hard to become a successful book dealer and book publisher, however, he had many strong competitors. Probably working as long and hard as he was. In Boston and other major cities at that time, many small businesses were run by booksellers who also published books and magazines. These businesses sprang up, flourished for a few years, merged with others, or died, that was a typical pattern.

The entrepreneurs moved from company to company. Putting their names on company publications at one place or another. Some of those publications survive today, therefore, we can tell who was working with whom at a given time.

By all indications, James Brown sought success and stability, he yearned for more than a few years' employment one place, then a few years somewhere else. He needed a way to stand apart from his competitors. Finally found a way to do exactly that. He used his personal interest in rare books, then he built a reputation for his extensive knowledge and sound judgment concerning rare books.

For sale in his store, Brown gathered an unusual stock of books, many of those works came from England and Europe. He watched for forced sales of books by impoverished nobility or for sales of valuable works for other reasons. The bankruptcy sales of those private libraries probably meant big losses to their owners, but correspondingly big gains for James Brown, he attended those sales himself, or he sent his well-instructed agents. Over time, his retail store stocked many valuable and unusual books he had found a distinctive market angle and one that paid off handsomely.

By the 1850s, Brown had earned a fortune in the book business. He invested a great deal of money in expanding the business, then he invested in a home in the country. There he experimented with fruit trees, he wanted good results. Discouraged, kept trying for trees hearty enough for northern climates. He devoted much effort to his amateur experiments in horticulture, but with little success. He knew the rewards of hard work, he had seen his business grow into a prosperous firm. But with too little knowledge of horticulture and too severe a climate to overcome, even the successful James Brown met defeat.

EXERCISE 7.   Repairing Fragments and Run-ons

A. *In the following passage, revise the fragments to create complete sentences.*
B. *Repair run-ons by using a comma plus a coordinating conjunction or a semicolon or by creating separate sentences.*
C. *Write your revisions between the lines.*

Biographers also write interesting accounts of Charles Coffin Little, another self-made man. Time and place, early nineteenth-century Boston. Like many other young men of his day, Little worked for a time as a printer's apprentice then he became a bookseller and publisher himself. For a few years, he joined the companies of others, for instance, in the early 1830s, his name appears on publications with Boston publishers Hilliard, Gray, and Wilkins.

A few years later, books appeared with his own imprint, namely, the Charles C. Little Company, then in 1837, publications appeared with a new name on the imprint, the partnership between Charles C. Little and James Brown had begun.

Little was described by associates as a thorough businessman and a gentleman. Known to be honorable in all his dealings. Little, Brown grew so much that by the 1850s, fifteen presses ran steadily. This number may sound small today, but in the 1850s, it represented the work of a sizable publishing company.

Around 1850, the company won a contract with the United States government to publish all the laws of the country. A large amount of capital was involved, consequently, Little, Brown stabilized and grew. The partners had seen their work flourish in previous years, but with that opportunity, the turning point had arrived for the business.

In 1852, Redding & Company, Boston, published a book entitled *The Rich Men of Massachusetts: Containing a Statement of the Reputed Wealth of about Two Thousand Persons* the book can still be found in research libraries. According to that book, Brown and Little had wealth estimated at $200,000 and $300,000, respectively. In 1986 purchasing power, those amounts equal approximately $3,700,000 and $5,500,000. Two self-made men had done well personally moreover they left a well-established company as a legacy.

EXERCISE 8. *Writing and Revising Your Sentences*

Write ten sentences on one of the following topics or on a topic suggested by your professor:

A. *You may have had the uneasy feeling that something was wrong, but you could not tell what it was, an experience similar to that of the neighbors described in Exercise 3 above. Or you may have felt uneasy in a new situation such as that experienced by the young hunter in Exercise 4 above. Describe a situation in which you were uneasy, indicating both the situation and your feelings.*

B. *You may know of someone who began modestly but succeeded beyond all expectations, as did James Brown and Charles Little. That person's success may be measured in money or fame or in some other way. Describe that person and that success.*

1. _____

2. _____

3. _____

4. _____

5. _____

6. _____

7. _____

8. _____

9. _____

10. _____

Now go back and review those sentences, revising them as necessary to correct such problems as comma splices, fragments, or fused sentences.

EXERCISE 9.   *Revising Student Sentences*

A. *In the following passages, correct all fragments and run-on sentences. Remember that semicolons, when used, separate complete, independent thoughts.*
B. *Examine compound sentences to determine whether the two independent thoughts are closely related. If not, create separate sentences.*
C. *Write your revisions between the lines.*

These examples were written by students in response to Exercise 8. As you read them, consider what is effective about these examples. Think, for instance, of the word choice. Is it exact and vivid? Consider the pacing of the stories being told. Is it rapid enough to hold your interest?

Example 1

One Sunday I was returning from the grocery store, and I was pulling out of the parking lot onto the street. A woman was coming toward me, she was turning into the parking lot. All the while honking her horn and pointing her finger. I turned to see if she was making those gestures at me, and she was. I had no idea why she was acting that way, so I frowned and started pointing at her. I finally pulled out onto the main street, I went straight home. But while I was driving, more cars started honking. Some of them flashing their lights on and off. I finally got home. I was still thinking about all the cars honking at me, then I found out that I didn't have my headlights on. I felt bad for all the people who were trying to help me, and I just thought they were crazy. I felt especially bad for the woman who first tried to help me.

Example 2

Last spring, I participated in the state hockey tournament. During the final game, in the third period, the score was two to two. Three minutes remaining. We had two people in the penalty box, and our opponents had a great chance to win with the two-man advantage. I was on the ice, skating all the while. If we made one mistake, they would win. Suddenly their defenseman lost the puck, it went over the blue line. As their team regrouped in their zone; I gambled and went after their defenseman with the puck. I had to make the play, they would have a four on two coming back. I got lucky, I stole the puck away. Suddenly I had a breakaway. It was just the goalie and me left in deciding if we would win or not. As soon as I crossed their blue line, I shot a low slapshot toward the corner of the goal, usually a slapshot on a breakaway isn't the smartest thing to do. However, the shot beat the goalie, we went on to win three to two.

Example 3

One night while living alone in an unsecured downtown apartment, I was awakened by a piercing shriek from one of my three cats. Startled, I jumped out of bed. In the living room I found three wide-eyed cats staring at me, the front door was wide open. I broke out in a cold sweat. Fearing an intruder. Flipping on the lights; I started to look around. After a thorough search, and finding no sign of an intruder, I concluded that the door must have been left unlatched. I felt better after that, however, it still did not explain the cat's odd behavior. Later while in the bathroom, I discovered a clump of fur along the rim of the toilet seat, the seat was closed. With this piece of evidence, I realized the seat must have fallen on one of the cats drinking out of the bowl. Feeling safe again, I gathered up the cats and comforted them, before going to bed again, I vowed to double-check the front door every night. Also to keep the toilet seat down from then on.

UNIT I PRACTICE TEST
Chapters 1, 2, 3

(70 POINTS)

Read each question carefully. Mark your answer to the left of the sentence. Check your answers with those at the back of the book.

A. TRUE-FALSE

_____ 1. When a linking verb is used, a subject complement usually is found in the sentence.

_____ 2. An adverb can modify verbs, adjectives, and other adverbs.

_____ 3. An adjective can modify nouns, prepositions, and conjunctions.

_____ 4. Because a proper noun names a specific person, place, or thing, it is capitalized.

_____ 5. The following words are typical prepositions: *not, never, always, quickly,* and *soon.*

_____ 6. A prepositional phrase consists of a preposition and its object, sometimes with modifiers.

_____ 7. A helping verb is always followed by a direct object.

_____ 8. The subject of a sentence must precede the verb.

_____ 9. A complete sentence must have either a direct object or a subject complement.

_____ 10. Sentence fragments occur when we remove prepositional phrases to find subjects, verbs, objects, or complements.

_____ 11. A sentence must have a subject and a verb, but sometimes the subject can be the understood *you.*

_____ 12. Comma splices consist of two or more separate independent thoughts put together with only a comma.

_____ 13. Pronouns change form according to their use; this quality is called *case.*

_____ 14. Typical action verbs include *is, are, was, were,* and *am.*

_____ 15. Typical helping verbs include *is, can, may,* and *shall.*

_____ 16. An indirect object can follow either an action or a linking verb, but it must come before a direct object.

_____ 17. A comma is always used with a coordinating conjunction.

_____ 18. Compound sentences consist of two or more separate, independent ideas, properly joined with a comma plus a conjunction or with a semicolon alone.

_____ 19. To find the direct object, ask these questions after a linking verb: To whom? For whom?

_____ 20. In the following sentence, the word *her* acts like an adjective, modifying the noun *test:* The student finished her test in forty minutes.

_____ 21. The sentence pattern in the sample sentence in Question 20 is S + AV + DO.

_____ 22. In the sample sentence in Question 20, there is only one prepositional phrase; it starts with the word *test.*

B. MATCHING

Examine the italicized words in the sentences below and identify them as one of the following:

    a. adjective   d. pronoun
    b. adverb   e. verb
    c. preposition

_____ 23. The *dancing* bear entertained the children at the fair.

_____ 24. *Who* could imagine such a sight?

_____ 25. It was *dancing* to a waltz played by the band.

_____ 26. As we watched, it waltzed faster *across* the floor.

_____ 27. Joan and Peggy are *nearly* finished with their lunch.

_____ 28. The *nearest* exit is near the aisle.

_____ 29. *She* and Kristina joined Hugh and me for lunch.

_____ 30. Surely the manager *would* accept a check with proper ID.

_____ 31. My check has *seldom* been turned down in restaurants.

_____ 32. The décor here is *lovely*.

_____ 33. Hugh *tasted* his soup and told us that it was excellent.

_____ 34. *Are* you ready to order dessert?

_____ 35. I have always *been* fond of desserts.

_____ 36. Carolyn skipped lunch to study for her *history* exam.

_____ 37. Her studying ran *beyond* lunch time, into the afternoon.

_____ 38. She had *never* studied so hard before.

C. MATCHING

For the following sentences, mark a, b, c, or d to correspond to the sentence pattern shown.

     a. S + AV   c. S + AV + IO + DO
     b. S + AV + DO   d. S + LV + SC

_____ 39. After the storm, the children played in the snow.

_____ 40. They ran after the dog and chased him away.

_____ 41. Then they built a snowman and a snow fort.

_____ 42. They gave the snowman a black hat to wear.

_____ 43. In the ice and snow, behind the garage and near the patio, there stands the abandoned barbecue pit.

_____ 44. How can we barbecue anything in the winter?

_____ 45. The patio is useless during the long months of winter.

_____ 46. Charcoal-broiled steak tastes wonderful anytime.

_____ 47. Flowers around the edges of the patio bloom beautifully in the summer and fall.

_____ 48. Steak, salad, and vegetables provide our guests a tasty meal.

_____ 49. The little girl on the swing looks straight ahead.

_____ 50. She and her brother are the neighbor's children.

_____ 51. They skate and ride their bikes past our house every day.

_____ 52. The wholesaler offers customers a discount for quantity sales of that product.

_____ 53. Will you return that book to the library soon?

D. MULTIPLE CHOICE

Read each of the sample sentences carefully. Then answer the questions that follow.

The small child near the street was in great danger, but his mother ran quickly and snatched him away.

54. The comma after the word _danger_ is
   a. correct
   b. incorrect

55. One subject-verb relationship is
   a. street/was
   b. street/danger
   c. child/was
   d. child/danger

56. Another subject-verb relationship is
   a. mother/ran
   b. mother/ran, snatched
   c. child/ran, snatched
   d. child/ran

57. One prepositional phrase is
   a. the small child
   b. ran quickly
   c. was in great danger
   d. near the street

58. The adverbs are
    a. small, quickly, away
    b. near, quickly, him
    c. quickly, away
    d. danger, away

59. The adjectives are
    a. small, great, his
    b. small, the, quickly
    c. his, quickly, away
    d. great, ran, his

60. The words *in great danger* are
    a. part of the compound subject
    b. part of the compound verb
    c. a prepositional phrase
    d. an interjection

61. The first part of the sentence contains a linking verb, but the second part contains
    a. action verbs without objects
    b. one action verb and one direct object
    c. an action verb, an indirect object, and a direct object
    d. two action verbs, one of which has a direct object

After the surprise birthday party, the guest of honor thanked the host and hostess.

62. How many prepositional phrases are in the sentence?
    a. one
    b. two
    c. three
    d. four

63. The subject complement is
    a. honor
    b. host, hostess
    c. party
    d. none of the above

64. The adjectives are
    a. surprise, honor
    b. after, surprise
    c. host, hostess
    d. surprise, birthday

65. The sentence pattern is
    a. S + AV
    b. S + AV + DO
    c. S + AV + IO + DO
    d. S + LV + SC

In the midst of the dangers of the raging battle, there stood the brave soldier with his country's flag.

66. How many prepositional phrases does the sentence contain?
    a. two
    b. three
    c. four
    d. five

67. What is the subject-verb relationship?
    a. there/stood
    b. battle/raging
    c. soldier/raging
    d. soldier/stood

68. What is the direct object?
    a. dangers
    b. soldier
    c. flag
    d. none of the above

69. How is the word *battle* used?
    a. object of a preposition
    b. direct object
    c. subject complement
    d. indirect object

70. What is the sentence pattern?
    a. S + AV
    b. S + AV + DO
    c. S + AV + IO + DO
    d. S + LV + SC

CHOOSING PRONOUNS AND VERBS

OBJECTIVES

Grammar and Sentence Structure

To choose correct pronouns for subjects and objects

To overcome common problems with verbs

To master subject-verb agreement

Writing

To put sentences together into unified paragraphs with topic ideas

To apply paragraphing principles in short memos and letters

4

Working with Subjects

Selecting Pronouns

Nouns are the natural choice to be subjects because they name the persons, places, or things about which we write or speak. As noun substitutes, pronouns can serve the same purposes as nouns. In the paired sentences below, notice that pronouns work as subjects just as nouns do. (Again, subjects are underlined once, verbs twice.)

Professor Martin began class with a summary of yesterday's lecture. Then she asked for the papers due today.

Jim lost his backpack this morning. He ran to the bookstore to buy another notebook before class.

Clouds passed by the window. They covered the sun for a few minutes.

Although these pairs of sentences express separate thoughts in separate sentences, there is a continuation of thought from one sentence to the next. In each pair of sentences, the pronoun at the start of the second sentence reaches across sentence borders and ties the ideas together by referring to a noun: the word *she* refers to *Professor Martin; he* refers to *Jim; they* refers to *clouds.*

In our writing, we want to tie ideas together to make smooth transitions from sentence to sentence. One way to build continuity was discussed in Chapter 3: connecting related ideas in compound sentences. Two methods of connecting those ideas were stressed: using a comma plus a coordinating conjunction and using a semicolon, with or without transitional words.

Using pronouns is not a substitute for those methods of connecting independent thoughts; it is merely another way to enhance continuity from sentence to sentence.

Join these sentences with a comma plus a coordinating conjunction or a semicolon. Add transitional words if you like.

   Example: We finished Unit 1, _so_ now we can begin Unit 2.

1. Professor Martin began class with a summary of yesterday's lecture

   _____ she asked for the papers due today.

2. Jim lost his backpack this morning _____ he ran to the bookstore to buy another notebook before class.

3. Clouds passed by the window _____ they covered the sun for a few minutes.

PRONOUN-ANTECEDENT CONNECTIONS

   The pronouns in the sentences above make sense because we know exactly to whom or to what they refer. The person or thing to which a pronoun refers is called an ***antecedent,*** which means that which goes before.

   If a pronoun has more than one possible antecedent, readers can become confused, or they may misunderstand. Consider, for example, this statement:

   When the car hit the truck, *it* rolled over.

   What happened? Here are two possible interpretations of that statement:

   1. When the car hit the truck, the car rolled over.
   2. When the car hit the truck, the truck rolled over.

   Either interpretation could be correct. We can't tell for sure what happened because the pronoun *it* has two possible antecedents, *truck* and *car.*

   Readers should not have to guess what writers mean; writers have a responsibility to make their meaning clear. We can avoid confusion over pronoun reference if we pay attention to the connections between pronouns and their antecedents.

Revise the following sentences to make the pronoun references clear. Write your revisions between the lines.

1. Parents of the seniors arranged the class party. They chose June 3 for the date. (Who chose the date?)

2. We need a mechanic or a service station attendant to reattach this hose. He should need only a few minutes. (Who needs only a few minutes?)

3. Scrambled eggs, granola muffins, pecan waffles, and blueberry pancakes were on the menu. They were Phil's favorite breakfast. (What is Phil's favorite breakfast—all of these items or just one?)

References after pronouns are less common, but possible. Then the word *antecedent* does not apply literally, though the pronoun still has a reference. Readers can connect the pronoun and its reference if the two words are reasonably close together. In these sentences, arrows connect the pronoun and its reference:

After *he* attended classes, Paul went to work.

Though *they* played a great game for the first three quarters, our team lost by two touchdowns in the last quarter.

PRACTICE 3

As in the previous examples, draw arrows from the italicized pronouns to their antecedents.

1. Because the Ohio River is formed where the Allegheny and Monongahela rivers join, *it* begins as a large river.

2. After *it* flows west and southwest for nearly a thousand miles, the Ohio River joins the Mississippi River at Cairo, Illinois.

3. The Allegheny and Monongahela rivers converge at Pittsburgh; at that point *they* form the Ohio River.

4. After *it* flows south about 2,350 miles through the middle of the continent, water from the Mississippi River enters the Gulf of Mexico.

AGREEMENT IN GENDER AND NUMBER

Regardless of their placement or order, antecedents and pronouns ordinarily connect easily, provided they agree in gender, number, and person—that is, singular with singular, plural with plural, masculine with masculine, and so forth.

As readers, we do not notice agreement between pronouns and their antecedents because the reading is smooth and easy to understand. Like travelers on a well-kept highway, we move along without thinking about the smooth ride. A mismatch or lack of agreement lurches us like potholes in the roadway.

You have seen many examples of agreement in gender and number (singular versus plural) in the past few pages. For instance, at the beginning of the chapter, the pronoun *he* was used to refer to *Jim*. The connection was smooth and natural.

By contrast, consider the lurching effect caused in the sentences below by the writer's shifting back and forth from singular to plural. These statements come from instructions given to cashiers. Notice the singular and plural words that are italicized:

> You have asked the *customer* how *they* are paying for this *purchase*. In the next line of your *sales slips*, you need to circle whether *it* is cash, check, or charge.

PRACTICE 4

Rewrite the two statements above, using singular or plural words consistently.

_____

_____

_____

Next, revise the following directions to use singular or plural words consistently. Make your revisions between the lines.

This memo provides you with detailed information on processing loan checks for students. When loan checks come in, take the following steps:

1. Find their blue cards in the files.

2. Write their ID number from the blue card and put it on the slip that is provided with the check.

3. Look up in the computer how many credits the student is taking.

4. Look up their name in the student loan book. Make sure their credits are matched with the loan application. If it says full-time, they must be taking at least twelve credits.

APPROPRIATENESS IN GENDER AND NUMBER

In addition to using clear antecedents and agreement in our writing, we want to make appropriate choices with respect to pronouns and other words. Two areas require special care: avoiding sexist references and avoiding misunderstanding over collective words.

Sexism in language creates resentment on the part of many readers. Writers may offend readers inadvertently, simply by following the tradition of using singular masculine pronoun forms to refer to human beings in general, as in this example:

> When a teacher makes assignments, *he* should give clear directions.

Though the pronoun *he* is traditional, it is sexist language and is best avoided. The idea is better expressed through different wording. Plural forms often provide an escape from sexist wording. Consider this version of the same sentence:

> When teachers make assignments, *they* should give clear directions.

Notice how smoothly the plural *they* avoids the use of the masculine singular form. Another option, suitable occasionally, is *he/she* or *he or she* (*he/his* or *his or her*), but that usage is awkward and soon becomes tiresome. For generalizations applying to many people, places, or things, plural statements are more graceful.

PRACTICE 5

Revise these sentences to eliminate sexism, to create agreement in number, and to make pronoun-antecedent references clear. Note that several changes in wording might be needed for agreement. Write your revisions between the lines.

Example: An author often works many years on a manuscript before *Authors often work on manuscripts many years before they are ready to submit them to publishers.* he is ready to submit it to a publisher.

1. Two British authors with the surname Lawrence lived from the 1880s to the 1930s, D. H. Lawrence and Thomas Edward Lawrence, but he used a different pen name.

2. Authors who want pen names select one, just as Thomas Edward Lawrence selected T. E. Shaw, and they use it as they like ever after.

3. A woman writer in the nineteenth century had good reason to use a masculine pen name, but they didn't always choose to do so.

4. American writer Harriet Beecher Stowe was one example of women using their own names.

Another problem can arise with **collective nouns,** which can complicate agreement in number. A collective noun refers to a single group made up of many individual members. Examples of collective nouns are *family, class, team, jury, faculty, crowd,* and *staff.* When a collective noun is the antecedent, we must first decide whether it is used in a singular or plural sense. However it is used, all references to it must agree, including other nouns, pronouns, possessive pronouns used as adjectives, and verbs.

Sometimes we can determine whether a singular or plural sense is implied by examining the context. If not, we must use common sense, using the following guidelines:

- When the group is acting as a unit, use a singular pronoun to agree with that single, unified group.

    The *jury* returned a guilty verdict after *it* had deliberated three hours.

- When members of the group act separately, use a plural pronoun to agree with the plural members.

    The *class* worked on *their* writing projects an hour because *they* wanted to create good papers.

CONSISTENCY OF PERSON

The most difficult pronouns to manage with respect to consistency are the second-person pronouns: the word *you* and all its forms (*your, yours, yourself*), used to designate the person written or spoken to.

Second-person pronouns are natural and useful. They make direct, immediate contact with the other person or persons, whether in speech or in writing. When we consistently address others in the second person, or when we deliberately move from general third-person statements to direct second-person statements, we are probably safe in using the second person.

By contrast, careless drifting into second person is confusing and illogical. Notice the jarring effects of shifts from third person (*students*) to second person (*you*) in this passage:

> To get the most from class, students should listen for the main points in the lecture and take careful notes. You can easily be lost if you let your mind wander. Students should try to review their notes soon after a lecture. You reinforce your memory by reviewing.

The entire passage is about students, not about you, the reader.

PRACTICE 6 _____

Revise the above passage to address the reader, or revise it to remain in the third person. Once you choose second or third person, use it consistently.

_____

_____

_____

_____

_____

In that passage, you had the choice of second or third person. Generally, second person is more casual and direct. It is ideal for giving instructions or advice, but because it is informal, second person is not appropriate in some business and professional settings.

Regardless of whether you choose second or third person, the principle of consistency is important. Do not shift carelessly, for no reason, from one person to the other. (Exercise 6, given later in this chapter, provides practice in spotting and correcting shifts.)

OTHER PROBLEMS OF PRONOUN SELECTION

The following two questions about pronouns are sometimes asked:

- When do we use pronouns ending with *self* and *selves*? (These words are called reflexive/intensive pronouns.)
- How are *this* and *that*, *these* and *those* used? (These words are called demonstrative pronouns.)

REFLEXIVE/INTENSIVE PRONOUNS

The word *reflexive* sounds like *reflecting*, a useful similarity because reflexive pronouns reflect back on the antecedent, as in the following examples:

> I hurt myself.
> He pushed himself too hard.

Think of *intensive* as similar to *intensifying*. Intensive pronouns add emphasis, thus intensifying meaning. In the following pairs of sentences, contrast the rather bland statements with the intensified statements:

> You must do it.
> You must do it yourself.

> That letter was written by George Washington.
> That letter was written by George Washington himself.

PRACTICE 7

Create two sentences using reflexive/intensive pronouns.

1. _____

2. _____

DEMONSTRATIVE PRONOUNS

Four words, all used to point out or demonstrate, belong in this category: *this, that, these,* and *those.* These words work as adjectives; *this* and *that* are used to modify singular nouns, and *these* and *those* are used to modify plural nouns:

> *this* book or *these* books
> *that* window or *those* windows

The words *this* or *that* are sometimes used vaguely in reference to the entire preceding idea. Here is an example:

> *Vague:*   After we had waited in line two hours, the concert was abruptly canceled without explanation. This made us angry.
> *Improved:* After we had waited in line two hours, the concert was abruptly canceled without explanation. This thoughtless treatment of fans made us angry.

Revise the following sentences to make the references of the italicized pronouns clear.

Example: The truck must be checked for fuel and oil as well as air pressure in the tires. *That* is very important.

The truck must be checked for . . . tires.

That inspection is very important.

1. The season tickets cost three dollars less than we expected. *This* was a happy surprise.

   _____

   _____

2. The new highway turns sharply to the east beside the water tower. *That* is a strange sight.

   _____

   _____

3. The fifty-foot tower was cleaned inside and out, then painted last summer. *That* was a hot, dangerous job.

   _____

   _____

Using Subject-Form Pronouns

Unlike nouns, which change forms only when changing from singular to plural, pronouns change forms according to their uses in sentences. This sentence from Chapter 1 illustrates the various forms of pronouns:

He gave *his* book to the student near *him.*

Though the pronouns *he, his,* and *him* all refer to the same person, no one pronoun would fit into all three positions in that sentence. Of the three, only the word *he* can work as a subject.

The following pronouns are commonly used as subjects:

I	you	he	it
we	they	she	who, whoever

These words are sometimes called *nominative case pronouns*, but if you think of them as subject-form pronouns, you will have a simpler label and one that reminds you of their use.

Although most of the time we have no difficulty choosing the proper pronouns for subjects, we may need reminders of several special uses which are covered in the following sections.

First, use subject-form pronouns whether the pronoun is part of the subject or is the entire subject:

> *He* walks too fast.
> *Michael, Joe, Carl, Paul,* and *he* walk too fast.
> *We girls* cannot walk that fast.
> The *cheerleaders* and *we spectators* cheered wildly.

When the pronoun is only part of the subject, as in the last three examples above, it helps to reverse the order of the subjects or to ignore the other parts of the subject. For instance, the last sample sentence could be changed to one of these versions:

> *We spectators* and the *cheerleaders* cheered wildly.
> *or*
> *We* cheered wildly.

By isolating the pronoun part of the subject, we can more easily select the right pronoun.

PRACTICE 9

A. Underline all parts of the subjects in these sentences.

> **Example:** <u>Book reviewers, critics, teachers, and we readers</u> enjoy well-told stories.

1. The Brontë sisters and Jane Austen were nineteenth-century British novelists, and they and their books are still read and respected.

2. Ann, Charlotte, and Emily Brontë all used the surname *Bell* as a pen name, but it is seldom remembered, except by literary scholars.

3. We readers and the book reviewers are less conscious of pen names than of the books themselves.

B. Underline the correct pronoun in these sentences.

4. Because Jane Austen lived about a generation ahead of the Brontës, (she, her) and (they, them) could never meet.

5. Like the Brontës, British novelist Mary Ann Evans used a pen name, but unlike them, (she, her) is still remembered by that name, George Eliot.

6. Several of my high school classmates and (I, me) dreamed of writing profes-sionally, but only Mona and (I, me) have published any writing.

The second point to remember is to use a subject-form pronoun as the subject of an incomplete comparison:

> He is taller than *I.*
> > (meaning: He is taller than I am.)
>
> We have worked as hard as *they.*
> > (meaning: We have worked as hard as they have.)

When we find incomplete comparisons, we find them at the ends of sentences. They begin with *than* or *as,* and a comparison is implied but not written or spoken in full, just as the sample sentences show. We think through the entire meaning first; then we put in the pronoun that fits. In the examples above, the subject-form fits perfectly as the subject of the implied verb.

PRACTICE 10 _____

Underline the correct choices in the following sentences.

1. The young golfer was surprised to learn that the caddie was older than (he, him).

2. The tournament sponsors disagreed with the golf pro, in that they wanted more publicity than (he, him).

3. Radio and television reporters wanted even more publicity than (they, them).

The third point is the following: when confronted with a choice between *who* and *whom,* use *who* if a verb needs a subject.

> *Who* left his car in the no-parking zone?
> *Whoever* left it there may get a ticket.

The alternative form *whoever* works exactly like *who,* just as *whomever* works like *whom.* These pronouns are often used in a part of the sentence called a **dependent clause** (to be discussed in detail in Chapter 9). For now, it is enough to know that a dependent clause is a second subject-verb unit inside a sentence, but that second unit is secondary in its importance and meaning.

The important thing to notice here is the use of the word *who* as a subject for a verb, even when the subject-verb unit is used within a larger structure.

Underline the subject of the "who" clause once and the verb twice in these sentences.

> **Example:** After the parking lot was full, a <u>driver</u>, who <u>arrived</u> late, left his car in a no-parking zone.

1. Officer Smith, who drove past the school, saw the car parked in the no-parking zone.

2. Mike Andrews, who had parked his car illegally, got a ticket.

3. We watched from the window and wondered who was getting the ticket.

Finally, remember to use subject-form pronouns as subject complements.

PRACTICE 12

In the following sentences, underline the subjects once and the verbs twice and circle the subject complements.

> **Example:** The <u>winners</u> <u>were</u> (Larry and she) ᔆᶜ

1. It is I.

2. The speaker was he.

3. The leaders were Dr. Mary Nichols and she.

These sample sentences follow one of the patterns learned earlier: S + LV + SC. Because the subject complement is so closely tied to the subject, it makes sense to use the same form of pronoun for both the subject and the subject complement.

Points to Use

- Treat individual complete thoughts (sentences) as separate units to be divided visually with a capital letter at the beginning and a period at the end. When individual sentences are closely related in thought, they can be joined by a comma plus a coordinating conjunction (FANBOYS) or by a semicolon (with or without a transitional word).

- Make sure each pronoun has a single clear reference.
- Make pronouns and their references agree in gender, number, and person.
- Use pronouns in ways that avoid sexist language.
- Avoid unnecessary shifts in gender, number, and person; pay special attention to the hazards of shifting from second- to third-person pronouns.
- Use reflexive/intensive pronouns to reflect on the subject or intensify meaning.
- Avoid using *this* and *that* vaguely in reference to an entire previous idea.
- Use subject-form pronouns as the subject of a sentence or the subject of an incomplete comparison.
- Use the subject-form pronouns *who* and *whoever* as subjects for verbs, whether the subject-verb unit is the main one in a sentence or a secondary one.
- Use subject-form pronouns as subject complements in formal usage.

Points to Remember

- Nouns and subject-form pronouns are used as subjects.
- When independent thoughts are closely related, they can be joined either with a comma plus a coordinating conjunction or with a semicolon.
- Pronouns tie ideas together by referring to nouns in other sentences or other parts of the same sentence.
- An antecedent is a noun to which the pronoun refers and from which it takes on meaning. Generally, the antecedent precedes the pronoun.
- Pronouns must match or agree with their antecedents in gender, number, and person.
- Subject-form pronouns are also called *nominative case* pronouns. The term *case* refers to the various forms of pronouns used within sentences.
- Subject-form pronouns are used as part or all of a subject, including subjects implied in incomplete comparisons.
- Subject-form pronouns include *who, he, she, they, I we, you.*
- Pronouns used as subject complements should be in subject form because of their close relationship with the subject.

EXERCISE 1.   Selecting Pronouns

Circle the letter of the better version, a or b, in the pairs of sentences below. Check your answers with those at the back of the book.

1. a. It must have been she who called me.
   b. It must have been her who called me.

2. a. The neighbors and we shared the cost of the fencing.
   b. The neighbors and us shared the cost of the fencing.

3. a. Us teachers insist on good grammar. This is only natural for teachers.
   b. We teachers insist on good grammar. This attitude is only natural for teachers.

4. a. John, Mike, Pat, and she were there.
   b. John, Mike, Pat, and her were there.

5. a. It was them who found the stolen car.
   b. It was they who found the stolen car.

6. a. Our family has fewer problems than them.
   b. Our family has fewer problems than they.

7. a. I think it was he that I saw.
   b. I think it was him that I saw.

8. a. Are we girls invited to the party?
   b. Are us girls invited to the party?

9. a. The witness said he was sure it was her.
   b. The witness said he was sure it was she.

10. a. As soon as the students left the rooms, the janitors searched them.
    b. As soon as the students left, the janitors searched the rooms.

11. a. Barbara and Tom dance better than Michelle and him.
    b. Barbara and Tom dance better than Michelle and he.

12. a. It is true that we students work hard in this class.
    b. It is true that us students work hard in this class.

13. a. Who was the one to leave first?
    b. Whom was the one to leave first?

14. a. When John talks with Paul, he always learns a lot.
    b. John always learns a lot when he talks with Paul.

EXERCISE 2.   Selecting Pronouns

Underline the correct choices in the following sentences. Check your answers with those at the back of the book.

1. Paul is a person (who, whom) is well qualified for that job.

2. But who can tell whether the best-qualified person is (he, him)?

3. Paul sent his letter to Mitchell Ross, Personnel Director, and (they, he) answered at once.

4. Few personnel directors answer as quickly as (he, him).

5. (We, Us) job applicants often wait weeks for replies.

6. Mike, Steve, and (he, him) began work on Monday.

7. Paul said, "(We, Us) beginners would have been lost without our supervisor's directions."

8. Do you know (who, whom) the new student is?

9. Jane and (she, her) have already become friends.

10. Because we are both new here, (she, her) and (me, I) have a lot in common.

11. Often (we, us) newcomers feel ill at ease.

12. A friendly student like Jane will have friends all (her, their) (life, lives).

13. When students are in new surroundings, (they, he, he/she) must work at getting acquainted.

14. Megan and (she, her) were more helpful than Arlene and (she, her).

15. It is (she, her) (who, whom) must make the first move.

16. The teacher said it was (they, them) (who, whom) should direct the newcomer to the cafeteria.

17. The student (who, whom) sits in the front row often contributes to the class discussion.

18. Laurie, Terry, Kevin, Andy, and (he, him) spend many hours working on their homework.

19. Some students spend less time on homework than (he, him) and (I, me).

20. It seems that Keith, Judy, Ken, and (she, her) get their work done in little time.

21. Neither Tim nor (he, him) got to school on time.

22. It was (he, him) working at the library yesterday.

23. The librarians found the newspaper articles Ken needed for his history report. (This, This assistance) helped him finish on time.

24. Reference librarians can find material quickly. (You, We, Students) really appreciate their skills.

25. It is reasonable that (we, us) students must spend a great deal of time in the library. (This, This effort) goes along with being a college student.

26. It was (they, them) whom we saw last night at the university library.

27. When Brad or (he, him) is absent, Molly takes notes for him.

28. The university libraries are open to all, and (it, they) serve thousands of users per year.

29. Specialized research libraries and archives are restricted to serious researchers with special permission, but it is (they, them) who need the facilities.

30. Scholars, writers, and (we, us) historians need specialized collections, like those at the Newberry Library in Chicago and the American Antiquarian Society in Worcester, Massachusetts.

EXERCISE 3.   Revising to Improve Sentences and Pronoun Choice

Revise the following letters, correcting pronoun choices, fragments, and run-ons. Replace compound sentences with separate sentences where appropriate. You may make other improvements in wording and in arrangement of ideas, if you find ways to do so.

These letters were written by college freshmen.

Letter 1

Dear Skip,

I am glad to hear from you, and you are smart to plan a vacation here. For those two weeks, you are in for the time of your life.

Before you come, let me tell you about Laguna. Nestled along the shore, among the cliffs, Laguna Beach is perhaps the most beautiful of all southern California cities, and it is bounded by beach for about five miles. As you enter the city, you will see one of the most enchanting views of the Pacific. Tourists like to stop at the Sunshine Cove roadside stand for the best date shake in the world. On the right of the highway is the crystal blue ocean, and the waves are coming in against the rocks. People like to look up at colorful homes set into the hills. Also remember to look for Irvine Cove and Emerald Bay.

Laguna Beach is known for its artists' colony, and you may want to see the Laguna Museum of Art. Even when there are no special events, there is always something to do. Maybe window shopping at the stylish boutiques, or eating at a restaurant, Mexican seafood or Hawaiian-style ribs. To just being lazy on the beach, catching sunshine and people watching.

I am looking forward to seeing you, take care for now, I have to get back to the beach.

Letter 2

Dear Craig,

I am happy to hear that you can come along with me to Winnipeg this summer. I will tell you about some of the things I found of interest there last year, later I can send more information about hotels and tourist attractions if you have questions.

The night of our arrival will be the first night of Folklorama, and it is one of the largest cultural celebrations in North America. Each cultural group has a separate pavilion, and there are about forty pavilions located throughout the city. A typical pavilion offers native food, drink, and entertainment. For a small fee, you can buy admission to all the pavilions, and you also get information about all of them in the form of a passport booklet. The fee also includes a shuttle service to each pavilion.

Another interesting attraction is Lower Fort Garry National Historic Park. The fort has been fully restored to resemble the mid-1800s fur trade period. Park employees dress in clothing of that era, and they act the roles of people who worked in the fort during that time. This provides a very authentic appearance of what life was like back then.

The new Assiniboia Downs Race Track has thoroughbred and harness horse racing nightly. Spectators can view the race from the grandstand; the indoor clubhouse with a dining room; or the Finish Line Sportsbar with a big screen TV. You can attend a concert at the track, if you are there the first Saturday evening of the month. During our visit, Roy Clark will perform at the track.

Winnipeg also has many fine restaurants, theaters, nightclubs, and parks to keep us well fed and entertained. You might also enjoy a river sight-seeing cruise, several are available. Let me know your wishes, and I'll make more definite plans.

EXERCISE 4.   Revising a Memo

A. *Correct the pronoun choice and sentence structure in the memo below, using the principles you have been studying.*
B. *Consider how you would react to this memo if you were Doris Jean Landin, the recipient. Revise the memo to improve its tone and attitude in order to help the reader (the customer) and maintain good will.*

Marysville Dental Clinic

To: Doris Jean Landin   Date: May 2, 1989
From: Marty Perkins
        Bookkeeping Department
Subject: Your Dental Bills

Your phone message was referred to my assistant, Joan Walters, and I yesterday morning. Your husband was coming into the office later that day, but neither Joan nor me had time to talk to him about your account. With the first of the month upon us, we were putting aside last month's work, I was getting new billings out.

We phoned your insurance company today to see if our March billing had arrived in their offices. It was sent on March 27, it shows clearly in our records.

Either Joan or me recorded the entry here. They said they got it on April 2, but neither Joan nor me heard from them until April 24. They were running late in their own paperwork, plus they lost three key employees mid-month. Putting them behind.

They sent two checks, one fully covering the March bill for your work. Another one for your son and you, February's work. Both you and him were covered, however you have 100% coverage. They cover only 80% for your daughter and he.

Now your balance due is $153.98. The deductible for your husband and you being satisfied for the year. The balance includes your husband's work yesterday, it's ready to be billed to the insurance company for $120.00, plus the 33.98 remaining on your son from February's work. His balance is not covered, the deductible for the year is not yet satisfied for he and your other child.

Please feel free to call again if you have questions, and Joan or me will gladly help you.

EXERCISE 5.   *Writing a Memo*

Write a memo in which you guide new employees through a routine task on the job. Choose one of the following suggestions or use an idea of your own:

A. *Writing up a bill of sale, invoice, or credit card purchase*
B. *Updating a patient's chart or relaying a doctor's or dentist's recommendations to a patient*
C. *Checking end-of-the-day cash register receipts*
D. *Taking phone messages*

Here are some specific guidelines to help you write effective memos.

- Use second-person pronouns. Statements with the understood subject *you* (discussed in Chapter 3) are ideal because they begin with the verb. Most of the directions in textbook exercises are written in that way; consider, for example, the directions in this exercise.
- Make your statements so clear and exact that they cannot be misunderstood. Remember that your readers need to know what not to do as well as what to do. At the same time, they do not need elaborate explanations

about why something is done a particular way. Stick to how the process is done.

- Number the steps if you believe that will help readers. Keep each step brief with enough open space on the page.
- Use the memo format shown in Exercise 4 (page 96).
- Type or word-process your memo. You may use letterhead stationery or not, as you like.

EXERCISE 6. *Staying Consistent*

A. *Revise the pronouns in the following student paragraphs so that first-, second-, or third-person pronouns are used consistently. Change person only when such changes make sense.*
B. *Improve the sentences by repairing comma splices, fragments, and fused sentences.*
C. *Combine these ideas into new, better sentences. Reword as you like, re-placing weak verbs and modifiers with stronger ones.*

Example 1

Little frustrations can make an ordinary day difficult. Last Friday I got up, as usual, at eight o'clock. I went to the kitchen and had my cereal, juice, and toast. Then I got ready for school. Putting on my school clothes is a ritual by now, you can do it without thought. I packed my books into my backpack, put on my coat, and I was off to school. My first class was sociology, that went smoothly. Then came communications, it also went well. Last came English composition, you really get challenged in that class. After school I started preparing for my date that night. Sometimes you can look in the closet and find nothing you want to wear. Well, I found something that would do. Then I went to take a shower. I turned on the faucets and to my surprise, there was no water. "Oh, no!" I screamed. "Why now of all times?" What can you do when something like that happens? This date I had looked forward to for a week. Well, after collecting my thoughts, I went to the health club, I took my shower there. You have to make do. I went home, got dressed, and finally was ready in time.

Example 2

You asked me how to ice fish, and this is my advice to you. The way to ice fish is to get a "house," which is really a small hut just big enough for two or three people and a wood heater. We set that hut out on the lake, preferably where the fish are biting. Now, get the heater going and drill holes in the ice for the lines. With the hardest work done, just set the lines and wait for the fish to come. This makes ice fishing better than fishing from a boat, we can sit in the house, play cards, reminisce about army days, or do whatever we want. You can rent a fancier "house" out on the lake with bunk beds, a stove, and a table, this can be quite comfortable. Sometimes we get food and other necessities and stay a couple of days out there. You don't have to worry about falling through the ice, it is about three feet thick during the dead of winter.

Example 3

I am standing high up in the mountains looking down on the desert. The sun is shining brightly in the sky. You can feel the heat from the afternoon sun, but as time passes, the sun sets in the west. It is now just below the mountain tops, and the sky is filled with shades of yellow, orange, and red. It looks like a huge fire is burning behind the mountain. Then as the sun sets, the sky is a brilliant red. You know the day is gone, and a peaceful darkness is upon the desert. Tomorrow the sun will rise again, and at nightfall, I can again experience another breathtaking Arizona sunset.

5

Working with Objects

Choosing Objects for Verbs

When an action verb is followed by a direct object, that object will be either a noun or a pronoun. It will answer these questions after the verb: "What?" or "Whom?"

PRACTICE 1

In the following sentences, underline the subjects once and the verbs twice, and circle the direct objects.

Example: The puppy chased the (ball)

1. The child saw a book on the table.

2. The work tired her.

An indirect object, found between the action verb and the direct object, will also be a noun or a pronoun. It will answer these questions: "To whom?" or "For whom?"

PRACTICE 2

In the following sentences, underline the subjects once and the verbs twice, and circle the indirect objects.

Example: The grateful customer left the (waiter) a generous tip.

1. The teacher gave him a tablet.

2. Jim offered her a dollar for that pen.

Only object-form pronouns can be used as direct or indirect objects for verbs. These words are *object-form* (also called *objective case*) *pronouns:*

me	him	you	it
us	her	them	whom

PRACTICE 3

Underline the correct choices in these sentences.

Example: Joan brought (she, <u>her</u>) the book.

1. The teacher gave (I, me) the papers.

2. The tornado missed (they, them).

3. The responsibilities worry (she, her).

Object-form pronouns fit in every instance: the word *me* is the indirect object of *gave* in the first sentence; the word *them* is the direct object of *missed* in the second sentence; and the word *her* is the direct object of *worry* in the third sentence. The other pronouns are all subject-form pronouns, which are fine when used as subjects or subject complements, but which are not appropriate as objects.

PRACTICE 4

We use object-form pronouns even if we have more than one object. In these sentences, circle the compound units, noting the pronouns within the units.

Example: Joan brought (Benjamin, Teresa, and her) the books.

1. The teacher gave Kristin and me the papers.

2. The tornado missed the Petersons and them.

3. The responsibilities worry Wade and her.

No matter how many separate direct or indirect objects a verb may have, the only pronouns to use as objects are object-form pronouns. If you are in doubt about the proper choice to make, ignore all the other parts of a compound unit and put the verb next to the pronoun. Then you will make the right choice.

PRACTICE 5

Write the correct choices in the following sentences.

Choosing Objects for Verbs   101

1. The teacher gave _____ (I, me) the papers.

2. The tornado missed _____ (they, them).

3. The responsibilities worry _____ (she, her).

PRACTICE 6

Underline the correct choices in the following sentences.

   Example: The travel agent sent Diane and (I, <u>me</u>) good information.

1. A ground cover serves the neighbors and (we, us) by preventing erosion on the hillside.
2. Aunt Mae offered Doris, Don, Jim, and (I, me) fresh apple pie.
3. The black bear frightened the hunters and (they, them).
4. The nurse provided Myrna, Dottie, and (she, her) first aid after the accident.

Occasionally, incomplete comparisons involve the S + AV + DO pattern. As noted in Chapter 4, incomplete comparisons begin with the words *than* or *as* and imply a comparison. Before making any pronoun choices, think through the entire meaning, because the pronoun choice can make a big difference. For example, consider this statement:

   The flood hurt the Smiths more than (we, us).

The statement means either

   The flood hurt the Smiths more than it hurt us.

or

   The flood hurt the Smiths more than we hurt the Smiths.

Which meaning is intended? Either one is possible, though the first is more likely. The point is that the meaning of the sentence depends on the pronoun used. More often than not, subject-form pronouns are used in incomplete comparison, but object forms are also possible, as the example above shows.

PRACTICE 7

Underline the correct pronouns in the following sentences.

1. Our guests enjoy herbal teas more than (we, us).

2. Few people like coffee as much as Jill and (he, him).

3. They buy more coffee each month than you and (I, me).

4. Caffeine affects some people more than (I, me).

To choose between the pronouns *who* and *whom*, as required in formal English, follow these steps:

1. Find the verb in the unit.
2. Find the subject that goes with that verb.

   - If there is no subject, use the pronoun *who*.
   - If there is a subject with an action verb, use *whom* as a direct object.
   - If there is a subject with a linking verb, use *who* for a subject complement.

Here that process is applied step by step:

> Our history teacher is the brightest person (who, whom) I have ever met.

1. The verb in the "who/whom" part of the sentence is *have met.*
2. The subject of that verb is *I.* Since there is already a subject, we can look for an object or subject complement. With this action verb, we want an object, *whom.*

> You can invite (whoever, whomever) you wish.

1. The verb in the "whoever/whomever" part of the sentence is *wish.* The subject of that verb is *you.*
2. Since there is already a subject, we can look for an object or subject complement. With this action verb, we want the object *whomever.*

> We will thank (whoever, whomever) plans the party.

1. The verb in the "whoever/whomever" part of the sentence is *plans.*
2. The verb has no subject, so we will select *whoever.* We don't need to analyze further, having solved the pronoun problem.

PRACTICE 8

Now examine this sentence and answer the questions below.

Our classmates, (who, whom) are not expecting a party invitation, will be surprised.

1. What is the verb in the "who/whom" part of this sentence?

---

2. What is the subject of that verb? _____

3. If the verb has a subject already, do you want the pronoun *whom* as an object of the verb or *who* as a subject complement? _____

PRACTICE 9 _____

Underline the correct choices in these sentences.

1. (Who, Whom) can we trust in a strange city?

2. Any person (who, whom) comes to class late may miss something important.

3. Shakespeare was one of the finest poets (who, whom) ever lived.

4. (Who, Whom) was the first man to discover electricity?

5. Peter is the one (who, whom) plays quarterback on our team.

Choosing Objects for Prepositions

To find the objects of prepositions, we use the same questions as for objects of verbs: "What?" or "Whom?" Here, as before, we can ignore other words in compound units. Pronouns used as objects of prepositions are in object form:

Dave stood *near* Jim, Kevin, and *him.*
(We can ignore Jim and Kevin and consider the preposition *near.* Near whom? Near him.)

Kathy stood *beside* Rochelle and *me.*
(We can ignore Rochelle and consider the preposition *beside.* Beside whom? Beside me.)

One unusual preposition is *between*, a preposition that takes two objects:

between him and me	between them and us
between you and me	between him and her

PRACTICE 10 _____

Underline the correct choices in these sentences.

1. The cherry pie was a treat for Doris, Don, Jim, and (I, me).

2. Aunt Mae baked for her children, grandchildren, and (we, us) that morning.

3. Lunch tastes good to hungry construction workers and office workers like (he, him) and (I, me).

4. One difference between (they, them) and (we, us) is the amount of physical labor in our jobs.

The correct use of the pronouns *whom* and *whomever* requires extra attention. When the pronoun immediately follows the preposition, it is easy to choose the right word. In the following examples the prepositional phrases are italicized:

> Ask not *for whom* the bell tolls: it tolls for thee.
> (John Donne, 1572–1631)
> He will go *with whomever* he pleases.
> I don't recall *to whom* I sent that letter.
> *To whom* should we speak about registration?

The last two examples may seem more natural with the words arranged in this way:

> I don't recall *whom* I sent that letter *to.*
> *Whom* should we speak *to* about registration?

In these last two examples, the preposition and its object are separated and their usual order is reversed: instead of the preposition preceding the object, it follows it.

To determine the correct pronoun choice, it is sometimes helpful to reword the sentence. Put the preposition and its object together in the usual order first; then select the pronoun.

PRACTICE 11

Underline the correct choices in these sentences.

1. (Who, Whom) shall I say phoned?

2. The receptionist asked me (who, whom) was expected this morning.

3. The receptionist's records indicate (who, whom) the phone messages are for.

4. The weekly staff bulletin publishes announcements from (whoever, whomever) submits them by the previous Thursday noon.

APPOSITIVES

As a final point about pronouns, we should consider the use of pronouns as appositives. Appositives are italicized in these sentences:

> The leaders, *Paula and Susan*, gave directions.
> The leaders, *Paula and she*, gave directions.
> The students listened to their leaders, *Paula and Susan*.
> The students listened to their leaders, *Paula and her*.

Appositives have the following characteristics:

- An appositive renames or identifies a noun (or pronoun) immediately preceding it.
- The appositive itself is a noun or pronoun, sometimes with its own adjectives.
- An appositive is normally set off with commas.
- An appositive saves words by offering information that would otherwise require an entire second sentence.

In this sentence the appositives are italicized and arrows connect them to the words they refer to:

> My friends, *Connie and Karen*, were invited to the
>
> party, *a birthday celebration*.

The same ideas could be expressed in three separate sentences:

> My friends are Connie and Karen. They were invited to a party. The party was a birthday celebration.

Or the ideas could be expressed in two separate sentences:

> My friends are Connie and Karen. They were invited to a birthday party.

By using appositives, we can combine ideas, forming more concise statements. In the example above, two or three separate sentences are combined into one, saving many words and saving time for both the writer and the readers. More importantly, by using appositives, we de-emphasize lesser ideas (those in the appositive) and emphasize the main idea in the sentence.

In the sentence above, the names of the friends are less important than the fact that they were invited to a party. The fact that the party is a birthday celebration is less important than the invitation. The hierarchy or priority of ideas is made clear by the structure of the sentence.

To be sure that the pronouns are in the same form as the words to which they refer, we follow rules that are entirely logical:

- If the pronoun used as an appositive refers to a subject or subject complement, use a subject-form pronoun.
- If the pronoun used as an appositive refers to an object of a verb or an object of a preposition, use an object-form pronoun.

PRACTICE 12

Examine the italicized pronouns in the following sentences. On the lines that follow the sentences, indicate whether those pronouns are subject or object form. Then circle the words to which the appositives refer.

Example: The radio (announcers,) Sharon, Phil, and *he*, shared the responsibility of reading the news.

_____subject form_____

1. They were our star athletes, John and *he*. _____

2. Two star players, John and *he*, played in that game.

   _____

3. Jennifer went to the party with them, Steve, Liz, and *him*.

   _____

4. Her friends, Joe and *he*, invited three people.

   _____

5. They invited three people, Sue, Terry, and *her*.

   _____

PRACTICE 13

Underline the correct pronouns in the following sentences.

1. The speaker addressed the faculty and (we, us) students.

2. Polly went to the game Friday night with all of them, David, Sharon, Keith, and (she, her).

3. The department leaders were our friends, Joyce and (she, her).

4. The chairpersons for our language departments are also teachers, Nancy, George, and (she, her).

A. *Using appositives, combine the ideas in the following sets of sentences into one sentence.*

1. Three Miami Dolphins fans watched the game with me Sunday afternoon. The fans are Pat, Joan, and Carl.

_____

_____

2. The fans most admired the two leading players. Those players were Walter and Nick.

_____

_____

B. *Now revise the sentences you wrote, adding a pronoun within each of the appositives.*

1. _____

_____

2. _____

_____

Points to Use

- Look for the S + AV + DO or the S + AV + IO + DO pattern in sentences with action verbs. Use an object-form pronoun for an indirect or a direct object.
- Ignore any nouns used as objects, and put verbs and the pronoun part of the object side by side. Generally, the correct choice will sound right when the two words are side by side.
- Look for all the objects that go with a preposition, knowing that there can be two or more. Use object-form pronouns as objects of prepositions.
- Be careful of the preposition *between*. It requires two objects, and if they are pronouns, they must be object forms, such as *between him and me.*
- Change the wording in a sentence if that helps you sort out *who/whom* usage.

- Solve *who*/*whom* problems with a step-by-step process, finding the verb first, then the subject, and finally an object or complement.
- Make pronouns that serve as appositives follow the same case as the words to which they refer. If they refer to subjects, use subject-form pronouns; if they refer to objects, use object-form pronouns.
- Use appositives to make sentences more concise and to show priorities of ideas.

Points to Remember

- Action verbs often take direct objects and sometimes take indirect objects. Direct objects answer these questions after the verb: "What?" or "Whom?" Indirect objects answer these questions after the verb: "To whom?" or "For whom?"
- Nouns and object-form pronouns can be direct objects, indirect objects, and objects of prepositions.
- To select the right pronoun as an object, ignore all other parts of the object.
- An appositive is a noun or pronoun (sometimes with adjectives) that renames or identifies the noun or pronoun immediately preceding it.
- A pronoun used as an appositive must be in the same case as the word to which it refers.

EXERCISE 1.   Selecting Pronouns

Underline the correct choices in the following sentences. Check your answers with those at the back of the book.

1. Between you and (I, me), college algebra is hard.
2. The assignments seem long to Sally, Peter, and (I, me).
3. With (who, whom) can we share our feelings?
4. The counselors ask (we, us) students for our opinions.
5. When they mention the long lines at registration, we speak candidly about (them, it).
6. Two students, Janet and (he, him), think that registration takes too much time.
7. We all missed Phil and (he, him) when they were absent.
8. It will be (he, him) who starts as quarterback in Friday's game.
9. (We, Us) students hear all kinds of stories about the faculty at our school.
10. We are not sure it was (she, her) that we saw downtown.
11. (Who, Whom) can help us repair a tire?
12. The map does not say to (who, whom) we can go for help.
13. Have you heard the news about Sherrie and (she, her)?
14. That story will amuse us more than (they, them).
15. We cannot believe (them, those, that) stories.
16. Our team has won as many games as (they, them).
17. It must have been (he, him) (who, whom) you saw there.
18. The neighbors, my cousins, and (we, us) went to the hockey game last night.
19. Yesterday's sociology lecture impressed Paul, Jennifer, and (I, me).
20. A few of the finer points were beyond Jennifer and (he, him).

EXERCISE 2.   Revising Pronoun Usage

In these sentences, some of the pronoun choices are correct and some are incorrect. Find all the instances of incorrect pronoun choice. Write the correct choices between the lines. Check your answers with those at the back of the book.

1. Seldom have I heard a more effective speaker than her.

2. It was him who drove carelessly through a red light.

3. The tea drinkers, Laurie and her, ordered pots of tea.

4. Can you guess who prefers coffee and who prefers tea?

5. He drinks coffee as often as I, but he likes tea also.

6. Coffee drinkers who use cream are Jean, Mike, and her.

7. Too much coffee gives my sister and I headaches.

8. My favorite TV star is a woman who has great talent.

9. Sally, Susan, and me all like to watch her perform.

10. From season to season, we cannot predict whom the leading TV stars will be.

11. Last night's TV special amused all of us, John, Jim, Doug, and I.

12. Anyone who watches TV often will form preferences.

13. Tonight it is Jim and I who will watch the late show.

14. There is agreement between Jim and I about TV shows.

15. If you watch much TV, you will understand why it is often boring to him and I.

16. If the editor had been there, she would have advised the writer to use this form: It is me.

17. The writer was careful to write these words in his report: Between them and us, there is mutual agreement.

18. The writer was the one who asked for directions today.

EXERCISE 3.   Reviewing the Uses of Pronouns

Match the italicized pronouns with their uses. Check your answers with those at the back of the book.

a. subject   d. subject complement
b. direct object   e. object of a preposition
c. indirect object   f. appositive

_____ 1. One September day, a small tiger-striped kitten came to live with *us*.

_____ 2. The Humane Society had kept *him* only a few days.

_____ 3. Someone had given *them* a litter of tiny kittens.

_____ 4. The litter included six babies, three black ones, two gray ones, and *him*.

_____ 5. The chief cat fanciers in our household are my older son and *I*.

_____ 6. I gave *him* the task of cleaning the litter box.

_____ 7. His brother and *he* eventually shared the chore.

_____ 8. Soon after the kitten arrived, we wondered aloud, "What can *we* name this cute baby?"

_____ 9. We could not let *him* be called "cat" indefinitely.

_____ 10. "Let *us* think hard and decide upon a clever name," I said.

_____ 11. We, the children and *I*, thought and thought.

_____ 12. Suddenly our four-year-old said, "I give *him* the name 'Spot.' "

_____ 13. "*Who* would call a cat 'Spot'?" we asked him.

_____ 14. "I call him 'Spot' because he has spots under his stripes," explained the child to his brother and *me*.

_____ 15. If you wanted to see a cat respond to a dog's name, it is *he* that you should have met.

_____ 16. Spot used at least eight of the nine lives allotted to *him* before his death four years ago.

_____ 17. Like all tabby cats, *he* had an *M* on his forehead, a detail that we explained to the children.

_____ 18. At least, that is what we have heard from people *who* know a lot about cats.

EXERCISE 4.   Reviewing Pronoun Choices

Circle the letter (a or b) of the correct choice. Check your answers with those at the back of the book.

1. a. Among we students, there is agreement about holidays.
   b. Among us students, there is agreement about holidays.

2. a. Columbus Day gives the faculty, the staff, and we students a holiday.
   b. Columbus Day gives the faculty, the staff, and us students a holiday.

3. a. A carefree weekend will be wonderful for all of us, my friends and me.
   b. A carefree weekend will be wonderful for all of us, my friends and I.

4. a. The first ones to leave for home will be Joe and I.
   b. The first ones to leave for home will be Joe and me.

5. a. My parents and we children get together often.
   b. My parents and us children get together often.

6. a. We invited our best friends, the Nicholsons and they, to dinner with the Sampsons and he.
   b. We invited our best friends, the Nicholsons and them, to dinner with the Sampsons and him.

7. a. Few people enjoy the weekend more than I.
   b. Few people enjoy the weekend more than me.

8. a. It was they who suggested a heavy coat of ski wax.
   b. It was them who suggested a heavy coat of ski wax.

9. a. Whoever he may be, he is probably right.
   b. Whomever he may be, he is probably right.

10. a. Between you and I, Presidents' Day is a welcome day.
    b. Between you and me, Presidents' Day is a welcome day.

11. a. Roy, Allen, and him will go skiing this weekend.
    b. Roy, Allen, and he will go skiing this weekend.

12. a. Valentine's Day is a happy day for Paul and she.
    b. Valentine's Day is a happy day for Paul and her.

13. a. Thanksgiving gives my family and me four free days.
    b. Thanksgiving gives my family and I four free days.

14. a. Us students face a long winter after Christmas.
    b. We students face a long winter after Christmas.

EXERCISE 5.   Creating Appositives

Change the italicized sentences into appositives and place them properly into the other sentences. Write new sentences, punctuating appositives correctly.

Example: I read the entire book last night. *I read a George Eliot novel.*

I read the entire book, a George Eliot novel, last night.

1. Silas Marner formerly was required reading for high school sophomores. *It is a novel by George Eliot.*

_____

_____

2. George Eliot is a pseudonym for Mary Ann Evans. *Mary Ann Evans was a nineteenth-century British author.*

_____

_____

3. Eliot's first novel appeared in 1859. *It was entitled Adam Bede.*

_____

_____

4. Silas Marner was a miserly weaver. *He is the protagonist in Eliot's most famous novel.*

_____

_____

5. In the novel, Silas's love for gold gives way to a new love. *He comes to love a golden-haired child.*

_____

_____

6. Middlemarch was published in 1871–1872. *It is Eliot's greatest novel.*

_____

_____

7. Dorothea is a central figure in <u>Middlemarch</u>. *She is a memorable example of Victorian industriousness.*

_____

_____

8. Paul, Brandon, and Tricia enjoy science fiction. *They are my students this year.*

_____

_____

9. Science fiction fans know about "Star Trek" and "Dr. Who." *"Dr. Who" is a television program on PBS.*

_____

_____

10. Gene Roddenberry was pressured by the Soviets to add a Russian to the "Star Trek" cast of characters. *Gene Roddenberry was "Star Trek"'s creator.*

_____

_____

11. Trekkies attend every "Star Trek" convention. *Trekkies are "Star Trek" fanatics.*

_____

_____

12. Followers of "Dr. Who" also have conventions. *These followers are called Whovians.*

_____

_____

EXERCISE 6. *Revising Sentences and Pronouns*

Revise the sentences and the pronoun choices in the letter below. Make your revisions between the lines.

93 First Avenue

Morris, TN 76500

May 30, 1989

Mr. Matt Williams

Editor, *The Rushville Bulletin*

27 East Main Street

Rushville, TN 76543

Dear Mr. Williams:

My friend, Mike Andress, and me need a job. Kate Saunders a copyreader for the *Bulletin* told him and I to apply. We really need work, we will do whatever jobs you have.

Mike and me can do almost any kind of work. In the army, our sergeant said he and I were good workers. Also Mike's a great guy to have around, he has a sense of humor, he makes other people feel great. Which is saying a lot.

Machines we are good at. We can handle things like presses. We can learn fast.

We plan on being in your area and will stop by to see you.

Yours truly,

Jenson L Blake

Jenson L. Blake

EXERCISE 7. *Revising Sentences and Pronouns*

As you read the letter below, write notes in the margins and at the end of the letter indicating what should be revised. Bring your notes to class for discussion. Some background information that will help you understand the letter is given first.

For many years, the Minnesota Twins and the Minnesota Vikings played in an open stadium in Bloomington, Minnesota, a suburb on the south side of Minneapolis. When serious discussion about building a new domed stadium began, its desirability and possible location were widely debated. Even more controversial were the possible economic consequences of various alternatives.

A resident with opinions on the controversy wrote the paragraphs below as part of a long letter to the *Minneapolis Tribune*. The letter was never published. Although the writer has views, those views are lost because the writing is crippled with many problems, including some of the ones you have studied so far in this book.

To the Editor:

Should the Twin Cities have a dome stadium? A question that has been raised several times. There are several good reasons why it is a good idea. There are many problems in this as well. I am for a dome stadium. Half the season is in the cold weather. When it is 20 below outside. The player and the fans are out there. Too cold and too wet.

They say Bloomington is a better place than downtown Minneapolis. One reason is traffic. There are several events downtown. And lots of traffic from events. That traffic is too much now. That traffic plus stadium events are really going to be a mess. A surprise to no one.

A stadium in the suburbs is more of an isolated area. Traffic is smoother. One more thing is the proposed liquor tax. The money made off a liquor tax is nowhere near enough to pay for half the cost of a new stadium which brings us back to the old one. Renovating is a lot less expensive. Maybe half as much. I am sure that there are many taxpayers who are ready to agree on remodeling the old stadium. It is a more economical decision. Hanging over your head is the liquor tax. One reason for not having a new stadium is not having the liquor tax hanging over your head.

One more question is what we should consider first, not last. Will the Vikings go to Los Angeles if they are not in a new stadium here? True, they had some poor seasons. But loyal fans here wanting to see games, going to be lost if they leave. One last point is the taxpayers. Is there a voice for the taxpayers? We need a voice. When you consider it is our hard earned money they are dealing with.

In closing I would like to add that this dome stadium issue will probably be solved when election time rolls around or there will be a lot of lawmakers out of a job.

EXERCISE 8.   *Writing an Opinion Letter*

Write a letter expressing your views on an issue that concerns you. Address your remarks to the editor of a newspaper, a city council member, an employer, a professor, a member of Congress or your state legislature, or some other figure. With a little research you should be able to find that person's exact name, title, and address.

Use the letter format shown below or another format as indicated by your teacher. Because this is your own personal statement, use good-quality plain paper with no letterhead.

Your street address
Your city, state   zip code
Date

Name of addressee (with title)
Name of company or organization
Street address
City, state   zip code

Dear _____:

xxxxxxxxxxxxxxxxxxxxxxxxxxxxxxxxxxxxxxxxxxxxxxxxxxxxxxxxxxxxxxxxxxxxxxxxxx
xxxxxxxxxx Keep your paragraphs short and single-spaced.   xxxxxxxxxxxxxxx
xxxxxxxxxxxxxxxxxxxxxxxxxxxxxxxxxxxxxxxxxxxxxxxxxxxxxxxxxxxxxxxxxxxxxxxxxx
xxxxxxxxxxxxxxxxx

xxxxxxxxxxxxxxxxxxxxxxxxxxxxxxxxxxxxxxxxxxxxxxxxxxxxxxxxxxxxxxxxxxxxxxxxxx
xxxxxxxxxx Double-space between paragraphs. xxxxxxxxxxxxxxxxxxxxxxxxxx
xxxxxxxxxxxxxxxxxxxxxxxxxxxxxxxxxxxxxxxxxxxxxxxxxxxxxxxxxxxxxxxxxxxxxxxxxx
xxxxxxxxxxxxxxxxxxxxxxxxxxxxxxxxxxxxxxxxxxxxxxxxxxxxxxxxxxxxxxxxxxxxxxxxxx
xxxxxxxxx

xxxxxxxxxxxxxxxxxxxxxxxxxxxxxxxxxxxxxxxxxxxxxxxxxxxxxxxxxxxxxxxxxxxxxxxxxx
xxxxxxxxxx Be brief, but be specific and courteous. xxxxxxxxxxxxxxxxxxxxxx
xxxxxxxxxxxxxxxxxxxxxxxxxxxxxxxxxxxxxxxxxxxxxxxxxxxxxxxxxxxxxxxxxxxxxxxxxx
xxxxxxxxxxxxxxxxxxxxxxxxxxxxxxxxxxxxxxx

xxxxxxxxxxxxxxxxxxxxxxxxxxxxxxxxxxxxxxxxxxxxxxxxxxxxxxxxxxxxxxxxxxxxxxxxxx
xxxxxxxxxx Three or four short paragraphs should be enough. xxxxxxxxxxxxx
xxxxxxxxxxxxxxxxxxxxxxxxxxxxxxxxxxxxxxxxxxxxxxxxxxxxxxxxxxxxxxxxxxxxxxxxxx
xxxxxxxxxxxxxxxxxxxxxxxxxxxxxxxxx

Yours truly (or some other complimentary closing),

Your name (typed)

EXERCISE 9. Considering How Language Skills Develop

Read the article below and compare Johnny's experiences with your own. How did you develop your language skills? Who helped you? What kinds of help did you get, both in school and elsewhere?

After class discussion, write a paragraph in response to this article. Take a position, either agreeing or disagreeing with the author's viewpoint.

Pity the pronoun snobs: There's no help for they

Suzanne Britt Jordan

I feel sorry for pronouns. Of all the parts of speech, pronouns take the most abuse. Prepositions get along fine. Conjunctions, adverbs and adjectives can manage. Granted, nouns are sometimes misspelled or misunderstood, and verbs can have trouble both coming and going. But still, it's the pronoun that suffers the most.

Everybody abuses pronouns, not just the illiterate crowd. In fact, the pronoun is more likely to take its licks from the high class, not the low; the college grads, not the high-school drop-outs; the socialites, not the hicks; the brains, not the brawns.

If you want to hear a pronoun misused, all you have to do is listen to college presidents, corporate executives, eminent theologians, scientists, graduate students and budding geniuses, in other words, anybody who might be likely to have a high socio or economic level. These particular pronoun-punishers learned good manners, which often is the same as learning ungrammatical manners. Manners and grammar don't mix. Manners and grammar have nothing to do with each other.

Consider: Along about the age of 6, Johnny, who was from a good family, started talking about going to the store with Joe. Johnny would say, "Me and Joe are going to the store." And Johnny's mother and father automatically said, "I. Joe and I." (To this sharp parental correction, Johnny always replied "Huh?" To which his mother said automatically, "I beg your pardon." But that issue is a whole 'nother ballgame.)

The point is that Johnny gradually acquired the idea that the word "me" was immoral and uncouth. No matter what happened, he must say "I." Johnny got the same idea about him, her and them—they all were bad. If Johnny said, "Me and her are going to the store," his mother automatically said, "She and I." If Johnny said, "Her and Joe are going to the store," his mother intoned, "She and Joe." If Johnny said, "Them and me are going to the store," his mother gasped, turned purple, and said, "They and I."

What Johnny's mother never explained was the concept behind the correction, probably because she did not know it herself. The error Johnny was making was using objective-case pronouns as subjects. And Johnny's mother was right to correct him. The catch is that Johnny picked up the erroneous conviction that objective-case pronouns were tacky and low class and that he should never, ever use them.

So Johnny grew up to be John, the classiest, most well-educated guy you ever saw, and here are some things he said around the country club: "Give the martinis to Estelle and I," "Just between she and I, Dirk's golf swing is lousy" and "That tennis pro is better than her." English teachers developed unfortunate little facial tics when they heard that one.

John went through life making fun of people who said correct things like "between her and me" and "for him and me" or "with them and me." Poor John: There's no snob like a grammatically incorrect snob.

6

Working with Verbs

In English, as in other languages, it is difficult to learn to use verbs correctly. A detailed discussion of verbs could take up many chapters of a book, many weeks in class, and many long hours of study outside class. This chapter does not offer a detailed analysis of verbs, but instead addresses common problems with verbs. Additional information about verbs is provided in Appendix A.

Handling Tenses

The word *tense* means time. To indicate time, verbs change form so that the word itself indicates the time. The most common tenses are past, present, and future, meaning exactly that—past, present, and future times. This example uses the verb *work:*

> *Past:*   Joe *worked* hard at his summer job.
> *Present:* Joe *works* long hours after school.
> *Future:*   Joe *will work* full-time again next summer.

The *present-tense* form of the verb might be considered the "regular" form of the verb. We create other tenses by adjusting the present tense. The present tense itself has the following four uses.

1. It indicates action or state of being in the present:

> Joe *is* a hard worker.
> Joe *works* after school every day.

2. It can be used to indicate future tense if other words in the sentence indicate that a future time is meant:

> Paul *leaves* for work in twenty minutes.
> Daniel *goes* to the dentist tomorrow.

3. It is used for the so-called timeless truth, a statement that does not change over time:

> My parents' names *are* Fred and Harriet.
> Lake Superior *is* the largest lake in the world.

4. It can be used to relate historic events in the "historical present." Here, for example, is the way the present tense could be used in a report or a television documentary:

> The United States prisoners of war *leave* North Vietnam and *fly* home by way of Hawaii. Cheering crowds *greet* them at the Honolulu airport. They *continue* their journey to the mainland a few hours later. . . .

PRACTICE 1

Write two sentences of your own, using the present tense.

1. _____

2. _____

The **past tense** has only one use: it indicates an action or state of being that began and ended in the past.

> Tammy *worked* at the hotel last summer.
> She *saved* money for college expenses.

Most past-tense verbs end with *ed*. The examples above use regular verbs (*work* and *save*). We form the past tense of regular verbs by adding *ed* to the present tense. There is no particular pattern for forming the past tense of irregular verbs. (Examples are discussed later in this chapter and in Appendix A.)

PRACTICE 2

Revise the two present-tense sentences you wrote in Practice 1 into past-tense sentences.

1. _____

2. _____

The *future tense* has only one use: it indicates action or state of being in the future. We form the future tense by adding the helping verbs *will* or *shall* to present-tense forms. Here are two examples of the future tense:

> Richard *will return* to construction work in June.
> The teachers *shall be* happy to rest this summer.

PRACTICE 3

Write two sentences of your own, using the future tense.

1. _____

2. _____

PRACTICE 4

Underline the verbs in the following sentences, and label them present, past, or future.

Examples: Madeline *past* sent an application letter and résumé to that

employer.

present
She expects a response within two weeks.

1. Megan wants a full-time summer job in the restaurant industry.

2. She will enroll in the hotel-motel management curriculum next fall.

3. Paula accepted a part-time job at the nursing home for the summer.

4. Paula and her sister are students in the nursing program at this college.

Note: The word *perfect* is used as part of the name of the next three verb tenses. The usual meaning, of being excellent or ideal, does not apply. Here *perfect* is merely part of a label.

The *past perfect tense* indicates an action or state of being that began and ended in the past before some other past action. In other words, there are two past actions (or states of being). The earlier one is in past perfect tense; the later one is in ordinary past tense. Past perfect tense thus indicates a sequence of events.

The past perfect tense requires the helper *had* plus the past tense of the verb. Consider the sequence of events in these sentences:

> After Judy *had worked* two weeks, she *received* her first check.
>> (Both actions are in the past, but the earlier of the two is in past perfect tense.)

> Although Dean *had been* busy all summer, he *was* even busier in school last fall.
>> (Both states of being are in the past, but the earlier of the two is in past perfect tense.)

PRACTICE 5

Underline the past-tense verbs and circle the past perfect verbs in the following sentences.

> **Example:** Because Michelle (had decided) to enter the premedical program, she <u>wanted</u> summer employment at the hospital.

1. Gary had considered computer technology for his career, but he decided on mechanical engineering instead.
2. After he had begun the mechanical engineering curriculum, he discovered the technical writing requirement.
3. He took that class after he had completed freshman composition.
4. Gary had investigated several career options before he entered college.

The past perfect tense serves writers in two ways. First, it makes the order of events clear. Contrast these two sentences:

> *Poor:*   Sally *remembered* that she *locked* the door.
> *Better:*   Sally *remembered* that she *had locked* the door.

PRACTICE 6

Use the past perfect tense to make the order of events clear in these sentences.

1. *Poor:*   Everything he *told* me about his job I *heard* before.

     Better: _____

2. *Poor:*   I already *knew* his feelings about that job because he *told* me.

Better: _____

In addition, past perfect tense eliminates the needless repetition of *would have.* Contrast these two sentences:

Poor: If Carla *would have worked* all summer, she *would have earned* twice as much money.

Better: If Carla *had worked* all summer, she *would have earned* twice as much money.

PRACTICE 7

Rewrite these sentences using the past perfect tense.

1. *Poor:*   If Sue *would have been* there during the summer, she *would have earned* enough for tuition.

Better: _____

_____

2. *Poor:*   If Brandon *would have remembered* his overparked car, he *would have moved* it in time.

Better: _____

_____

The **present perfect tense** is formed by adding *have* or *has* to the past form of the verb. This tense has two uses:

1. It indicates actions or states of being that have occurred at some indefinite time in the past.

   Larry *has worked* on various jobs over the years.
   The newspaper editors *have seen* many angry letters.
   Sandra *has been* my student several times in various classes.

2. It indicates actions or states of being that began in the past and have continued into the present.

   Heidi *has been* my student for six weeks.
   Tim *has worked* as a landscape designer for three years.

The editors *have read* six angry letters since printing a controversial story yesterday.

PRACTICE 8

Create two examples of your own, one illustrating the first use of the present perfect tense and the other illustrating the second.

1. _____

_____

2. _____

_____

The **future perfect tense** uses *will have* or *shall have* with the past form of the verb. This tense indicates a future action or state of being that will come to pass at a fairly definite time in the future. That future time will be clearly indicated in the context (either in the same sentence or nearby).

Here are two examples of the future perfect tense:

Brett *will have completed* his first year of college by June 10.

By next fall, Cheryl *will have been* a college student for a year.

PRACTICE 9

The two examples above set up the pattern of the future perfect tense. Finish the following sentence yourself:

By this time next year, I *will have finished* _____

_____

Summary

Past perfect + past:

After Brad *had worked* for three weeks, he *received* his first check.

Present:

Brad *works* the evening shift.

Present perfect:

Brad *has worked* after school every day during the school year.

Future:

Next summer, Brad *will work* thirty hours a week.

Future perfect:

By next fall, Brad *will have worked* two full summers at the same job.

PRACTICE 10

Write complete sentences below, using the six tenses of study. *Do not use* to study *or the* ing *form,* studying. *The parts of the verb are* study *(present),* studied *(past), and* studied *(past participle, to be used with a helper).*

1. Present: _____

   _____

2. Past: _____

   _____

3. Future: _____

   _____

4. Past perfect: _____

   _____

5. Present perfect: _____

   _____

6. Future perfect: _____

   _____

Tenses customarily are shown in dictionaries and other reference works in a set order, usually in this manner: *lie (lay, lain)*. Here is an explanation with examples:

Present tense (used alone)	Past tense (used alone)	Past participle (used with helpers)
walk	walked	walked
drink	drank	drunk
think	thought	thought
lie	lay	lain
lay	laid	laid

(For other examples, see Appendix A.)

The examples above remind us of irregularities in the language. The first verb, *walk*, is considered "regular" because it uses *ed* endings for the past and the past participle. The verbs *drink* and *think*, which look and sound so much alike, not only are "irregular" but differ from each other in the way their principal parts are formed.

The irregular verbs *lie* and *lay* are often confused, even though they have very different meanings:

> lie = to rest or recline
> lay = to put or place

Confusion between the two verbs is perhaps as inevitable as confusion between identical twins. The present form of *lay* can be viewed as an identical twin of the past form of *lie: lay* (as part of *lay*) and *lay* (as part of *lie*) look exactly alike, but they are two entirely different entities.

In these examples using *lie*, notice the tenses and the meanings:

> Patrick *lies* down to rest after finishing work.   (PRESENT)
> Last Sunday, he *lay* in bed until 10 A.M.   (PAST)
> Most weekend mornings, he *has lain* in bed late.
>   (PRESENT PERFECT)

People can rest or recline involuntarily or against their wishes:

> People *lie* in hospital beds, eager to get well.   (PRESENT)
> After falling on the ice, Fay *lay* still, unable to get up.   (PAST)

Objects can also rest or recline:

> The towel *lies* on the kitchen table.   (PRESENT)
> The plates *lay* on the table until Joan got home from work.
>   (PAST)
> The silverware *has lain* in the drawer, untouched since
>   lunch.   (PRESENT PERFECT)

Create four sentences in which you use forms of lie. *Use any tense you like.*

1. _____

2. _____

3. _____

4. _____

Another distinction between these two verbs, *lie* and *lay*, is that *lay* takes a direct object and *lie* does not. Certain action verbs can have objects, but others cannot. The technical terms for this distinction are *transitive* (taking an object) and *intransitive* (not taking an object).

Notice that the verb *lie* (in any of its tenses) has no direct objects. The verb *lay* (in any of its tenses) has direct objects, circled in the examples below:

Sheila *lays* her (books) on the desk.   (PRESENT)

Last night, she also *laid* her (notes) on the desk.   (PAST)

She *has laid* her (schoolwork) there daily all fall.

(PRESENT PERFECT)

PRACTICE 12

Lie and lay *are used in their various forms in the following sentences. Note again the presence or absence of direct objects. Circle the direct objects in these sentences.*

1. The book *lies* where Melanie *had laid* it.

2. The notes *have lain* on her desk because she *laid* them there before she *lay* down to rest.

3. Winter-weary students *lay* their books aside on spring days and *lie* in the warm sunshine.

4. Because they *laid* their work aside to soak up sunshine, evenings of study *lay* before them.

One final caution about verb tense is needed: be consistent and logical with verb tense. Within a given passage, verbs should stay in the same tense unless there is good reason for changing. Pointless changes are confusing.

Consider, for instance, this passage in which the writer shifts back and forth between past and present, apparently for no reason:

> Craig *worked* long hours in the kitchen, but he *makes* good money and *enjoys* being there with other employees, many of whom *were* his age. He *wants* a better job and *looked* but *found* nothing good.

PRACTICE 13 ────────────────────────────────

Replace the present-tense verbs with past-tense verbs in the example above. Write the revised sentences below.

_____

_____

_____

_____

_____

Handling Mood and Voice

In addition to having tense, verbs have qualities called **mood** and **voice.** Here we are concerned only with those special situations in which these qualities make a difference in our writing.

When expressing a wish or a condition contrary to reality, use the **subjunctive mood.** Most commonly, the subjunctive mood simply means that *were* replaces *was* in those few special situations:

> If Tim *were* taller, he would be a basketball star.
> As though one summer *were* not enough, Mona has agreed
>   to work at the nursing home again next year.
> If Peggy *were* here, she would tell us about her trip.

Usually the subjunctive mood verb appears in dependent clauses (to be studied in Chapter 9). Some of these word groups begin with words suggesting conditions contrary to reality or wishes, such as *if, as though, though, as if.*

Write three sentences using the subjunctive mood.

1. _____

   _____

2. _____

   _____

3. _____

   _____

With *voice,* we have two choices, *active* and *passive.* Generally we use active-voice verbs rather than passive-voice verbs. Here is the distinction:

- **Active voice.** The subject is the doer of the action:

   Bill earned a thousand dollars last summer.

- **Passive voice.** The subject is the receiver of the action:

   A thousand dollars was earned last summer.

      or

   A thousand dollars was earned last summer by Bill.

The active voice is more common; it is also more direct, easier to understand, and more concise. The passive voice requires a helping verb, and this automatically adds an extra word. Here are more examples:

Active: Stuart and Tony won athletic scholarships for

             college.

Passive: Athletic scholarships for college were won.

             or

             Athletic scholarships for college were won by Stuart

             and Tony.

Notice that the doer may disappear entirely in the passive voice, or the doer may be mentioned in a prepositional phrase, one of the weakest spots in a sentence.

_____

Label the following examples either active or passive.

_____ 1. The door was blown shut by the gust of wind.

_____ 2. Weather forecasters had warned us about this storm.

_____ 3. The dinner menu was brought to us promptly.

_____ 4. Most of us ordered the specialty of the day.

Although in some situations, the passive voice is preferred, it should be used deliberately, not carelessly. Passive voice should be reserved for these special situations:

- When the doer is unknown:

    Nancy's <u>car</u> <u>was stolen</u> last night.

    The <u>package</u> <u>was left</u> by my door.

- When the doer is obvious, unimportant, or less important than the recipient of the action:

    The <u>package</u> <u>was delivered</u> at 3 P.M.

    <u>Fred</u> <u>was bitten</u> by the snake.

- When it is more tactful not to mention the doer:

    A <u>mistake</u> <u>was made</u> on my monthly statement.

    The wrong <u>directions</u> <u>were given</u> to me.

PRACTICE 16 _____

Rewrite the following statements, using the passive voice. You may omit the doer.

Example: You rang up the wrong numbers on this cash register.

The wrong numbers were rung up on this cash register.

1. You sent me the wrong blade for this lawn mower.

_____

2. The postman brought us the notice of the overdue tax bill.

_____

3. The mortgage company paid the tax bill from an escrow account.

_____

4. They mailed the payment on time, but a clerk in the treasurer's office mislaid the payment.

_____

Points to Use

- Use the most appropriate tense, given the choice of six useful tenses (present, past, future, past perfect, present perfect, and future perfect). The right tense saves words because time can be indicated in the verb itself, and the sequence of actions (or states of being) can be clarified by verb tenses.
- Use the past perfect in "if" units to avoid the wordy, boring repetition of _would have._
- Choose carefully between forms of _lie_ and _lay,_ using the presence or absence of a direct object and—most important—the meaning intended.
- Stay consistently in the same tense, or change tenses only when you have reason to do so.
- Use the subjunctive mood to express wishes or conditions contrary to reality.
- Make the active voice the norm; use the passive voice only when you have a good reason to do so.
- Use your knowledge of the active and passive voices to help unravel difficult reading material. Find the doer(s) and the action first to determine the meaning.

Points to Remember

- The present tense indicates an action or a state of being in the present, but it can also be used to indicate future actions, timeless truths, and the historic present.
- The past tense indicates an action or a state of being in the past. Generally, the past tense is created by adding _ed_ to the present-tense form of the verb.

- The future tense indicates an action or a state of being in the future. This tense requires the helper *will* or *shall.*
- The past perfect tense indicates an action or a state of being that began and ended in the past, before some other past action. It uses the helper *had.*
- The present perfect tense indicates an action or a state of being at some indefinite time in the past or one that began in the past and continues into the present. It uses the helpers *have* or *has.*
- The future perfect tense indicates an action or a state of being that will come to pass at a fairly definite time in the future. It uses the helpers *will have* or *shall have.*
- Verb forms are usually shown in reference books with three principal parts, in the following order: present, past, and past participle.
- *Lie (lay, lain)* means to rest or to recline. This verb does not take a direct object. *Lay (laid, laid)* means to put or place. This verb takes a direct object.
- The subjunctive mood expresses a wish or a condition contrary to reality. It generally means that *were* is used in place of *was.*
- The active voice means that the subject is the doer; passive voice means that the subject is the receiver.
- In the passive voice, the subject may not be mentioned, or the subject may be mentioned in a prepositional phrase. The passive voice requires a helping verb.

EXERCISE 1. Choosing Verbs for Consistency and Tense

Underline the correct choices in the following sentences. Check your answers with those at the back of the book.

1. Paul (lies, lays) in bed until 9 A.M. on Saturdays.

2. When Dale had to go to early classes all week last year, on Saturdays he often (lay, laid) in bed late.

3. (Lie, Lay) that package on the dining room table.

4. If Sam (had gone, would have gone) to the play, he would have enjoyed every minute of it.

5. The teacher who (directed, has directed) plays at our school since 1985 is directing this production.

6. When he (finished, had finished) work on the fall production, he (concludes, concluded) that it was well done.

7. The starring role in the Oscar-winning movie is played by an actor who sings, dances, and (acts, acted) well.

8. In Shakespeare's plays, there (were, are) many comedy parts.

9. If I (was, were) a great actress, I would like to play Cordelia in Shakespeare's *King Lear.*

10. Shakespeare's plays (have been, were, are) popular from his day to the present.

11. After baseball practice last night, Gary (lay, laid) his baseball cap on the front hall table.

12. He (played, has played) baseball every day since spring began, including today.

13. Todd (laid, has laid, lays) carpet for Brown's Furniture Store for several years and still works there.

14. He works forty hours a week and (earned, earns) a good living.

15. Like many workers, he has often (lain, lay, laid) down for a nap between work and dinner.

16. Sometimes he has (lain, laid, lay) on the couch for an hour.

17. Last night, when he (finished, had finished) his evening paper, Todd (lay, laid) down for a short nap.

18. After Kathy (studied, had studied) for her algebra test, she phoned Kim.

19. By tomorrow at this time, Kathy (will finish, will have finished) her first year of college algebra.

20. While Kathy studies, she underlines, makes marginal notes, and (wrote, writes, will write) in her notebook.

EXERCISE 2. Recognizing Active and Passive Voice

Indicate whether the verbs in the following sentences are in active or passive voice. Check your answers with those at the back of the book.

_____ 1. Joe enjoyed his work at the restaurant.

_____ 2. He was greeted each day by the manager.

_____ 3. He worked eight hours in each shift.

_____ 4. Generous tips were received by many of Joe's coworkers.

_____ 5. Because Joe worked in the kitchen, he received no tips.

_____ 6. He laid the dirty towels in the laundry basket.

_____ 7. Towels were thrown there by all the kitchen workers.

_____ 8. Glasses and dishes were piled high by the hard-working busboys.

_____ 9. Silverware was dropped in a special basket.

_____ 10. Waitresses carried heavy food trays.

_____ 11. Joe learned how hard restaurant work is.

_____ 12. His friends were told many of the details.

_____ 13. After a long, hard summer, Joe wanted to quit and return to school.

_____ 14. A surprise party was given for him the last day.

_____ 15. The waitresses had planned the party.

_____ 16. New landscaping has been added in front of the restaurant this fall.

_____ 17. Joe enjoys an occasional visit to the restaurant as a patron.

_____ 18. His friends give him extra attention.

_____ 19. Coupon specials are also offered to him as a college student.

_____ 20. Restaurant work attracts many teenagers and college students.

EXERCISE 3. Creating Sentences Using Tenses, Moods, and Voices

Write complete sentences that use the following features.

1. Present tense of *lie:*

   _____

   _____

2. Past tense of *lie:*

   _____

   _____

3. Present perfect tense of *lie:*

   _____

   _____

4. Present tense of *lay:*

   _____

   _____

5. Past tense of *lay:*

   _____

   _____

6. Past perfect tense of *lay:*

   _____

   _____

7. Future perfect tense of *save* (the principal parts of this verb are *save, saved, saved*):

_____

_____

8. Active voice, using any verb you want:

_____

_____

9. Passive voice, using any verb you want:

_____

_____

10. Subjunctive mood:

_____

_____

EXERCISE 4.   *Revising for Consistent, Logical Use of Tenses*

On a separate piece of paper, revise the following essay to make verb tenses logical and consistent. Use several tenses, but make sure that the time sequence throughout is logical. Rearrange the order of sentences as you choose, and eliminate any sentences you feel are irrelevant.

Survival on the Prairie

Early settlers on the midwestern prairies faced two main challenges in the winter: getting food and staying warm. The same challenges confront people in northern climates today, but we are better able to deal with them. Often the pioneers turned to the Indians for solutions to problems. The Indians had learned how to handle winter.

The first problem is that very little fresh food can be found on the frozen prairie. Ice fishermen could catch fresh fish, and hunters brought home rabbit or deer. Other food had been grown in the summer and preserved for winter. Large amounts of wheat, corn, rice, barley, and oats were dried and stored for long winters. Some of the grain is used by animals, and the rest is ground into flour or cereal. All summer and fall, when food is abundant, settlers canned fruit, vegetables, and meat.

Storing food sufficient for five or six months creates a challenge, too. Most pioneers lived in small cabins or dugouts that offer little storage space. Food supplies had to be stored elsewhere. Caves provide a convenient solution if they are located close enough to the dwellings. Some usable caves had been in existence for centuries, but others had to be dug by the pioneers. Newly created caves designed for food storage are called root cellars because root crops (such as potatoes, turnips, and carrots) will keep for months in the cool, damp cellars. Many settlers had root cellars for their harvest of root crops, squash, pumpkins, and melons, plus canned and dried grains and meat.

A second major problem is staying warm. Fuel is hard to find on a frozen prairie, just as food is, and fuel supplies must be gathered when available and stored. In this respect, too, settlers had storage problems once they got what they needed. In wooded areas, settlers could find firewood in all seasons, but many parts of the prairie do not have enough woods to provide sufficient fuel. The native prairie grass burns well, but gathering and storing sufficient grass to heat a cabin all winter is impractical.

Many settlers bought coal to supplement their wood supplies. Of course, coal comes into the Midwest by way of trains or barges and is sold in towns. Settlers on the prairies had to plan ahead, buy the coal in good weather, move it to their farms or ranches on wagons, and store it for winter.

Today we spend very little time preparing food and fuel supplies for winter; we generally can buy all we need as we go along. Modern transportation and distribution systems changed the way people acquire necessities for surviving winter.

EXERCISE 5.   *Revising Verb Usage and Sentence Structure*

A. *Revise the following paragraph of a student's essay, writing between the lines and in the margins. Replace weak* be *verbs with action verbs, and make tenses consistent and logical.*
B. *Repair fragments and comma splices.*
C. *Use compound sentences to connect related thoughts.*
D. *Reword as you like to make the paragraph read better, but preserve the original meaning.*

It was about six months ago. But it seems like only yesterday. I was in an odd situation, I was on the way to the pediatrician's office in the city. My son, Jeremy, was with me. My daughters came along. Sharon and Megan. I was eager to see a friend who worked at the doctor's office. Her name was Stacie, I went to high school with her. At the office, I found out she has that day off. So I phoned her after Jeremy had his appointment. She said to come over. On the way to her house, Jeremy, Sharon, Megan, and I had lunch. Then we left the restaurant to go to Stacie's house. After driving twenty minutes, I was lost. I found a phone booth near the highway. Stacie is easy to understand

and gives great directions. After talking a few minutes. I hung up the phone. Then I tried to open the door. It would not budge. I tried again. No use. I was stuck. Three young children were left alone in a nearby car.

EXERCISE 6. Revising to Use Active and Passive Voice

A. Revise these sentences to use the active voice.

1. It was believed by our accounting department that payments should be made before January 1.

   _____

   _____

2. We were advised by the tax specialist that the Internal Revenue Service should be consulted before any changes are made in our filing procedure.

   _____

   _____

3. The arrival of the shipment was scheduled by us for November 15.

   _____

   _____

4. The date on the invoice was arranged by us so that deferred payment could be sent by you.

   _____

   _____

5. The date for the exam is being postponed by the professor because the impression given to her by the students is that the material is not understood.

   _____

   _____

   _____

B. Revise these sentences to use the passive voice.

6. Your salesman promised us a 10 percent discount, but you show only a 5 percent discount on the invoice.

_____

_____

7. I do not understand why you do not honor your company's promises.

_____

8. The typist typed the contract and mailed it yesterday.

_____

9. The mail service delayed the arrival of the contract.

_____

10. The recipient signed the contract and returned it within two weeks.

_____

EXERCISE 7. Writing About Your Own Experience

On a separate piece of paper, write a short account of a situation in which your life was moving along as usual, only to be interrupted by an unexpected situation or problem, such as getting stuck in a phone booth or losing a wallet or passport. Write at least ten sentences.

EXERCISE 8. Revising Student Writing

In response to Exercise 7, students wrote the following accounts of their experiences. Read these accounts for discussion in class. As you read them, mark passages that need improvement concerning verb choice and sentence structure.

The students wrote these accounts before studying topic sentences for paragraphs. Although these accounts deal with single, specific events, each one lacks a central focus. What is the central idea in each of these paragraphs? Summarize that central idea in one sentence.

Example 1

One afternoon last summer I was on my way to a repair shop. I was picking up my motorcycle tire, it was repaired. I had just turned off the freeway and was looking for the right street. I drove about four blocks but couldn't find it. I decided to keep driving and finally came to a familiar street, there I decided to turn left. The light was green, and I waited for a car to pass, then I turned. What a surprise. I was horrified to find that I turned the wrong way onto a one way. I sat up straight, like an arrow, in the seat, after I dodged a few cars, I was able to get over to the right side of the road. I stopped and took a deep breath and heard my heart beat wildly. I shook off all forms of embarrassment, then I made my turn and went on my way. The right way this time.

Central idea: _____

Example 2

After an unsuccessful hunting season last year, I was so frustrated I didn't know what to do. I knew I had to do something because I love hunting, another season like that was more than I could face. So I looked around for solutions. Finally I bought a piece of hunting land that should solve the problem. The land is five hundred acres, it consists of a field that is mainly for planting corn. A mile and a half one way and a half mile across the other way. The field was enclosed by woods with many small trails, just dirt paths, still hunters will be able to get through to the field. The woods have some clear spots for hunting. The land is all fairly hilly with many ridges, and the ridges looked like they were traveled by a lot of deer. The woods and field will be good for hunting because of the many food sources, corn, acorns, and a little pond for water are the main food sources for the deer. Sounds good, doesn't it?

Central idea: _____

Example 3

While I was at work last week, a very unusual girl walked into the office. She was wearing a tight mini skirt, patterned hose, spike heels, and a daring low-cut sweater. Her hair was blond with streaks in it, and it was cut in a punk style. The most surprising part of her appearance was what I saw dangling from her nose. It was an earring! I couldn't imagine what she wanted in our office. We sell real estate and arrange for rentals. Maybe she wants to rent an apartment, I thought. She didn't say anything; just stared at me for what seemed like a long while. I began to get uneasy. Then she said she wanted change for a dollar. Wow, was I ever relieved! Luckily I had change in my purse, and after I gave her that, she left.

Central idea: _____

7

Working with Sentences

Matching Subjects and Verbs

Subjects and verbs must match or agree in number.

- Singular subjects take singular verbs:

    The <u>train</u> <u>is</u> often late during rush hour.

    <u>I</u> <u>wait</u> patiently.

- Plural subjects take plural verbs:

    The <u>trains</u> <u>are</u> full of passengers during rush hour.

    <u>We</u> <u>look</u> for empty seats, but often we must stand.

FINDING THE SUBJECT

In earlier chapters, we found subjects more easily by following these steps:

1. Eliminating nonessential parts of the sentence.
2. Relying on standard word order.

Nonessential parts of the sentence include prepositional phrases, adjectives, adverbs, and interjections. The remaining words will constitute the essential parts of the sentence: subjects, verbs, objects, or complements.

PRACTICE 1

Draw a line through the prepositional phrases and the other modifiers in the sentence below. Then underline the subject once and the verb twice.

In the fall with the bright-colored leaves on our trees, the scene between our house and our neighbors' houses reminds us of pictures of the rural New England countryside in autumn.

Sometimes punctuation gives us visual clues about nonessentials. When a group of words comes between the subject and the verb, it is often set off with commas on each side. A word group enclosed in parentheses or dashes—like this example—can be ignored; no essential sentence elements will be found inside those marks.

Many kinds of nonessential word groups can be enclosed in punctuation marks, including appositives (introduced in Chapter 5) and word groups that begin with such expressions as *together with, as well as, along with, including,* and *in addition to.* Such units are generally set off with commas.

PRACTICE 2

Draw a line through the nonessential word groups in the following sentences. Then underline the subjects once and the verbs twice.

Example: Paul Simons, ~~my neighbor across the street~~, enjoys hockey.

1. Mr. Simons, along with his wife and daughter, attends most of the professional hockey games in this city.

2. Another neighbor, John Michaelson, as well as his family, prefers football over hockey.

3. Sports fans, in addition to supporting their favorite teams, bring revenue into the cities.

4. The regular concert series and special concerts, including those featuring guest artists, attract many music lovers.

When setting aside nonessentials, watch for the adverbs *here* and *there.* These words cannot be subjects even though they can be used at the beginning of a sentence. When a sentence begins with that wording, the subject is delayed:

There is the student's history textbook.

Here are his class notes.

Sometimes introductory phrases delay the start of a sentence. These units are often set off with commas.

Since Monday, we have learned a great deal.

With good guidance, we can learn a great deal.

PRACTICE 3

Draw a line through the nonessential word groups in the following sentences. Then underline the subjects once and the verbs twice.

Example: ~~There~~ <u>are</u> ~~many dedicated~~ <u>historians</u> and <u>anthropologists</u> ~~at~~ ~~work on gaining understanding of our past~~.

1. In coming years, there will be further research into the Neanderthal era.

2. In 1856, in a valley near Düsseldorf, West Germany, evidence of an extinct human species was found.

3. After the discovery in that valley, the name of the valley, Neanderthal, was applied to that extinct species.

4. Over the generations since 1856, the word *Neanderthal* assumed several meanings, including the connotation of a crude, boorish person.

Relying on word order (subject first, then verb) can also help us find subjects. Rearranging words into standard word order is especially useful with questions.

<u>Was</u> the <u>party</u> <u>postponed</u>?

becomes

The <u>party</u> <u>was</u> <u>postponed</u>.

Sometimes it helps to ask yourself what the sentence is really about: Who is doing what? Even when a sentence is long and complicated, the subject and verb can usually be found by answering that question. It may help to reword the statement, using standard word order, along with your own words. Then you should be able to see the subject and verb at once.

PRACTICE 4

Rewrite the following sentences in your own words. In your new sentences, underline the subjects once and the verbs twice.

Example: Slowly, steadily, gently, without a whisper to break the silence falls the snow.

The <u>snow</u> <u>falls</u> softly, gently, without a whisper.

1. Out of the mist and fog across the lovely valley arose a whiff of smoke.

_____

_____

2. Because of the importance of the discovery, there will be extensive news coverage about this vaccine.

_____

_____

3. "Get back," the officer shouted at the crowds; therefore, "get back" they did.

_____

_____

SELECTING THE VERB

Having located the subject, we can select a verb. The principle makes sense: use a singular verb with a singular subject, a plural verb with a plural subject. But one peculiarity should be noted first: Singular third-person, present-tense verbs often end with s; the corresponding plural verbs (third person, present tense) do not end with s.

Singular: The girl *walks, talks, dances, sings.*
Plural: Girls *walk, talk, dance, sing.*

Present-tense, third-person verbs are among the most commonly used verbs. To make matters a bit more confusing, subjects of these verbs often end in the opposite way; that is, singular subjects don't usually have s endings, plural subjects usually do.

PRACTICE 5

Create your own examples, adding present-tense verbs to these third-person subjects.

1. The student _____.

2. The student _____ and _____.

3. The students _____ and _____.

4. They _____.

The verbs you used almost certainly fit the patterns described above. The patterns seem natural, even though the rules describing them sound contradictory.

Various situations can create special problems in matching subjects and verbs. For example, collective nouns can be either singular or plural, depending on the intended meaning. As we did in Chapter 4 when choosing pronouns to agree with a collective noun antecedent, we use the entire context and common sense to determine whether a singular or plural meaning is intended. Then we make the entire sentence singular or plural, including pronouns, verbs, and any other references.

The jury returns its verdict before it leaves court.

(Notice the many singular words: *its, it, leaves.*)

The jury then return to their jobs and their homes.

(Notice the many plural words: *their jobs, their homes.*)

To select the right verb, first determine whether the collective noun has a singular or a plural meaning. Then use singular or plural words consistently throughout the sentence.

PRACTICE 6 _____

Underline the correct verbs in the following sentences.

1. The staff (plan, plans) for its annual conference at a resort on the lake.

2. The team (run, runs) around the football field three times to warm up before it begins practice.

3. The team (celebrate, celebrates) its winning season with a parade through the city streets.

4. At dinner time in many households, the entire family (sit, sits) down together.

_____

In addition, words pertaining to quantity can be singular or plural, depending on the situation. Words such as *most, half, some,* and *part* take on their meaning when we have more information: Most of what? Half of what? Some of what? Part of what?

The answers to these questions usually come immediately, often in prepositional phrases. Of course, the words in these phrases cannot be subjects of sentences, but the phrases do color the meaning, as in these examples:

Most of the pie is on the kitchen table.

Most of the pies are on the kitchen table.

Half of the dessert is gone.

Half of the desserts are gone.

Picture the subject mentally. One part of a singular entity will be singular (*most of the pie*); part of a plural entity will be plural (*most of the pies*).

PRACTICE 7

Underline the correct verbs in the following sentences.

1. Part of the letter (is, are) typed neatly.

2. Most of the business letters (is, are) word-processed.

3. Two-thirds of our correspondence (come, comes) from advertisers or bill collectors.

4. A quarter of our friends (write, writes) notes on their holiday greeting cards.

Another item to keep in mind is that compound subjects joined with *and* are considered plural. Nevertheless, there are a few rare exceptions in which the two parts of the unit are thought of as one, not two:

Ham and eggs is my favorite breakfast.

The bow and arrow was used by that deer hunter.

Ordinarily we use a plural verb when the two parts of a compound subject are joined with *and:*

Dogs and cats please their owners.

Kristin and Kevin attend all the football games.

Compound subjects joined with the words *or* or *nor* are considered separately, creating three possibilities:

1. Both parts of the subject are singular. Then the verb is singular, as in this example:

Either Mary or Sue drives that red car.

2. Both parts of the subject are plural. Then the verb is plural, as in this example:

Neither the drivers nor the mechanics find any problems with that car.

3. One part is singular, the other plural. Then the verb agrees with the part of the subject that is closer to the verb, as in these examples:

> Neither the <u>driver</u> nor the <u>mechanics</u> <u>find</u> any problems with that car.

> Neither the <u>mechanics</u> nor the <u>driver</u> <u>finds</u> any problems with that car.

PRACTICE 8

Underline the subjects once and the correct verbs twice in the following sentences.

Examples: Either the <u>teacher</u> or the <u>students</u> <u>shut</u> the door.

Either the <u>students</u> or the <u>teacher</u> <u>shuts</u> the door.

1. Neither the doctor nor the patients (see, sees) all the insurance forms.

2. Either the nurses or the clerical workers (fill, fills) in the forms.

3. Dr. Teresa Grant and her nurse (handle, handles) about thirty patients per day in the office.

4. Neither Dr. Grant nor her assistants (want, wants) an increased patient load.

Indefinite pronouns require special attention. They are considered singular, but are easily mistaken for plural. The first two on this list present particular problems:

everyone	one
everybody	each
someone	no one
somebody	nobody
anyone	anybody

It may help to think of *everyone* and *everybody* as meaning each and every individual one or each and every individual body. Use singular references throughout the sentence when one of these pronouns is the subject. Compare these singular and plural examples:

> <u>Everyone</u> <u>comes</u> to class with (his) or (her) (paper) done.

> <u>Students</u> <u>come</u> to class with (their) (papers) done.

Subject complements do not have to agree with the subjects and verbs, as these examples show. (The subject complements are labeled SC.)

SC
The <u>reason</u> for her anxiety <u>was</u> family problems.

SC
Family <u>problems</u> <u>were</u> the reason for her anxiety.

SC
Tracy's favorite <u>gift</u> <u>was</u> new sweaters.

SC
Ron's new sport <u>shirts</u> <u>were</u> his favorite gift.

Also keep in mind that certain words with *s* endings are always singular or always plural, and others can be either singular or plural, depending on their use. Singular words include *mathematics*, *civics*, *economics*, *physics*, *measles*, *mumps*, *news*. In these sentences, notice that the verbs agree with the singular subjects:

The <u>news</u> <u>was</u> all bad yesterday.

<u>Economics</u> <u>is</u> an interesting field of study.

<u>Mathematics</u> <u>belongs</u> in many college students' programs.

Plural words include *scissors*, *trousers*, and *eyeglasses* (or *glasses*). In these sentences, notice that the verbs agree with the plural subjects:

Cory's <u>glasses</u> <u>are</u> on the desk.

Gary's <u>trousers</u> <u>were</u> on the chair last night.

PRACTICE 9

Underline the correct verbs in the following sentences.

1. Brent's sunglasses (lay, lays) on the kitchen table.

2. The problem with the glasses (was, were) scratched lenses.

3. Kirk's good news about his grades (make, makes) his parents happy.

4. Physics (is, are) his most demanding class and lab work.

Amounts are considered singular, as in an amount of money or ingredients. Blocks of time can be considered singular or plural. Note the following examples:

Twelve dollars is too much to pay for lunch.

Three cups was enough flour for that recipe.

Four years in college goes by quickly.

or

Four years in college go by quickly.

PRACTICE 10

Underline the correct verbs in the following sentences.

1. The new glasses (cost, costs) ninety dollars.

2. Ninety dollars (is, are) a reasonable price for eyeglasses.

3. Neither the glasses nor the eye exam (is, are) covered by our insurance.

4. Five bags of driftwood chips (cover, covers) the space between the shrubbery and the flower bed.

5. Either the shrubbery or the trees (require, requires) pruning every season.

6. Three bushels of fruit (come, comes) from that small tree each year.

Using Sentences in Paragraphs

A paragraph is a group of sentences related in thought and arranged in a visual block on the page. Every paragraph has one central idea, and all the sentences in that paragraph should relate to that main idea. Putting ideas together if they are related in thought is the principle underlying compound sentences. The same principle, by extension, applies to paragraphs.

Consider, for instance, sentences 11 and 12 and 14–19 on pages 38–39 (Chapter 2, Exercise 2). As they stand in that exercise, those sentences are set apart so that you can analyze them individually. Here, with slight modification, the same ideas are put together in a paragraph.

The War of 1812 had been very unpopular in New England. Some leaders in New England had advocated secession from the union. But before secession became a real possibility, the war ended with representatives of England and the United States signing a peace treaty on Christmas Eve, 1814. When the United States Congress ratified the treaty on February 16, 1815, the mood in New England changed over-

night. Talk of secession was dropped instantly with the arrival of peace, and in Boston, the pace-setting city of its
region, musicians and orators staged festive public celebrations.

The individual ideas in that paragraph belong together because
they all concern one central thought:

The ending of the War of 1812 changed the mood in New
England overnight.

As the paragraph above stands, this central idea is not as forceful
or as clear as it would be if that central idea were stated openly at the
start. A good way to make sure that a paragraph establishes a central
idea in readers' minds is to begin with a **topic sentence**—a summary
statement that establishes a central idea in readers' minds.

A topic sentence establishes both the topic to be discussed in the
paragraph and the limits of that topic. For instance, let us begin the
sample paragraph about the War of 1812 with the suggested topic
sentence. Now, the paragraph opens with a statement of its topic,
namely, the end of the war. In addition, that broad topic is limited to
one specific feature, namely, the changing mood in New England.

The ending of the War of 1812 changed the mood in New
England overnight. The war had been very unpopular in that
part of the country. Some leaders in New England had advocated secession from the union. But before secession became a real possibility, the war ended with representatives of
England and the United States signing a peace treaty on
Christmas Eve, 1814. When the United States Congress
ratified the treaty on February 16, 1815, talk of secession
dropped instantly. With the arrival of peace, musicians and
orators in Boston—the pace-setting city of its region—staged
festive public celebrations.

This revised version of the paragraph emphasizes the change in
mood in New England; the topic sentence directs our attention to that
idea, and all the sentences that follow pertain to that idea. This is just
one example of a well-known and practiced principle: starting a paragraph with a topic sentence gives the writer a central idea to focus on
while writing and the reader a central idea to focus on while reading.

PRACTICE 11

A. Combine sentences 7, 8, 9 in Exercise 4, Chapter 8, page 189, into a
short paragraph beginning with this topic sentence: "The song 'My Country 'Tis of Thee' has a long history." Revise the sentences and rearrange
their order as you like, but keep the facts accurate. (Write on a separate
piece of paper.)

B. *Create topic sentences for the student paragraphs in Chapter 6, Exercise 8, pages 141–142.*

How can we tell whether ideas are related or whether they belong in the same paragraph? Generally, ideas are related if they support the same central idea. An effective paragraph is said to have unity (oneness) because it deals with one central idea, an idea generally stated in the topic sentence.

In the paragraph below, some of the ideas do not belong because they do not relate to the central idea. The first sentence is the topic sentence; it states the central idea.

PRACTICE 12

Draw a line through the sentences that do not belong in this paragraph.

Students in the two-year medical assistant program must meet certain requirements. They must complete three courses in medical lab fundamentals and then three courses in clinical procedures. These courses must be taken in sequence. Nutrition Care I, II, and III are taken in sequence by dietetic technology students. At the same time, courses in typewriting and business communications must be completed by the students in the medical assistant program. Meanwhile, medical technology students are required to take organic chemistry, general biology, and zoology in preparation for the rest of their four-year degree program. But the hard work is worthwhile because graduates of the medical assistant program find good jobs.

PRACTICE 13

A. *Find the course requirements for a program that interests you. Your college catalogue will list these requirements.*
B. *Create five sentences in which you describe the requirements.*
C. *Use a topic sentence patterned after the first sentence of the paragraph above.*
D. *Write your five sentences on a separate piece of paper.*

In writing the paragraph in Practice 13, you probably combined certain ideas in order to cover the requirements in only five sentences. For instance, you could have combined individual math courses by stating that math is required through calculus or through the second year of analysis, including vector analysis.

Although there is no "right" length for paragraphs, we need adequate support for the topic idea. Assuming that the topic idea is limited and therefore manageable in one paragraph, five to seven sentences should be enough. Paragraphs vary greatly in length because they vary greatly in their content, audience, and purpose.

Points to Use

- Find the subjects and verbs in your sentences by eliminating nonessential parts and rearranging words into standard word order: subject first, then verb.
- Use standard word order unless you have a good reason not to. Readers will follow your ideas more easily if you use typical sentence patterns, the ones readers know and expect.
- Avoid confusing extra words or phrases with the subject. Word groups between the subject and the verb often are not part of the subject, but rather are extra elements set off with commas.
- Use your own examples as reminders of the *s* endings on third-person, present-tense, singular subjects: He *talks, walks, dances,* and so forth. Contrast those examples with the plural forms: They *talk, walk, dance,* and so forth.
- Be aware of those few special situations in which subject-verb agreement requires special care. Two common pitfalls involve indefinite pronouns (e.g., *everyone, everybody*) and compound units.
- Treat indefinite pronouns as singular words, including *everyone* and *everybody.*
- Use plural verbs for compound subjects joined by *and.*
- Consider compound subjects joined by *or* or *nor* separately. Use a singular verb if the parts are singular, a plural verb if the parts are plural. If one part of the subject is singular and the other part is plural, the verb should agree with the part that is closer to the verb.
- Combine sentences into paragraphs when the individual ideas are related. Do not combine sentences into paragraphs when the individual ideas are unrelated.
- Develop paragraphs around one central idea.
- Use a topic sentence to express the central idea. A good place for the topic sentence is the beginning of the paragraph.
- Back up your topic idea with supporting sentences—perhaps five to seven of them—so that the central idea is clear to the reader.

Points to Remember

- Singular subjects require singular verbs; plural subjects require plural verbs.
- Eliminate nonessential parts of the sentence and use standard word order to help find subjects.

- Collective nouns can be singular or plural, depending on their use. The entire sentence must be singular or plural for consistency.
- Subjects pertaining to quantities can be singular or plural depending on the context, but a total sum of money or material is singular. Amounts of time can be singular or plural.
- Use plural verbs for compound subjects joined by *and.* Compound subjects joined with *or* or *nor* are considered separately.
- Indefinite pronouns—such as *everyone, everybody, no one, nobody, someone, somebody,* and others—are considered singular.
- Subjects and verbs must agree, but subject complements do not need to be in agreement.
- In some special cases, nouns are simply classed as singular or plural. Words classified as singular include *mathematics, measles,* and *news.* Words classified as plural include *trousers, scissors,* and *eyeglasses.*
- A paragraph is a group of related ideas combined visually in a block of print. This concept extends the principle of combining related ideas into a compound sentence. Within the paragraph, individual sentences are combined visually because they are related in thought.
- Sentences in a paragraph should all pertain to one main idea.
- A topic sentence, often placed at the beginning of the paragraph, expresses the main idea of the paragraph. Other sentences should support that main idea.
- Paragraphs vary in length, depending on their content, audience, and purpose.

EXERCISE 1. Selecting the Correct Verb

Underline the subjects and circle the correct verbs or other word choices in these sentences. Check your answers with those at the back of the book.

1. Each of the many restaurants in our area (has, have) something distinctive to offer.

2. Half of the nearby restaurants (is, are) fast-food places.

3. There on the northwest corner of that busy intersection (stand, stands) my favorite restaurant.

4. The restaurant, because of all the traffic on those streets, (get, gets) a lot of business.

5. Neither the food nor the service (need, needs) improvement there.

6. Both the cooks and the waitresses (is, are) quick.

7. Lisa Williams, together with Joyce Sampson, (work, works) there after school every day.

8. Neither Lisa nor the other waitresses (take, takes) many days off.

9. Everyone in that restaurant (work, works) hard during (his, his/her, their) (shift, shifts).

10. The specialty of the day (is, are) fresh berry pies.

11. Blueberry pie, especially with ice cream, (top, tops) off a meal perfectly.

12. (Does, Do) Jim and I want dessert today?

13. Someone in your family with a big appetite (like, likes) cherry pie.

14. Four dollars (is, are) a reasonable price to pay for a simple, nutritious lunch.

15. After lunch, Dave's glasses (was, were) still lying on the lunch counter, and he could not see well without (it, them).

16. Mathematics (is, are) difficult enough for Dave when he has his glasses.

17. Classes in physics and economics (run, runs) right before noon on that campus.

18. Half of the sandwich (is, are) enough for me.

19. Half of the sandwiches (look, looks) delicious today.

20. Neither of these menus (tell, tells) the price of a bowl of clam chowder.

21. The complete menu (take, takes) three pages.

22. Three-fourths of the menu selections (is, are) available at noon.

23. Our favorite waitress, Marcia Paulson, or one of her friends (serve, serves) us regularly.

24. Everyone in our group (appreciate, appreciates) Marcia's quick and friendly service.

25. A bowl of soup or two sandwiches (make, makes) a satisfying lunch.

26. For a gourmet dinner, there (is, are) several excellent local restaurants.

27. Thirty dollars per person (seem, seems) expensive, but everyone at the company party (pay, pays) that amount to enjoy the festive occasion.

28. Either elegant food or outstanding service (attract, attracts) patrons to the expensive restaurants.

29. Neither friendly waitresses nor a pleasing atmosphere (compensate, compensates) for poor food.

30. The family (is, are) eager to celebrate Jim's birthday.

31. The family, along with his grandparents, Uncle Ted, and Aunt Martha, (dine, dines) out every year on that day.

32. Most of us (enjoy, enjoys) those family gatherings.

33. Most of the dinner (arrive, arrives) under candlelight in the quiet, elegant restaurant.

34. The nine-year-old guest of honor, unlike his parents, (dislike, dislikes) candlelight.

35. After he had waited a year for this birthday party, (was, were) it fair to take him there for his dinner?

36. There (is, are) many reasons for and against candlelight dining.

37. Neither our car nor the cars of our relatives (was, were) large enough to take all of us to the dinner.

38. Their cars and our car (was, were) used.

39. Everyone in the family (enjoy, enjoys) the boy's birthday and (like, likes) the dinner out.

40. The time for farewells for another year (come, comes) too soon.

41. Either the waiter or the waitress (bring, brings) the check.

42. (Was, Were) the food, the service, and the atmosphere satisfactory?

43. Jim's answers to that question (change, changes) our plans for next year.

44. The restaurant staff (listen, listens) to suggestions for improvements in (its, their) work.

45. Jim, as well as other members of the family, (is, are) happy to be remembered on special occasions.

46. (Is, Are) Mr. and Mrs. Smith home this evening?

47. On the back porch, there (stand, stands) a picnic table with six chairs.

48. The team, along with the coach and the cheerleaders, (is, are) coming to the party after the game.

49. The committee on political action (hold, holds) its meetings on our campus each month.

50. Half of their discussion (go, goes) toward resolving local issues.

51. Half of their members (go, goes) to the meetings regularly.

52. Two hours, especially in late afternoon, (make, makes) a tiring session.

53. Forgotten by the students and overlooked by the teacher, there (lie, lies) an extra copy of the test.

54. None of the students (take, takes) extra time to look for lost copies of tests.

55. Most of this exercise (is, are) easy and obvious.

EXERCISE 2. Completing Sentences with Subjects and Verbs

A. *Add present-tense verbs to complete these sentences. Underline the subjects once and the verbs twice.*

Example: Either the senior class <u>president</u> or the other <u>officers</u>

<u><u>will</u> organize</u> the class party.

1. For just a few moments, the horse and its rider _____

_____

2. The silvery light of dawn over the trees behind our house _____

_____

3. The safety inspector, along with his newly appointed assistant and his experienced secretary, _____

_____

4. After a few introductory remarks, enough to get the children's attention for a moment, the junior high school principal _____

_____

5. On the back of the postcard, beside the return address, a blurred message _____

_____

6. Neither the head football coach nor the assistant coaches _____

_____

7. The Houston Astros games on television _____

_____

8. After the game but before dinner, the guests who joined us for the afternoon _____

_____

9. For the wedding reception and dinner, forty dollars per person _____

_____

10. After watching the afternoon races at the track, everybody _____

_____

B. *Add subjects to complete these sentences. Underline the subjects once and the verbs twice.*

Example: ___*allen*___ seldom misses the horse races on the weekends.

11. _____ immediately run away in panic at the very sight.

12. _____ calls to the suspect and chases after him.

13. _____ take the suspect back to the station in the patrol car and book him.

14. _____ usually goes to the school cafeteria and eats between classes, then leaves after class for work.

15. _____ often select cold sandwiches and salads in the early fall but order soup or chili on cooler days.

16. _____ become dental hygienists after long, careful training on our campus.

17. _____ either work at law enforcement agencies immediately after graduation or continue their education in four-year institutions after two years here.

18. _____ hopes to transfer to a private college after two years at this school but needs financial aid.

19. _____ often work twenty or more hours per week and do most of the preparation for college classes during the weekends.

20. _____ fully understands the heavy demands of long work hours and many study hours.

EXERCISE 3. *Writing Original Sentences*

Create two original sentences following the patterns listed below. Underline the subjects once and the verbs twice.

1. Sentences with singular subjects and verbs:

a. _____

b. _____

2. Sentences with compound subjects:

 a. _____

 b. _____

3. Sentences with collective nouns as subjects:

 a. _____

 b. _____

4. Sentences with indefinite pronouns as subjects:

 a. _____

 b. _____

5. Sentences with subject complements:

 a. _____

 b. _____

EXERCISE 4. *Revising Sentences and Pronoun and Verb Choices*

On a separate piece of paper, rewrite the following memo to repair subject-verb agreement, pronoun choice, and sentence structure. In addition, the memo needs appropriate tone and logical order. Add and omit details so that the ideas are expressed in an orderly and effective way.

To: Ms. Lynn Sparta   Date: October 17
From: Eddie Peters
Subject: Why We Haven't Gotten Raises

We all talked about it over last night and nobody is satisfied with the answer you gave us about our raises, everybody says the same thing, we earned them.

Working here is hard, we have long hours and people like Pete, Michelle and Joel is really hurting from extra shifts. Then low wages besides. The ones who are like Doug and Barb, single and working few hours, has no complaint.

Last month a cook and busboy and two waitresses, here a long time and every one of them a good worker has given notices, they just can't wait longer for raises. Now three more want to quit.

In August Tim said he asked you and you said we'd get maybe around 45 cents an hour increases before the end of summer, now this is October. No increases yet. Not for me or Sharon, not for anybody I know of around here.

Another thing. We asked for the vents over the dishwasher to get cleaned in July, you said, sure, no problem, right away. On hot days all summer better airflow through there would of helped. Did we get it, no, and it is still stuffy in that end of the kitchen. Plus the dishwasher leaks and makes the floors slippery.

EXERCISE 5. *Creating Sentences*

On a separate piece of paper, create ten complete sentences using the information given below. You may use any of these facts in any order. Double-space your sentences, and underline the subjects once and the verbs twice.

> The five Great Lakes, east to west, Ontario, Erie, Huron, Michigan, Superior.
> Largest Superior; smallest Ontario.
> Formed by glaciers during the Ice Age.
> Many glaciers advancing and retreating. Over two million years.
> Hollowed valleys, created basins, left lowlands.
> Final forms recent. From 15,000 to 10,000 years ago.
> Great cities around the lakes. Chicago, Detroit, Toronto, Cleveland, and others.
> Deepest lake, Superior, 1,330 feet maximum depth.
> Lake Erie, maximum depth of 210 feet.
> Used for sports. Recreation. Transportation.
> Shores for parks and wilderness areas.
> System forms largest expanse of fresh water in the world.
> Connected to form a waterway. Valuable to Canada and the United States. For commerce, transportation, recreation.
> Total of 94,460 square miles of water in the lakes.

EXERCISE 6. *Creating Short Paragraphs from Sentences*

You have just returned from a trip that included the Great Lakes region. Now you want to describe that region to a friend. Naturally you would not simply list facts, though you will use some facts and state them accurately.

On a separate piece of paper, arrange the information from Exercise 5 into two paragraphs, one describing the lakes and the other summarizing their importance.

EXERCISE 7. *Building Paragraphs from Isolated Facts*

Imagine that you are a medical assistant in a family practice clinic. As part of your job, you must prepare a one-page fact sheet on toxemia. Your writing must be well organized so that patients can grasp the information easily and find specific points for reference later.

On a separate piece of paper, arrange the information given below into two short paragraphs. In one paragraph describe toxemia and its dangers. In another describe its symptoms and treatment.

Can appear in last three months of pregnancy
Shows first in sudden rise in blood pressure
Can cause spontaneous abortions and stillborn infants
Unknown causes
Fairly common
Treated like high blood pressure
Salt-free diet and rest
Diuretics and other medications useful
Requires careful monitoring by doctors
A reason for regular checkups throughout pregnancy

UNIT II PRACTICE TEST
Chapters 4, 5, 6, 7

Part 1 (50 POINTS)

Read each sentence carefully. Mark a, b, or c on the line next to each sentence, depending on whether you have selected the first, second, or third choice for a given question. (Some of the questions have only two choices; for them, simply mark a or b on the answer line.) Check your answers with those at the back of the book.

_____   1. When the phone rang, Tom, David, and (he, him) all ran to answer it.

_____   2. They all wondered (who, whom) would be calling them.

_____   3. "Could it be (he, him)?" David asked aloud.

_____   4. The call must be for Tom or (I, me), he thought.

_____   5. Tom will get to the phone first because he is faster than (I, me).

_____   6. The caller asked to speak to Tom or (he, him).

_____   7. Between you and (I, me), I think they were sorry to find that the caller was conducting a phone survey.

_____   8. (We, Us) consumers are often asked our preferences.

_____   9. Companies want to give (they, them, their) customers good service.

_____   10. Manufacturers give hospitals, businesses, and (we, us) housewives a wide choice of detergents.

_____ 11. (Who, Whom) buys on the basis of price alone?

_____ 12. Mother, Jan, and (she, her) enjoy quality clothing.

_____ 13. These fashion lines impress Sara, Jill, and (she, her).

_____ 14. They seemed to like those lines as much as (I, me).

_____ 15. Perhaps it was (she, her) who first discovered them.

_____ 16. If we are dissatisfied with a product, to (who, whom) should we complain?

_____ 17. Most companies stand behind (there, their, they're) products, ensuring customer satisfaction.

_____ 18. The customers, Lynn, Barbara, and (she, her), endorsed that product.

_____ 19. Looking through the screen door, Dan called to Alissa, "It is (I, me). Please open the door."

_____ 20. Alissa keeps the door locked except for the children and (he, him, himself).

_____ 21. (Whoever, Whomever) comes to the door must knock.

_____ 22. Locking the door gives the children and (she, her) a sense of security.

_____ 23. If it (was, were) a safer neighborhood, Alissa would not be so concerned.

_____ 24. After Dan (entered, had entered) the house, Alissa locked the door again.

_____ 25. She (has locked, locked) her house every day since she moved there three years ago.

_____ 26. The handbag, along with her scarf and shoes, (lie, lies) beside the suitcase.

_____ 27. Laurie and her sisters (enjoy, enjoys) traveling.

_____ 28. Laurie thinks that two hundred dollars (is, are) too much to pay for a plane ticket to Chicago.

_____ 29. Neither Laurie nor her sisters (pay, pays) that much for most of their Minneapolis-to-Chicago plane tickets.

_____ 30. Our tickets (lie, lay) on the counter in front of us yesterday while we talked to the ticket agent.

_____ 31. Someone had (lay, laid, lain) them there by mistake.

_____ 32. Neither my ticket nor the children's tickets (belong, belongs) on that counter.

_____ 33. Sometimes a misunderstanding on the part of the airline employees (cause, causes) confusion.

_____ 34. Everyone in the store (like, likes) wide aisles.

_____ 35. Shannon, together with her mother and the saleslady, (find, finds) that her favorite handbag is expensive.

_____ 36. The saleslady, in addition to her managers, (was, were) happy to sell the handbag to Shannon.

_____ 37. The family (spend, spends) their time at a shopping center where each person can find things of interest.

_____ 38. Anyone who has a chance to go to the National Zoological Park in Washington, D.C., (enjoy, enjoys) the experience.

_____ 39. The Zoological Park, along with art galleries, museums, observatories, and other agencies, (form, forms) a part of the Smithsonian Institution.

_____ 40. Neither the employees nor the tourists (find, finds) parking near the main buildings.

_____ 41. After battling congested traffic for more than an hour, one of the frustrated tourists (park, parks) in a ramp.

_____ 42. Most of the tourists (feel, feels) frustrated about parking problems.

_____ 43. Most of their time (has been, have been) spent visiting interesting and impressive places.

_____ 44. A main attraction at the zoo (is, are) the tigers.

_____ 45. (Was, Were) the white Indian tiger or the orange Bengal tiger outside his lair when you visited the zoo?

_____ 46. The baby monkey, either one of the spider monkeys or one of the golden marmosets, (scamper, scampers) to the front of the cage.

_____ 47. An aviary (is, was) a large enclosure designed to hold a large number of birds in confinement.

_____ 48. How can an elephant (lie, lay) down in such a small room?

_____ 49. After the giraffes (ate, had eaten) the hay in a trough ten feet up the wall, they drank water from a trough nearly that high.

_____ 50. The Minnesota Zoo in Apple Valley, Minnesota, along with a few other major zoos, (feature, features) beluga whales.

Part 2 (50 POINTS)

Write complete, correct, original sentences to illustrate any ten of the following twelve items.

1. Present perfect tense of the verb _lay:_

_____

_____

2. Active-voice use of the verb _save_ (in any tense you wish):

_____

_____

3. Passive-voice use of the verb _save_ (in any tense you wish):

_____

_____

4. A subject-form pronoun as a subject complement:

_____

_____

5. An object-form pronoun as a direct object:

_____

_____

6. The past tense of the verb *lie:*

_____

_____

7. A pronoun used as part of a compound subject:

_____

_____

8. Use of the subjunctive mood:

_____

_____

9. The past perfect use of the verb *lay:*

_____

_____

10. The future perfect use of the verb *earn:*

_____

_____

11. A pronoun used as an appositive:

_____

_____

12. A collective noun used as a subject:

_____

_____

USING PHRASES AND CLAUSES

OBJECTIVES

Grammar and Sentence Structure

To understand and use phrases

To understand and use dependent clauses

To understand and use subordination to combine ideas

Writing

To combine sentences using subordination

To arrange sentences into short paragraphs

To revise paragraphs

To plan a writing project

8

Recognizing and Using Phrases

Handling Verbal Phrases

Before you start a journey into unknown territory, you probably look at a map to get a sense of where you are going and which roads you are taking. You could think of this chapter as a journey into unknown territory, though you will see familiar landmarks, such as prepositional phrases and appositives.

Before this journey begins, you will find an overview of the road ahead helpful. The following terms provide a map to what lies ahead:

- A *phrase* is a group of words acting together as a unit, having neither subject nor verb. A prepositional phrase, consisting of a preposition plus an object, is an example of a phrase.

   Your book is *on the table.*

- A *verbal* is a structure that looks like a verb and is derived from a verb, but does not work like a verb. The three types of verbals are the gerund, the infinitive, and the participle. A *gerund* is a noun derived from a verb and ending with *ing.* It often functions as a subject.

   Swimming relaxes me.

An *infinitive* is a noun, an adjective, or an adverb created from a verb, using the word *to* plus a verb. (No words should come between *to* and the verb.)

   To swim relaxes me.

A *participle* is an adjective derived from a verb and ending with *ing* (the present participle) or *n, en, d, ed,* or *t* (the past participle).

the *falling* rain	a *torn* shirt
the *frozen* lake	*fried* rice
the *bent* twig	*popped* corn

- A *verbal phrase* is a phrase that begins with a verbal and is followed by other words (its objects, complements, or modifiers). This structure is simpler than the description suggests. Examples of verbal phrases are given below.

Note the similarity and simplicity in these patterns:

prepositional phrase = preposition + (modifiers) + object
verbal phrase = verbal + modifiers, objects, or complements
   or
verbal phrase = verbal + other words forming a unit with the verbal

EXAMPLES OF VERBAL PHRASES

The three types of verbal phrases are gerund phrases, infinitive phrases, and participial phrases. Examples of these phrases are given in sentences below. Note that prepositional phrases are sometimes included within the verbal phrases. The use of the phrase in each example is given in parentheses after the example.

In the following discussion, note the guidelines for punctuation for each type of verbal phrase.

Gerund Phrases (Nouns).   Punctuation of gerund phrases depends on usage:

- Nouns used as subjects, objects of verbs, or subject complements—all vital parts of sentences—are not set off with commas.
- Nouns used as appositives—nonessential elements of a sentence—are set off with commas.

1. *Swimming a few laps after work* relaxes me.   (SUBJECT)
2. I enjoy *swimming in the outdoor pool.*   (DIRECT OBJECT)
3. My favorite recreation is *skiing in Colorado.*   (SUBJECT COMPLEMENT)
4. My favorite recreation, *skiing in Colorado,* gives me many hours of pleasure.   (APPOSITIVE)

PRACTICE 1

Write a sentence containing a gerund phrase. Underline the gerund phrase and indicate in parentheses the use of the phrase.

_____

_____

_____

Infinitive Phrases (Nouns, Adverbs, or Adjectives). Punctuation of infinitive phrases depends on the part of speech and on placement:

- Infinitive phrases used as nouns are not set off with commas (see examples 1 and 2 below).
- Infinitive phrases used as adverbs or adjectives are set off with commas when they are introductory. If they appear in the middle or at the end of a sentence, they are not set off (see examples 3, 4, and 5 below).

   1. *To swim a few laps after work* relaxes me.   (SUBJECT)
   2. I love *to swim in the outdoor pool.*   (DIRECT OBJECT)
   3. Dave went home *to read travel brochures about skiing in Colorado.*   (ADVERB, TELLING WHY HE WENT HOME)
   4. *To make money for the skiing trip,* Mark worked extra hours all fall.   (ADVERB, TELLING WHY HE WORKED)
   5. Everyone has some advice *to give to the new skier.*
      (ADJECTIVE, MODIFYING ADVICE)

PRACTICE 2

Write a sentence containing an infinitive phrase. Underline the infinitive phrase and indicate in parentheses the use of the phrase.

_____

_____

_____

Participial Phrases (Adjectives). Punctuation of participial phrases depends on placement:

- When the participial phrase is introductory, it is set off with a comma (see examples 1 and 2 below).
- When the participial phrase is in the middle of the sentence and gives extra, nonessential information, it is set off with commas (see examples 3 and 4 below).
- When the participial phrase is in the middle of the sentence and gives necessary information, it is not set off with commas (see examples 5 and 6 below).
- When the participial phrase is at the end of the sentence, it is set off with commas only when it refers back to the subject at the beginning of the sentence (contrast examples 7 and 8 below).

   1. *Fishing through the ice,* Todd and Brian caught enough fish for a tasty dinner.
   2. *Frozen solid by the severe cold,* the lake was perfect for ice skaters and ice fishermen.

3. The careless student, *writing too fast*, produced an illegible exam paper.
4. His puzzled math teacher, *frowning at the 7's resembling 4's*, gave the student a low grade.
5. Exam papers *written legibly* earn better grades.
6. The textbook *lost in the student center* had no name in it.
7. The owner must have regretted the loss, *considering the book's cost and its value in the course*.
8. Textbooks often cost many dollars *earned through long hours of hard work*.

PRACTICE 3

Write a sentence beginning with a participial phrase. Underline the participial phrase.

_____

_____

Write a sentence with a participial phrase in a position other than the beginning of the sentence. Underline the participial phrase.

_____

_____

PROBLEMS THAT ARISE WITH VERBAL PHRASES

Punctuation.   The rules discussed above follow two general principles:

- Commas set off nonessential elements with sentences, such as participial phrases and appositives.
- Commas set off introductory elements, such as phrases that lead up to the main subject and verb.

Dangling Modifiers.   Dangling modifiers can be various types of phrases, but most often they are participles. ***Dangling participles*** are participles that have nothing or no one to refer to; they are poised in mid-air, truly dangling. Consider the opening phrases here:

Running for the train, the suitcase was lost.
(Who was running? the suitcase?)

Approaching unknown territory, the map was essential.
(Who was approaching the territory? the map?)

Generally, words in sentences connect to the words that are closest to them. The dangling modifier is no exception; by mere proximity, these modifiers attach to the words nearby, even though the connection makes no sense.

In the following sentences, the dangling phrases are italicized and connected by arrows to the words to which they are attached (illogically attached, but attached nonetheless):

Driving down France Avenue, an accident occurred.
(Was the accident driving down France Avenue?)

Watching the game on television, the doorbell rang.
(Was the doorbell watching the game on television?)

Avoiding dangling modifiers is simple, once we recognize the problem. A sentence with a dangling modifier is revised so that the modifier is given a logical reference, something or someone to refer to. Note that these revised sentences use the active voice:

Driving down France Avenue, Joel saw an accident.

Watching the game on television, we heard the doorbell ring.

PRACTICE 4

Revise the following sentences to eliminate the dangling modifiers. Add details as needed and use active-voice verbs.

Example: Driving home on the freeway, the radio played my favorite song.

Driving home on the freeway, I heard my favorite song playing on the radio.

1. *Expecting to win the tournament,* a victory party was planned.

   _____

2. *Failing to follow directions,* Ellen's cake was flat and tough.

   _____

3. *To keep the scholarship,* a "B" average must be maintained.

   _____

4. *Approaching unknown territory,* the map was essential.

   _____

5. *Running for the train,* the suitcase was lost.

_____

_____

Our examples so far have shown dangling modifiers at the beginnings of sentences, where they most commonly occur. The opening modifier attaches to the subject of the sentence with good reason because the subject is usually the main element at the start of the sentence. The subject draws the modifier to itself like a magnet drawing in loose particles.

Sentences that end with dangling modifiers also require revision. The problem is the same, though perhaps less noticeable:

1. The suitcase was lost, *running for the train.*

2. A winning lottery ticket must be presented *to claim the prize.*

3. The game got off to a great start, *scoring six times in the fourth inning.*

PRACTICE 5

Revise the three sentences above to eliminate the dangling modifiers.

1. _____

_____

2. _____

_____

3. _____

_____

In summary, we can avoid dangling modifiers by making sure our modifiers actually refer to what we want them to. A common pattern is as follows:

opening modifier, subject + verb

This pattern works well, provided the opening modifier connects logically to the subject that follows. Of course, we need logical connections between modifiers and their references in all sentences. Finally, we can avoid dangling modifiers by using the active voice; sentences in active voice seldom contain dangling modifiers.

Handling Other Phrases

Besides verbal phrases, three other phrases occur in English:

- The prepositional phrase
- The appositive phrase
- The noun-participle (absolute) phrase

PREPOSITIONAL PHRASES

Although prepositional phrases are so familiar from previous chapters that they need no introduction here, we should consider their proper handling.

As a general rule, prepositional phrases are not set off by commas. If they appear at the beginning of a sentence, however, they can be, particularly if they consist of three or more words:

In the spring the narcissus are the first flowers to bloom.

or

In the spring, the narcissus are the first flowers to bloom.

Phrases of three or more words should be set off by commas to divide the opening phrase and the main sentence elements that follow:

Despite the cool nights, the mums continue blooming in the fall.

Authorities differ on the use of commas with introductory prepositional phrases. Some recommend that we use commas sparingly; others feel that we can use them more generously. Yet there is agreement on the intent behind the rules: to make the writing clear and easy for readers to understand.

PRACTICE 6 ────────────────────────────

Which sentences do you find easier to read and understand, those in Set A or those in Set B? Write your choice on the lines below Set B, stating why one set seems better to you. There is no right or wrong answer.

Set A

In English the most frequently used letter is *e*.
In written and in spoken English the least frequently used letter or sound is *z*.
To the surprise of many English-speaking people the second least frequently used letter is *j*.

Set B

In English, the most frequently used letter is *e*.

In written and in spoken English, the least frequently used letter or sound is *z*.

To the surprise of many English-speaking people, the second least frequently used letter is *j*.

_____

_____

_____

On the basis of this comparison, perhaps you can understand your readers' task a little better. If commas will help your readers, use them to set off opening prepositional phrases; if they will not help your readers, leave them out.

Although prepositional phrases create no special problems, as a matter of style, avoid using long strings of prepositional phrases. Sentences carelessly put together with many back-to-back prepositional phrases lumber along like long freight trains; after the powerful engine passes by—the subject and verb—the rest of the cars clatter down the track monotonously:

> After breakfast, our waitress gave directions to us about the best route from that restaurant to the nearest entrance to the interstate highway.

That sentence could be simplified in this way:

> After breakfast, the waitress gave us directions to the interstate highway.

Generally, two or three prepositional phrases back to back should be enough in one sentence. The rest can be dropped, or the ideas can be combined in other ways.

PRACTICE 7 _____

Revise the following sentences to eliminate long strings of phrases.

Example: Baseball fans watch the performance of their favorite team in the fall during the playoffs before the World Series.

Baseball fans watch their favorite team's performance during the fall playoffs before the World Series.

1. Our team was on the road for almost a week during the fall for playoff games with the winner of the opposing league.

   _____

   _____

2. The team won the playoff series of games in Detroit on a Monday afternoon in October at about 5 P.M.

   _____

   _____

3. Many radio and television commentators were surprised at the sight of our team's winning in those playoffs in Detroit at the end of that season.

   _____

   _____

APPOSITIVE PHRASES

The *appositive* was defined in Chapter 5 as a noun or pronoun unit that identifies the noun or pronoun immediately preceding it. You saw the following example on page 106:

My friends, *Connie and Karen*, were invited to the

party, *a birthday celebration.*

By using appositives, writers can add information quickly and easily with very few words. Like prepositional phrases, appositives are easy to use. Punctuation is simple: set off appositives with commas, with a few rare exceptions (to be noted in Chapter 13).

In the three sentences below, notice that the appositive phrases vary in length, depending on the modifiers. The number of modifiers to be included depends on the writer's purpose. Writers must decide how much detail is needed and include the appropriate amount. For instance, each of the following sentences is appropriate in its place:

The student, *a tall young man*, worked hard in college.
The student, *a tall young man with a pleasant smile*, worked hard in college.
The student, *a tall young man with a pleasant smile and a pleasing manner*, worked hard in college.

Write three versions of one basic sentence. Use an appositive, but change it from sentence to sentence by adding modifiers, as shown in the examples above.

1. _____

   _____

2. _____

   _____

3. _____

   _____

NOUN-PARTICIPLE PHRASES

The *noun-participle phrase*, the least common of the phrases, consists of a noun followed by a participle. Other words can be added as modifiers, but the essential structure consists of the noun and then the participle, in that order.

> *His hands clutching the wheel*, the driver swerved to avoid the motorcycle.

Sometimes more than one participle is used in the phrase, but in all cases the verbal part(s) will appear after the noun.

> *A tornado having been spotted*, classes were dismissed.

The noun-participle phrase stands apart from the sentence; it has absolutely no grammatical connection with it. Perhaps for this reason, the phrase is sometimes called an *absolute phrase.* These phrases are set off with commas, since they constitute nonessential or extra units attached to the sentence.

PRACTICE 9 _____

Underline the noun-participle phrases in the following sentences.

Example: The office clock having stopped, Beverly had to rely on her wristwatch.

1. Their classes canceled, the students watched weather reports on television.

2. My students, their assignments completed, relaxed for a long weekend.

3. The tornado warnings were canceled, the storm having dissipated.

Points to Use

- Use phrases to add information with just a few words. Appositives are especially useful in this regard.
- Use verbal phrases, appositives, and noun-participle phrases to add variety to your writing.
- Set off an introductory phrase with a comma, unless it is a two- or three-word prepositional phrase (and even then, you have the option of using the comma).
- Be moderate in the number of prepositional phrases used back to back. Rather than stringing four or more of these phrases together, try to combine ideas in other ways.
- Make sure your opening verbal phrases have logical references so that you avoid dangling modifiers.
- Use the active voice rather than the passive voice to avoid creating dangling modifiers.
- Set off nonessential parts of sentences with commas to clarify the meaning for your readers. Setting aside the nonessential parts calls attention to the core of the sentence.
- Try to avoid splitting an infinitive by putting a word or words between the two parts of the infinitive. Sometimes a split infinitive reads smoothly, but more often it is awkward. It is usually better to reword the sentence.
- Use verbals to add the liveliness of verbs to your writing. Contrast the static adjective here with the verbal (participle) adjective: *bright* face versus *glowing* face.

Points to Remember

- A phrase is a group of words acting together as a unit; it has no subject or verb.
- There are six types of phrases: (a) three verbal phrases—gerund, infinitive, and participial—and (b) three others—prepositional, appositive, and noun-participle (absolute).
- Verbals are derived from verbs and look like verbs, but they cannot do the work of verbs. They can begin phrases, and they can be nouns, adverbs, or adjectives.
- Gerunds are verbals that end with *ing* and act as nouns. Gerund phrases usually are vital parts of the sentence and therefore are

not set off with commas; the only exception is the gerund phrase used as an appositive.

- Infinitives are verbals that consist of the word *to* plus a verb. Infinitives and infinitive phrases work as nouns, adverbs, and adjectives. When an infinitive phrase comes at the beginning of a sentence, it is set off with a comma unless it is the subject. Elsewhere in the sentence it generally takes no commas.

- Participles are verbals that work as adjectives. Several endings are possible on participles: *ing* for the present participle and *n, en, d, ed,* or *t* for the past participle.

- A dangling modifier has no word to which it can attach logically. Instead, it automatically attaches to the nearby reference, typically the subject of the sentence. An opening phrase must logically connect with what follows in the sentence.

- An appositive is a noun or pronoun unit that renames or identifies the noun immediately preceding it. Ordinarily appositives are set off with commas.

- The noun-participle phrase consists of a noun followed by a participle. Modifiers can be included. The phrase is set off with commas because it is nonessential.

EXERCISE 1.   Identifying Phrases

Match the italicized phrases below with the following choices. Check your answers with those at the back of the book.

a. gerund	d. prepositional
b. infinitive	e. appositive
c. participial	f. noun/participle

_____ 1. *Studying the history of the alphabet* interests me.

_____ 2. Authorities differ *in their interpretations.*

_____ 3. The final tail of the R was added *to avoid confusion with the letter D.*

_____ 4. *Lying on its side (like this ⊀),* the Phoenician A (10th century B.C. or earlier) is an ancestor of the modern A.

_____ 5. *Seeing the resemblance to our A* is easy.

_____ 6. *To some* of us, the letter C is special.

_____ 7. *Modified by the Romans,* the letter C dates from about the third century B.C.

_____ 8. Frederick W. Goudy, *an impressive scholar,* worked on the history of our alphabet.

_____ 9. *His scholarship unchallenged,* Goudy's writings were reprinted and released anew after his death.

_____ 10. *To be a typographer,* one must be an artist as well as a printer.

_____ 11. Goudy (1865–1947), *the most prolific type designer in American history,* designed more than 100 typefaces.

_____ 12. Typographers arrange type attractively *for printing books and other materials.*

_____ 13. The letter L, *changed many times over the ages,* has had its present form since about 900 B.C.

_____ 14. *Designing new lettering styles* takes patience.

_____ 15. The alphabet itself, *one of mankind's greatest achievements,* has remained in its current form for centuries.

_____ 16. Have you ever stopped *to notice type styles?*

_____ 17. *Thinking about their design,* you will appreciate more fully their creators' talent and ingenuity.

EXERCISE 2.   *Reviewing Phrases*

Complete the following statements in your own words.

1. A phrase is _____

   _____

2. A verbal is _____

   _____

3. Verbals differ from verbs in these two ways:

   a. _____

   b. _____

4. Verbals resemble verbs in the following ways:

   a. _____

   b. _____

   c. _____

5. The three kinds of verbals are _____,

   _____, and _____ .

6. An appositive is _____

   _____

7. A verbal that functions as a noun is a _____ .

8. A verbal that functions as an adjective is a _____ .

9. A verbal that can function as a noun, an adverb, or an adjective is an

   _____ .

10. Examine the following sentence and answer the questions below:

Spring having come to Montana, there were no more freezing rains.

    a. What is the subject? _____

    b. What is the verb? _____

    c. How many infinitive phrases are there? _____

    d. How many gerund phrases are there? _____

    e. How is the word *there* used? _____

    f. What part of speech is *freezing?* _____

    g. What type of phrase is *Spring having come to Montana?* _____

EXERCISE 3. *Identifying the Correct Handling of Modifiers*

For the following pairs of sentences, circle the letter (a or b) of the better version. Check your answers with those at the back of the book.

1. a. To become a good artist, practice is necessary.
   b. To become a good artist, a student must practice.

2. a. The young painter worked for subtle effects, concentrating on soft color combinations.
   b. The young painter worked for subtle effects concentrating on soft color combinations.

3. a. The art of printing having changed greatly since Gutenberg's day, now uses computer technology.
   b. The art of printing, having changed greatly since Gutenberg's day, now uses computer technology.

4. a. Gutenberg, a German experimenter credited with inventing movable type, lived from about 1398–1468.
   b. Gutenberg a German experimenter credited with inventing movable type, lived from about 1398–1468.

5. a. Having developed movable type, his books were more beautiful than those of his competitors.
   b. Having developed movable type, he created books more beautiful than those of his competitors.

6. a. To call Gutenberg the inventor of printing, is not exactly accurate.
   b. To call Gutenberg the inventor of printing is not exactly accurate.

7. a. The Chinese had developed a printing method by the eighth century A.D., using wood blocks.

b. The Chinese had developed a printing method by the eighth century A.D. using wood blocks.

8. a. Gutenberg had no way of knowing about printing methods developed centuries earlier in Asia.
   b. Gutenberg had no way of knowing about printing methods, developed centuries earlier in Asia.

9. a. Dying impoverished after a life of creative work is a sad ending to Gutenberg's biography.
   b. Dying impoverished after a life of creative work, is a sad ending to Gutenberg's biography.

10. a. The art of printing with movable type spread to most of Europe by 1500, advanced by German craftsmen.
    b. The art of printing with movable type spread to most of Europe by 1500 advanced by German craftsmen.

EXERCISE 4. *Creating Appositives*

Combine the following paired sentences into single sentences using appositives. Remember that commas set off appositives. (Note: Song titles are set off in quotation marks; book titles are italicized.)

Example: "The Star Spangled Banner" is our national anthem. It uses the tune of an old British drinking song.

"The Star Spangled Banner," our national anthem, uses the tune of an old British drinking song.

1. *The Bay Psalm Book* was the first book published in the British colonies of North America. It was published in 1640.

   _____

   _____

2. *The Bay Psalm Book* offered new translations of the Old Testament Psalms. This book was used by New England colonists for several generations.

   _____

   _____

   _____

3. The popular meter of that era was used in *The Bay Psalm Book.* It used the pattern of alternating lines of eight and six syllables.

_____

_____

4. Psalm 23 opens with a typical example of that popular meter. It reads "The Lord to mee a shepheard is, want therefore shall not I."

_____

_____

5. An introduction to *The Bay Psalm Book* advised the colonists to use the music in a book by Thomas Ravenscroft. Ravenscroft was a British musician and book compiler.

_____

_____

6. In London in 1621, Ravenscroft published a psalter with a long title. It was *The Whole Booke of Psalmes, with the Hymnes Evangelicall and Songs Spirituall.*

_____

_____

7. "My Country 'Tis of Thee" uses the tune of the British national anthem. "My Country 'Tis of Thee" is an American patriotic song.

_____

_____

8. Samuel F. Smith wrote the words for "My Country 'Tis of Thee." Smith was a young Massachusetts clergyman.

_____

_____

9. "My Country 'Tis of Thee" was first sung July 4, 1831, at Boston's Park Street Church. It is a church that still stands across from the Boston Commons.

_____

_____

10. "Dixie" was written by Dan Emmett in 1859. It became the battle song of Confederate soldiers during the War Between the States.

_____

_____

11. Two composers of Civil War songs wrote music that captured the mood of the era especially well. They were George F. Root and Henry Clay Work.

_____

_____

_____

12. The lyrics of "The Battle Hymn of the Republic" were written by Julia Ward Howe. She was a prominent social leader in Boston.

_____

_____

EXERCISE 5. Combining Sentences Using Phrases

Combine the following paired sentences by changing the italicized sentence into the kind of phrase indicated in parentheses at the end of the line. Write the new sentence, punctuating it correctly. Your new version should preserve the meaning of the original sentence. You may reword if you like, so long as you preserve the basic meaning. For each problem there may be more than one correct answer.

Example: I stood on the sidelines happily. *I watched our team win the game.* (participial phrase)

I stood on the sidelines happily, watching our team win the game.

Watching our team win the game, I stood on the sidelines happily.

1. Many fans gathered around the triumphant team. *The fans were congratulating them on their victory.* (participial phrase)

_____

_____

2. They need to win one more game. *Then they would become the state champions.* (infinitive phrase)

_____

_____

3. *Mr. Williams is our coach.* He has been at this college for nine years. (appositive phrase)

_____

_____

4. The team plays on a high school football field. *It is located about a mile from the college campus.* (participial phrase)

_____

_____

5. *The team may win the state championship again this year.* That would be a great achievement for the team and the coach. (gerund phrase)

_____

_____

6. Kim does not understand football very well. *She is one of my best friends.* (appositive phrase)

_____

_____

7. *She could attend more games and watch the plays closely.* Then she would understand football better. (prepositional phrase with gerunds)

_____

_____

8. Linda attends nearly every basketball game. *She likes seeing her friends there.* (infinitive phrase)

_____

_____

9. Racquetball is now a popular sport. *It has gained popularity in recent years.* (participial phrase)

_____

_____

10. The college has several racquetball courts. *They are located in the new addition to the gym.* (participial phrase)

_____

_____

11. *Karla Robbins is our tennis coach.* She also teaches swimming. (appositive phrase)

_____

_____

12. Tennis players need great dexterity. *They need dexterity for playing well.* (infinitive phrase)

_____

_____

EXERCISE 6. *Writing a Memo About a Writing Project*

On a separate sheet of paper, complete the following writing assignment.

Think of a problem at work, at school, or in your community, a problem that you can help solve through writing. As part of your work later in this course, you will write an appropriate letter or report addressing that problem.

You know better than anyone which problems need attention around you. You may need to prepare information on a new product in connection with an advertising campaign at work. You may need to gather data for a report, or you may need to write instructions to help new employees in your department, store, or office. These problems and others like them confront workers daily; resolving such problems requires writing.

You may have a problem closer to home. Perhaps your children cross a dangerous intersection on the way to school. You believe that a stop sign is needed on that corner. A letter to the city council might focus attention on the danger and result in a stop sign being put on the corner. Or perhaps you have water, air, or noise pollution problems in your community. A letter to the newspaper editor or to a council member might get some attention and bring action.

You may be required to prepare a report or some other piece of writing for another class this term, perhaps a report requiring documentation (footnotes and bibliography). Your college work outside this class may give you many reasons to write.

Obviously this class cannot deal with all the details involved in all these kinds of writing. But it is practical to devote some time here to writing that focuses on real concerns in your life.

One purpose of this memo is to let your teacher know about your need to write in other parts of your life. Your teacher can direct you to sources of specific information that will help you (e.g., regarding report, letter, or memo formats or using footnotes and bibliographies).

Write a memo to your professor answering the following questions:

1. What problem do you need to solve through writing? (Be as specific as possible.) To whom would you be writing?
2. What would you hope to accomplish by writing? Do you want to call attention to the problem or suggest solutions or action—or both?
3. Do you need specialized forms or other specialized information in order to complete this writing? (Be specific.)

EXERCISE 7.   Considering How Writing Can Help Solve Problems

The examples below were written by students in response to Exercise 6. Read these examples and be prepared to discuss them in class. Your discussion should focus on the following points:

- Why would writing work better than phoning in these situations?
- Why do clear, attractive, carefully written letters and memos tend to get better results than sloppy ones? (Pretend you are the receiver of these students' communications; what would you notice, and how would you react?)
- What specific information should each writer include in order to make his or her message strong and effective?
- Why would the tone of a writer's communication be important in these situations? What tone should these writers use?

Example 1

I need to solve a problem at work concerning my wages and hours. I am going to write to my supervisor and ask him for a raise. I am also going to tell him I want more hours.

I hope to get more money and hours, for I am a good worker, and the work I do is very hard and strenuous at times. I think writing is a better way of telling my supervisor what I want to say because he is not always around, and if he is around, he is usually very busy.

Example 2

The problem I need to solve is with the apartment I live in. There are only four apartments in the building. The building is run down and not up to standard living.

One problem is the lighting in the hallway. The light sometimes doesn't come on at night. Second, the fire extinguishers are not updated. The last time they were checked was six years ago. The third problem is that the bathrooms are a health hazard. Tiles are falling down, and paint is peeling.

I will write to the landlord and the city housing department. I spoke with the landlord, but I got nowhere, and I have to do something. We have children to protect. The way things are going, the place will not be safe for anyone pretty soon.

Example 3

The problem I need to solve is that my car insurance is too expensive for my circumstances. I'm insured under my parents' policy, and so is my ten-year-old car. I drive back and forth to college five days a week. With only one minor speeding ticket on my record and with the good student discount, I still have to pay $100 a month. Talking to other students, I've found that they pay about half of what I do.

I have to explain my situation to the insurance company. Maybe there is a mistake. If that company can't do any better for me, I will have to check around with others.

Example 4

I need help from the company manager about a problem that comes up every once in a while. I work at a rental company. We rent all kinds of stuff, furniture, tools, equipment, small vans, etc.

The trouble is some customers abuse the things they rent. It's not always obvious right when they bring things back. Then we get stuck fixing things up, and some of these same people keep coming back. I know what they did before. I don't want to rent to them again, but I don't know how to tell them "No!"

One example came up last week with our bobcat. This guy had reserved it before. The minute I heard his name, I remembered last time he used it to clean out his barn. One other time he reserved it, but never showed up and never paid. This time he got pushy, and I ended up writing down his name in the reservation book.

Later the same day another man came in, wanting the bobcat. That was a new customer, and he said he would even pay more to have it. Chances are he would take good care of it. But it was too late. The other guy's name was on the book.

So I need to know what to do about reserving to customers if they abuse things and come back again. Also I want to know how much I can stand up to people who've been lousy customers in the past.

9

Recognizing and Using Subordinate Clauses

Recognizing Subordinate Clauses

A *clause* is a group of words that act as a unit; it has both subject and verb. We have two kinds of clauses:

- Main or independent clauses
- Subordinate or dependent clauses

In this chapter, we will concentrate on subordinate clauses and their uses. These clauses are used as parts of sentences. If they are left to stand alone, they will not make sense even though they do have a subject and verb. Consider these examples:

When the time comes.

If our friends arrive today.

Because we had no money with us.

As soon as we left home.

PRACTICE 1

Create complete sentences by adding main clauses to these subordinate clauses.

Example: When the time comes, *we will enjoy vacation.* .

1. If our friends arrive today, ———————————————————.

2. Because we had no money with us, ————————————————.

3. As soon as we left home, ————————————————————.

As we can see in the examples above, subordinate clauses depend on the rest of the sentence to make sense. For this reason, these clauses are often called dependent clauses. The words *dependent* and *subordinate* are both appropriate terms for these types of clauses.

Subordinate clauses are identified according to how they fit into sentences: as adverbs, adjectives, or nouns.

ADVERB CLAUSES

Adverb clauses qualify as clauses according to the definition above, and they qualify as adverbs according to several familiar hallmarks. Recall what was discussed about adverbs in Chapter 1.

- Adverbs are often movable.
- An adverb modifies a verb, adjective, or other adverb.
- Adverbs answer these questions: When? Where? How? How much? How well? Why? To what extent? Under what circumstances?

As another clue, adverb clauses begin with **subordinating conjunctions.** Here are some examples:

after	if	unless
although	since	until
as	so that	when
as if	before	where
as though	because	while
though	whenever	even though

Perhaps the most frequently used subordinating conjunctions are *if, though, although, because, when, since,* and the combinations *even though, so that,* and *as soon as.*

Because these words connect adverb clauses to main clauses, the word *conjunction* fits. Nevertheless, these words differ from the seven conjunctions mentioned earlier (remembered as FANBOYS). These conjunctions are called *subordinating.* Unlike *coordinating* conjunctions (the FANBOYS), these conjunctions do not connect equal units; rather, they connect subunits to main units.

The terms matter less than the principle: subordinating conjunctions show relationships between the ideas in dependent and independent clauses.

For instance, in the four sentences below, note that the main subject (*John*) and the main verb (*works*) do not change. The adverb clauses are italicized. The words *because, so that, before* and *if* make the connection between the clauses clear.

John works *because he needs the money.*
John works *so that he can go to school.*
Before he comes to his classes, John works.
If his boss needs him at night, John works.

We can change the placement of adverb clauses in sentences without affecting meaning. The sentences will be equally clear and strong whether adverb clauses appear at the end or the beginning of the sentence. Compare these two versions of the same idea:

Because he needs the money, John works.
John works *because he needs the money.*

These two examples show us that adverb clauses are movable. We can also see how to punctuate them:

- If the adverb clause appears at the beginning of the sentence, set it off with a comma.
- If the adverb clause appears at the end of the sentence, do not set it off with a comma. Note, however, these few exceptions: clauses beginning with *though, although, even though,* or *whereas* can be set off with commas even when they are used at the end of the sentence.

PRACTICE 2

Change the placement of the clauses in the following sentences, rewording if necessary. Write the new sentences and punctuate correctly.

Example: When lines intersect, they cut across or through one another.

Lines cut across or through one another when they intersect.

1. Streets intersect when they cut across or through one another.

_____

_____

2. We will have vanilla ice cream for dessert because our dinner guests prefer vanilla over other flavors.

_____

_____

3. Seed pods are removed from the vanilla plant so that they can be processed for the flavored extract.

_____

_____

4. Although the vanilla plant yields the best extract, good vanilla flavoring can also be made synthetically.

_____

_____

_____

ADJECTIVE CLAUSES

Adjective clauses qualify as both clauses and adjectives. Recall what was discussed about adjectives in Chapter 1.

- An adjective modifies a noun or a pronoun.
- Adjectives answer the following questions about nouns or pronouns: Whose? Which one or ones? What kind or kinds? How many?

Unlike the movable adverb clauses, adjective clauses are fixed in place, and they appear in predictable spots, directly after the words they modify. Adjective clauses usually begin with one of these pronouns: *who (whom, whose), which,* and *that.* Because these words are all pronouns, they can work as subjects and objects, and in adjective clauses they sometimes do exactly that. At the same time, they connect the dependent clause to the rest of the sentence. Think of these pronouns as doing double duty and as being more versatile than the subordinating conjunctions, which merely connect clauses.

In the sentences below, the adjective clauses are italicized, and the words they refer to indicated by arrows. Notice that the clauses refer to words immediately preceding them:

The announcer *who described the game* was excited.

The programs *that were delayed* were later televised in their entirety.

The newscaster *whose program was delayed* praised the Miami Dolphins victory.

PRACTICE 3 _____

Underline the adjective clauses in the following sentences and draw arrows from the clauses to the words they modify.

1. The fans look forward to the Super Bowl game that is played at the end of the season.

2. The players whom we see in every game are the ones who played most of the game today.

3. The snacks which the fans consumed made money for the concession stands.

We use *who* (*whom, whose*) to refer to people. We use *which* to refer to animals or things, but we can also use *that* to refer to people, animals, or things. For instance, in sentence 2 of the practice above, the reference is to people; therefore, a form of *who* is used. In the other sentences, the references are to things, making *which* or *that* possible choices.

PRACTICE 4

Underline the correct choices in the following sentences.

1. The calendar (who, which) we use was introduced in 1582.

2. The calendar is used by most of the world, including Americans, (who, which) adopted the calendar in 1752.

3. A calender is a machine (that, who) makes paper or cloth smooth by pressing it through rollers.

4. The verb *calender* means to press material through a machine (that, who) is called a calender.

The choice between *who* (subject) and *whom* (object) is a step-by-step process, beginning with finding the verb, as discussed in Chapter 5. If the verb needs a subject, *who* is correct; if the verb has a subject and needs an object, *whom* is the right choice, as shown in these examples:

S   AV

The announcer who described the game was enthusiastic.

DO S AV

The players whom we see in every game are here today.

Occasionally the words *when* and *where* begin adjective clauses. Although we generally associate these words with adverb clauses, *when* can start an adjective clause modifying a time, and *where* can start an adjective clause modifying a place:

January 1 is the day *when the bowl games are played.*

Pasadena, California, is the city *where the Rose Bowl game is played.*

The opening pronouns *that* or *which* are sometimes understood and not spoken or written. Even when an opening pronoun is omitted, the adjective clause can be complete. Compare these paired examples, noting that the meaning is clear with or without *that* (or *which*):

The dog *that Mike owns* bit my neighbor.

The dog *Mike owns* bit my neighbor.

PRACTICE 5

Underline the adjective clauses in the following sentences.

1. The television show I most enjoy is on Friday evening.

2. The late movie comes at a time when I am asleep.

3. The local theater where the recent movies appear has a Wednesday night special.

4. On the night we went to the movies, the tickets were the regular price.

Adjective clauses are set off with commas if they are nonessential. The handling of adjective clauses follows a principle that should be familiar: generally, we do not set off any part of a sentence if it is essential to the structure or meaning.

As a general rule, we protect the core of the sentence—subject + verb + object or complement—from disruption. If there is an interruption, we have a unit with commas on both sides, setting the disrupting element apart in total, like this:

subject, *other unit*, verb + object

To punctuate adjective clauses, follow these basic rules:

1. If the clause is essential to point out exactly what is meant, it is called **restrictive.** It restricts the meaning and is not set off with commas.

The calculus class *which is held at 11 A.M.* has only three more seats available.

Restrictive clauses restrict the meaning; they help identify subjects or other key sentence elements. In the sentence above, the italicized clause identifies the subject, indicating which calculus class has only three more seats available. Other sections of calculus may or may not have seats available.

2. If the clause merely adds additional information, it is called *nonrestrictive* and is set off with commas.

> The calculus class, *which is held at 11 A.M.*, has only three more seats available.

Nonrestrictive clauses add extra information. In the second version of the sample sentence, the main point is that only three more students can enroll in calculus. Incidentally, the class meets at 11 A.M.

Whether a clause is restrictive or nonrestrictive is sometimes obvious, sometimes obscure, and sometimes arguable. The punctuation gives readers clues to the meaning and importance of the clauses; whether clauses are restrictive or not is a distinction made by writers.

PRACTICE 6

Underline the clauses in these sentences. In the margin, label them either restrictive or nonrestrictive.

> **Example:** The symphony concert, which is televised on Friday
>
> evening, is my favorite program.   *nonrestrictive*

1. The woman who owns that duplex advertised for a caretaker.

2. Ms. Lynn and her business partners, who own the apartment house on our corner, advertised for a caretaker.

3. The prizefight that had been postponed twice was held last Saturday.

4. The prizefight, which had been postponed twice, was held last Saturday.

Punctuation reflects both the writer's understanding and the intended meaning. For instance, in sentence 3 in the practice above, the restrictive clause identifies the particular prizefight held last Saturday. Because the clause is treated as restrictive, the writer apparently thinks that readers need the clause in order to know which fight was held on Saturday. The writer of sentence 4 presumes that readers know which fight was held last Saturday; the fact that it had been postponed twice is nonessential information.

Sometimes writers have difficulty distinguishing between restrictive and nonrestrictive clauses. But this much we can be sure of: clauses are always one or the other, restrictive or nonrestrictive. Therefore, either we do not separate them from the rest of the sentence with commas, or we set them off entirely. We cannot use one comma as a compromise between none and two. In this instance, a compromise makes no sense.

NOUN CLAUSES

Everything we know about nouns applies equally well to noun clauses. Like other nouns, these clauses can be subjects, direct objects, objects of prepositions, or subject complements. As nouns, they play important roles in our sentences; because they are important, they are not set off with commas.

Noun clauses usually begin with one of these words: *that, who, whoever, what, whatever, whether.* Occasionally *when, where, why,* and *how* are used.

You use noun clauses every day, often without realizing that you are doing so. As soon as you begin a sentence with words like *I believe,* you are about to use a noun clause as a direct object. Think about how you might complete this statement:

        S   AV   DO
        I believe _____.

When filling in the blank line, you would almost certainly create a noun clause, probably one that starts with the word *that,* either written or implied. Here is a typical example:

        S   AV   DO
        I believe that our team will win.

The noun clause is *that our team will win;* the entire clause is the direct object of the action verb *believe.*

PRACTICE 7

In the following sentences, the noun clauses are italicized. On the blank line, indicate how the clause is used: as a subject, direct object, subject complement, or object of a preposition.

    Example: *How a football team can play with snow on the field* is difficult for me to understand.

        subject of "is"

1. *Whether the snow interferes with the game* is a matter of opinion.

_____

2. I believe *that your school has a good basketball team.*

_____

3. Alaska offers many opportunities for *whoever can endure the climate.*

_____

4. The question is *how Alaskans adapt to the long, hard winters.*

_____

As the previous examples show, the noun clause is an essential element in the sentence, working as a subject or object or subject complement. Unlike adverb and adjective clauses—both of them modifiers added to the sentence pattern—noun clauses are generally part of the basic sentence pattern.

Using Subordinate Clauses

SUBORDINATION

By using subordinate (or dependent) clauses, we can combine ideas and show relationships between ideas. These relationships may pertain to cause and effect, time, or condition (with the clauses working as adverbs), or these relationships may modify nouns or pronouns (with the clauses working as adjectives).

Using subordinate clauses allows us to include ideas that neither require nor deserve the weight of a full sentence; we subordinate certain ideas by using subordinate clauses. By using subordination, we show the relative importance of ideas, playing down lesser ideas and emphasizing main ideas.

To understand how important subordinating can be, see what happens without it. Notice the effect when every idea—no matter how important or unimportant—is presented in a separate sentence:

> We stood on the corner for an hour. We waited for the bus. It did not come. We were frustrated. We were angry. We would be late for work. Finally the bus came. We were thirty minutes late.

Although these sentences are complete and correct, the passage is boring because all the sentences are short, simple, and structured the same way. All the ideas receive equal attention because they are all cast into full sentences, but many of those ideas should be subordinated—that is, played down through the use of subordinate clauses or phrases.

Here is one revision of the passage above. Some of the ideas have now been absorbed into full sentences (italicized and identified in parentheses).

Although we stood on the corner for thirty minutes (adverb clause) *waiting for the bus* (participial phrase), it did not come. *Frustrated and angry* (participial phrase), we thought *that we would be late for work* (noun clause). *When the bus finally came* (adverb clause), we got to work thirty minutes late.

In the revised version, cause-and-effect relationships and time relationships come through clearly. Because there are fewer main ideas, those few stand apart, emphasized by contrast with the ideas subordinated in clauses and phrases.

PRACTICE 8

Revise the following passage, using clauses and phrases to subordinate lesser ideas. You may reword if you like, and you may rearrange the order of the ideas. (Write on a separate piece of paper.)

I remember the first day of school. The parking lots were full. The ramp was full. No parking was allowed on most of the side streets near campus. I had a math class at 9 A.M. I was almost late. Finally I found a parking spot. I parked the car. I ran across the lot. I dashed up the sidewalk and through the door. I found the right room. The sign beside the door caught my attention. It announced a change of room for my class. I had to run back down two flights of stairs. I found the right room. I went in and sat down. It was 8:59.

SENTENCE TYPES

Besides subordinating ideas for more interesting and effective writing, we can use subordinate clauses to add variety to our sentences. Here are the four sentence types, based upon the presence or absence of dependent clauses:

Simple: one independent clause
Compound: two or more independent clauses
Complex: one independent clause plus one or more dependent clauses
Compound/complex: two or more independent clauses plus one or more dependent clauses

PRACTICE 9

In the sentences below, indicate the correct sentence type, according to these four choices:

a.	simple	c.	complex
b.	compound	d.	compound/complex

Examples: _C_ Sandra, who won many honors as a high school athlete, has become a leading athlete on our campus.

_d_ Because Amy plays tennis so well, she has many invitations to play, but she must decline most of them during the school year.

_____ 1. Tracy swims well, and she is on the college swimming team.

_____ 2. Because Tracy swims well, she is on the college swimming team.

_____ 3. Tracy, who swims well, is on the college swimming team, and she must practice with the team every afternoon.

_____ 4. Tracy, who won medals for swimming while she was in high school, swims and dives every day.

_____ 5. The swimming coach at our high school praised Tracy and the team for their accomplishments.

___

Notice that it is the structure of a sentence, not its length, that indicates the sentence type. We will now examine each of the sentence types in greater detail.

Simple sentences can be long and involved. They may have many modifiers, and they may be far from simple in the ideas expressed. In other words, the word *simple* does not mean easy or simple-minded; rather, it is merely a label for a certain type of sentence structure.

The following sentences are both simple sentences:

Chocolate ice cream appeals to people of all ages.
Wanting to please the children, their grandparents put a swingset in the back yard.

PRACTICE 10 _____

Create two original simple sentences:

1. _____

_____

2. _____

_____

Compound sentences are appropriate when two or more related ideas deserve equal attention. Like items balanced on a scale, compound sentences must be balanced because of their equal weight (in importance, not necessarily in length). Compound sentences must be joined properly so that they do not create such problems as comma splices or fused sentences. The way to avoid these problems is to join independent clauses either with a semicolon or with a comma plus a coordinate conjunction.

Notice the equal weight of or the balance between the clauses in these compound sentences:

> My older brother is a barber, and his wife is a pharmacist.
> First I'll do my homework; then I'll watch the game.

PRACTICE 11

Create two original compound sentences.

1. _____

   _____

2. _____

   _____

Complex sentences typically are preferred over other sentence types because they are so flexible and expressive, showing relationships between ideas. Some authorities believe that most of our sentences should be complex sentences.

Although the compound sentences in the examples above are correct as they stand, we would have to turn them into complex sentences in order to show connections between ideas or to emphasize one idea over the other, as in these examples:

> My older brother, who is a barber, is married to a pharmacist.
> (emphasis on his marriage)

> My older brother, whose wife is a pharmacist, is a barber.
> (emphasis on his career)

PRACTICE 12

Revise the compound sentences you created in Practice 11 into complex sentences.

1. _____

   _____

2. _____

_____

_____

Compound/complex sentences combine the advantages of compound and complex sentences. The only hazard of this sentence type is that the relationships between the various clauses can become complicated. Nevertheless, that need not be the case. Here are some examples in which the relationships are clear:

> Because they are ashamed of their big feet, some people will not admit their real shoe sizes, yet they complain when salespeople sell them shoes that do not fit.
> Because I enjoy cheesecake, I often order it for dessert, but last night the restaurant had run out.
> The waiter suggested that I try bread pudding with rum sauce, so I agreed and discovered that it is delicious.

PRACTICE 13 _____

Create an original example of a compound/complex sentence.

_____

_____

_____

Points to Use

- Follow these general principles for punctuation of clauses as well as phrases:

  1. Use commas to set off nonessential elements.
  2. Use commas to set off introductory elements—that is, those leading up to the main clause (the main subject and verb).

- Use subordinate clauses to add supportive information to main ideas.
- Put lesser ideas into phrases and subordinate clauses; put the most important ideas into main clauses.
- Use phrases and subordinate clauses to combine ideas, playing down the less important ideas so that the more important ones stand out.

- Remember that complex sentences are usually stronger than compound sentences because the priority and relationship of ideas are built into the complex sentence.
- Use compound sentences when the two (or more) main ideas are related in thought; the sentence structure will convey that they are balanced and equally important.
- Be sure to join separate independent thoughts either with a comma plus a coordinate conjunction or with a semicolon.
- Vary sentence structure by using all four kinds of sentences: simple, compound, complex, compound/complex.

Points to Remember

- A clause is a group of words acting as a unit, having both subject and verb. Main (independent) clauses are sentences. Subordinate (dependent) clauses depend on the rest of the sentence because they cannot stand alone.
- Subordinate clauses act as adverbs, adjectives, or nouns.
- Adverb clauses begin with subordinating conjunctions, words that signal the use of clauses. Like other adverbs, adverb clauses are often movable; they can modify verbs, adjectives, and adverbs.
- Adverb clauses are set off with commas when they begin sentences.
- Adjective clauses begin with pronouns—namely, *who* (*whom, whose*), *which, that*—that sometimes are used as subjects or objects within the clauses. Adjective clauses immediately follow the words they modify.
- Adjective clauses are set off with commas if they are not essential (nonrestrictive). If they are essential to the meaning (restrictive), they are not set off with commas.
- Noun clauses work as other nouns do—as subjects, direct objects, subject complements, and objects of prepositions. Because they are essential elements of sentences, noun clauses are not set off with commas.
- Using subordinate clauses helps us combine ideas. By showing relationships between ideas, we make our writing more appealing.
- Subordination allows us to emphasize main points by putting them in main clauses and to de-emphasize lesser points by putting them in subordinate clauses.
- The four sentence types are simple, compound, complex, and compound/complex. Although all these types are useful, the complex sentence may be the most useful because it lets us show relationships between ideas.
- Compound and compound/complex sentences must be joined either with a semicolon or with a comma plus a coordinate conjunction.

EXERCISE 1. Creating Sentences

Consider the use of clauses within the sample sentences and notice the punctuation. Then write your own original examples, using these patterns. Underline the clauses in your sentences.

1. Begin a sentence with an adverb clause, using the subordinating conjunction *because.*

    Example: <u>Because the roads were icy</u>, I drove slowly.

    _____

    _____

2. End a sentence with an adverb clause, using the subordinating conjunction *after.*

    Example: I went to the store <u>after the sale was over</u>.

    _____

    _____

3. Modify a subject with a restrictive *who* clause.

    Example: The player <u>who sprained his ankle in practice</u> cannot play in Saturday's game.

    _____

    _____

4. Modify a subject with a nonrestrictive *who* clause.

    Example: Dan Michaels, <u>who played in last week's game</u>, will be in the opening line-up this week.

    _____

    _____

5. Use an adjective clause that does not modify the subject. The clause can be either restrictive or nonrestrictive; use commas appropriately.

    Example: Our friends built the cabin <u>that they use for weekend retreats</u>.

    _____

    _____

6. Use a noun clause as a direct object.

    Example: He believes <u>that our team will win.</u>

_____

_____

7. Use a noun clause as a subject complement.

    Example: Jane's complaint is <u>that the pay is too low for such hard work.</u>

_____

_____

8. Use a noun clause as the subject.

    Example: <u>How the employer can expect Jane to work so hard for so little money</u> puzzles me.

_____

_____

9. Use two adverb clauses, one at the beginning and the other at the end of a sentence.

    Example: <u>As soon as he arrived</u>, Sally left the party <u>because she did not want to see him.</u>

_____

_____

10. Begin a sentence with a *who* clause used as a subject.

    Example: <u>Who the man was</u> remains a mystery.

_____

_____

11. Use a clause that could begin with either *that* or *which*.

    Example: The fence <u>that (which) we built around our back yard</u> is now painted white.

_____

_____

12. Use an adverb clause and an adjective clause in the same sentence, punctuating correctly.

   Example: The designer <u>who planned our landscaping</u> was pleased with it <u>after she saw the results.</u>

   _____

   _____

13. Use a noun clause and an adverb clause in the same sentence, punctuating correctly.

   Example: <u>After we had walked for hours,</u> we realized <u>that we could not cover the entire amusement park.</u>

   _____

   _____

EXERCISE 2.   *Identifying Subordinate Clauses*

In the following sentences, match the italicized clauses with the following choices. Check your answers with those at the back of the book.

   a. adverb
   b. adjective
   c. noun

_____   1. *When people wanted to write thousands of years ago,* they used bark, stone, animal skins, or clay.

_____   2. Among the Chinese, woven cloth was used for many centuries *before paper was invented.*

_____   3. *What they knew about weaving cloth* helped them develop the first paper.

_____   4. The first paper *that was developed by the Chinese* grew out of their interweaving fibers into cloth.

_____   5. The first paper must have been made in a similar way *because they knew about the weaving process.*

_____   6. Paper making, *which developed around 100 A.D. in China,* spread westward by way of the Middle East.

_____   7. *Why the Chinese were the first to develop paper* is not known.

_____ 8. The ancient Egyptians created papyrus from a plant *that grew in the delta of the Nile River.*

_____ 9. The plant, *which grew to a height of about three feet,* was used for many purposes besides papyrus.

_____ 10. Strips of stem from the plant were laid side by side *after they had been cut to a desired length.*

_____ 11. *After a second layer of strips had been laid over the first at right angles and interwoven,* the sheet was soaked in the Nile.

_____ 12. *Whether the river water caused the strips to adhere* is not certain.

_____ 13. More likely, the water dissolved a sticky substance in the plant *so that the strips stuck together.*

_____ 14. The Roman scholar Pliny (23–79 A.D.) mentioned *that papyrus varied considerably in quality.*

_____ 15. Papyrus was made only in Egypt, *although a variety of the plant also grew in Sicily.*

_____ 16. The Egyptians exported the writing material to countries *where the paper plant did not grow.*

_____ 17. *Although the Mediterranean climate tended to destroy papyrus over the years,* some medieval Latin manuscripts in papyrus are still extant.

_____ 18. Papyrus was superseded by parchment and vellum after the fourth century A.D. *because raw material for those substances was more abundant.*

_____ 19. By the eighth century A.D., the Arabs had learned to make paper *so that papyrus was no longer needed.*

_____ 20. It seems *that paper making spread to Europe by about 1100 A.D.;* then the making of papyrus ceased.

EXERCISE 3.   *Finding and Identifying Subordinate Clauses*

In the following sentences, underline the subordinate clauses and identify them as adverb, adjective, or noun clauses. (Some sentences contain more than one subordinate clause.) Check your answers with those at the back of the book.

Example: *adj, adj*   Animal skins, <u>which had been used for writing material for centuries</u>, were mentioned by Roman historians <u>who wrote about their times.</u>

_____ 1. Historians suggest that animal skins were used as early as 200 B.C.

_____ 2. Although papyrus was a common writing material for the ancient Romans, skins became more important in the early years A.D.

_____ 3. Examples that date from about 100 A.D. are still extant.

_____ 4. Skins of sheep, goats, and calves came into more use until eventually they superseded papyrus.

_____ 5. The word *parchment* means the skin of sheep or goats, though other skins were sometimes used.

_____ 6. Vellum, which is made from the skins of younger animals, is of finer quality.

_____ 7. Authorities believe that the skins of younger animals were considerably better in quality.

_____ 8. In the Middle Ages, animals were sometimes taken prenatally so that their skins could be used for superb vellum.

_____ 9. Processing skins became a big industry since there was much demand for writing material.

_____ 10. Because vellum and parchment were expensive, medieval scribes wrote tiny letters squeezed together.

_____ 11. Their page layout was designed so that every bit of the surface was used.

_____ 12. By the late Middle Ages, the lettering style was Gothic, which uses narrow letters with little space between them.

_____ 13. You may wonder what the ancient scribes used for pens.

_____ 14. The Egyptians used a plant stem that could be sharpened to a point.

_____ 15. The Greeks used a stone, metal, or ivory stylus which made marks on wax-covered tablets.

_____ 16. Hollow reeds, which grew in many countries, also made good pens.

_____ 17. How the quill pen became popular is not known, but in the Middle Ages, quill pens that were made of goose, crow, or swan feathers were common.

_____ 18. The word *pen* comes from a Latin word, *penna,* which means feather.

_____ 19. Because quill pens worked so well with parchment, they remained popular for many centuries.

_____ 20. Quill pens were superseded when metal pens were introduced in the 1700s.

EXERCISE 4.   *Subordinating with Clauses and Phrases*

In the following examples, combine the two sentences into one and write the new sentence. Change the italicized sentence into the structure indicated in parentheses. Follow the punctuation rules discussed in this chapter and underline book titles. There may be more than one correct answer.

> **Example:**   *The clouds looked dark and the wind became gusty.*
> Mother shut the windows. (adverb clause)

Because the clouds looked dark and the wind became gusty, Mother shut the windows.

Mother shut the windows because the clouds looked dark and the wind became gusty.

1. Dave and Martha went to lunch. *The class was over.* (adverb clause)

_____

_____

2. The class has studied subordinate clauses. *The material is presented in Chapter 9.* (adjective clause)

_____

_____

3. *Friday morning's lecture was about adjective clauses.* I spent an hour reviewing adverb, adjective, and noun clauses. (adverb clause)

_____

_____

_____

4. *Cervantes was a Spanish novelist of the sixteenth century.* He is best known for Don Quixote. (appositive phrase)

_____

_____

5. Cervantes was a Spanish novelist of the sixteenth century. *He is best known for Don Quixote.* (participial phrase)

_____

_____

6. Dr. James went to the world's leading research laboratory. *She would get information there for her research project.* (infinitive phrase)

_____

_____

_____

7. *Dr. James could find valuable data there.* That was her belief. (noun clause)

_____

_____

8. That player was home with a torn ligament. *We did not see him today.* (adjective clause)

_____

_____

9. *Michael is the quarterback for our team.* Last year he won an award as the best football player in the local high school league. (appositive phrase)

_____

_____

_____

10. The evening news broadcast was delayed. *The Celtics game went into overtime.* (adverb clause)

_____

_____

11. Linda Williams is a cancer researcher. *She works at the university laboratories.* (participial phrase)

_____

_____

12. Linda believes in her work. *She thinks that a cancer cure will be found during her lifetime.* (noun clause)

_____

_____

13. *Evan Ransom spoke at the garden club last week.* He described the best ways to preserve rosebushes through the winter. (adjective clause)

_____

_____

_____

14. Evan Ransom spoke at the garden club last week. *He described the best ways to preserve rosebushes through the winter.* (participial phrase)

_____

_____

_____

15. *The gardeners got valuable tips for preserving rosebushes.* The tips helped the gardeners. (gerund phrase used as a subject)

_____

_____

EXERCISE 5. Subordinating with Clauses and Phrases

On a separate piece of paper, revise these short, choppy sentences by combining ideas into appropriate phrases and clauses. Write complete, correct sentences, consistent in tense, person, and number. Preserve the original meaning as much as possible.

Examples: Allan wants a new sport jacket. It must complement his shirts and ties. He needs the jacket for the school party. The party will be held Saturday night.

Allan wants a new sport jacket to complement his shirts and ties. He needs the jacket for the school party Saturday night.

There are supplies in the storeroom. They are high-quality supplies. Use those. Don't buy any more until you have used those.

Use the supplies in the storeroom before you buy any more. You will find that these are high-quality supplies.

1. The ice fishermen build small houses on the lake. They drive their cars out onto the ice, and they sometimes misjudge the ice, and the ice breaks, and they fall in.

2. I wrote three reports. They were all detailed. Then I turned them in to my boss, and she read them, and she approved them.

3. Parents of small children seldom go out for an evening. They cannot afford baby-sitters, or they cannot find good baby-sitters. Grandparents can be very good sitters. Grandparents are not always nearby. They may have no time. They may not want to baby-sit.

4. The new cars look different. They are shorter. They look less streamlined. The bodies are brought out flush with the fenders.

5. The station wagon came from the north, and the van came from the east, and the driver of the van didn't see the stop sign. The station wagon had the right of way. The cars collided in the intersection. The driver of the station wagon was pinned inside the car.

6. The rain came for five days without stopping. It let up a bit for a few hours the third day. The river rose to its banks the fourth day. The fifth day it spilled over the banks. It began to flood houses and businesses. People moved out.

7. Doug had a good trip. That is what he said. He began in England. He went to Paris for a week. Then he spent a few days in Switzerland. Then came his eight days in Italy. After that he went to Austria. Then he visited Germany. Then he went back to London.

8. Reading poetry helps a reader in many ways. It is a pleasure to read. It gives rich, vivid descriptions. It expresses emotions, and it brings an appreciation of the language, and it can tell entertaining stories, or it can stimulate thinking on moral issues.

EXERCISE 6. Subordinating with Phrases and Clauses

On a separate piece of paper, write or type improved versions of the sentences below, using subordinate clauses and phrases. You should first decide which ideas deserve greater emphasis. In some cases, alternate versions are possible, depending on the emphasis.

Example: The U.S. Constitution went into effect in 1789, and it is one of the world's greatest governmental documents.

> *The U.S. Constitution, which went into effect in 1789, is one of the world's greatest governmental documents.*
>
> *The U.S. Constitution, one of the world's greatest governmental documents, went into effect in 1789.*

1. Andrea studied hard during her senior year in high school, and she wanted to go to college.

2. Mr. Carter is a fine speaker, and he is the minister at an active church in our community.

3. Steve has taken guitar lessons for only six months, and already he is a good performer.

4. The heavy fog made driving hazardous, and it did not lift until noon, and we had to get to school.

5. Joan is driving to the airport to meet a friend, and he is coming from Chicago.

6. You want me to help you with your algebra problems, so you must help me with my history report.

7. Their principal crop was potatoes, and the potato harvest was poor, so the farmers went into debt.

8. Stuart was an experienced detective, but he could not solve the arsenic murder case, and he was frustrated.

9. The violin was an old instrument with a beautiful tone, and it belonged to my grandfather.

10. Uncle Bill is my mother's brother, and he invited me to visit his ranch last summer, and I wanted to go.

11. The tanker was full of gasoline, and it narrowly missed a collision with a truck full of explosives.

12. The breakfast menu was long, and it included eggs, toast, French toast, and pancakes, and it named three kinds of juice, and it mentioned cereal.

13. I saw the Danish rolls on the counter, and they looked delicious, and then I knew what to order.

14. The title of that book was appealing, but the book turned out to be boring.

15. Professor Drake has been head of the chemistry department for five years, and she died yesterday.

16. Benjamin Franklin was a statesman and a writer, and he also experimented with electricity.

17. Music in American public schools goes back to 1838, for in that year, music was accepted into the Boston Public Schools.

18. The first school music classes were singing classes, and they were for children about eight to fourteen.

19. A Boston musician worked to get music accepted into the Boston school curriculum, and his name was Lowell Mason.

20. Lowell Mason wrote many popular hymn tunes, and some of them are well known to Americans to this day.

EXERCISE 7.   Creating a Paragraph

On a separate piece of paper, write a paragraph based on the information provided in the passage below. Combine sentences, rewording them if you wish, and subordinate lesser ideas. Make sure you punctuate so that your sentences make sense to the reader.

The year was 1837. It was fall in Boston. The school board approved music classes in four of the city's grammar schools. Grammar schools enrolled students from about age eight through fourteen. Some private schools had music classes. Public school students had no chance to learn music in school. But the city council did not approve funding for music in the schools. Music teachers were disappointed. Many parents were disappointed. All fall newspapers carried stories about music in the schools. Some papers also wrote editorials. Some people favored music in the schools. Other people were opposed. Music classes began in December. A music teacher volunteered to teach for a year without pay. His name was Lowell Mason. He had many years of experience teaching music. He wanted to prove that public school children could learn music.

EXERCISE 8.   Revising Paragraphs

On a separate piece of paper, revise the paragraph in Exercise 5, Chapter 6 (pp. 139–140), using sentence combining. Add a second paragraph, using the passage below as a source of information. (Note: This episode is a true story as related in a student's paper.)

I tried the door again. It really was stuck tight. I looked in my purse for more change. I thought about it. Maybe I could phone someone to come rescue me. But I had no more change. Several people passed by. I was pounding on the phone booth by now. They didn't seem to pay attention to me. Finally I waved to a man. He was headed my way. I waved and pounded and screamed. He noticed. He tried to open the door. It would not open. He walked away. I screamed again. He motioned that he was going to get help. I watched him go into a nearby building. Soon he was back. He had phoned the telephone company. They arrived in a few minutes. They opened the door. The children were safe in the car. I had been locked in the booth only a few minutes. It had seemed like an eternity.

EXERCISE 9.   Forming Topic Ideas and Organizing Paragraphs

Look again at the sentences in Exercises 2 and 3, Chapter 9 (pp. 211–214), and Exercises 1 and 4, Chapter 8 (pp. 185–186, 188–190). Many of those sentences deal with the same idea or with closely related ideas. Find several sentences (at least four or five) that pertain to a central idea. Then, on a separate piece of paper, create a paragraph based on the information in those sentences.

Your first step is to write an original sentence that sums up that central idea—that is, a topic sentence. Then arrange four or five sentences you selected from the exercise to form a paragraph. You may reword the sentences if you wish, but preserve the original meaning.

For example, here is a student paragraph based on some of the information in Exercise 4, Chapter 8 (p. 189).

The song, "My Country, 'Tis of Thee," has a long history. Though it is an American patriotic song, it uses the tune of the British national anthem. Samuel F. Smith, a young Massachusetts clergyman, wrote the words. The piece was first sung over 150 years ago. It was first sung on July 4, 1831, at Boston's Park Street Church, which stands across from the Boston Commons.

UNIT III PRACTICE TEST
Chapters 8 and 9

Part 1 (50 POINTS)

Read each question carefully. Mark your answer on the line to the left of each question. Check your answers with those at the back of the book.

A. PHRASES

Match the italicized word groups with the following items:

a. prepositional phrase   d. gerund phrase
b. infinitive phrase   e. appositive phrase
c. participial phrase

_____ 1. Paragraphs, *modern typographical devices*, are an outgrowth of printers' practices.

_____ 2. Medieval scribes, *needing every bit of their writing material*, could not waste space on indentations.

_____ 3. *To show breaks in the material*, the scribes made small marks in the text or in the margin beside the text.

_____ 4. *Making marks in the margin* became the common practice.

_____ 5. The sign *used by scribes in those days* has survived to this day as a symbol meaning "paragraph."

_____ 6. The word "paragraph" is derived *from "para" meaning "beside" and "graphos" meaning "to write."*

_____ 7. The mark *written in the margin beside the text* became known as the paragraph mark.

_____ 8. *To make the printed page more appealing visually*, printers separated blocks of material into paragraphs.

_____ 9. Gutenberg, *the German inventor of the fifteenth century*, devised a means of using movable type.

_____ 10. Modern photocopying has improved people's ability *to reproduce printed matter quickly*.

_____ 11. *Using modern techniques*, libraries can store and retrieve vast amounts of material efficiently.

_____ 12. Have you ever read centuries-old material *from a microfilm reader?*

_____ 13. *Collecting and filming medieval manuscripts* would be a difficult and expensive project for any institution.

_____ 14. A world-famous center *devoted to filming medieval documents* is St. John's University, Collegeville, Minnesota.

_____ 15. Can you imagine *looking at a manuscript that has lain untouched for centuries?*

_____ 16. Many medieval manuscripts were written in uncial lettering, *a style of the early centuries* A.D.

_____ 17. Uncial letters are entirely capital letters because they predate the distinction *between capital and small letters*.

_____ 18. *Named for the Roman word <u>uncia</u> (meaning "inch")*, uncial letters varied in size and shape over time.

B. CLAUSES

Match the italicized word groups with the following items:

    a. adverb
    b. adjective
    c. noun

_____ 19. Jacques Barzun, *who has had a long career as a teacher, scholar, and writer*, offers good advice to writers.

_____ 20. He says *that clear, straightforward English is no one's native tongue.*

_____ 21. *Though he assures his readers that such clarity can be achieved,* he reminds them that it must be worked for.

_____ 22. *That good writing should sound natural, not stuffy or pompous,* is another of his excellent observations.

_____ 23. Hernando Cortez, *who was a Spanish explorer of the 1500s,* conquered the Aztecs.

_____ 24. *When exploration of the New World was taking place,* the Spanish played a major part.

_____ 25. *How John Cabot became an English explorer* is an interesting story.

_____ 26. Did you realize *that he was born Giovanni Caboto (1450), a native Italian?*

_____ 27. *Because Columbus is credited with discovering the New World,* few people recall other explorers.

_____ 28. A project *that interests Americans* involved John Cabot and his crew, sent westward to find a route to Japan.

_____ 29. The result was *that Cabot discovered the North American mainland in 1497 by reaching part of what is now Canada.*

_____ 30. His second voyage, in 1498, brought him southward *so that he arrived near what is now called Chesapeake Bay.*

_____ 31. *Because he failed to find rich cultures with goods to trade with England,* Cabot went home disappointed.

_____ 32. King Henry VII, *who had no idea of the size or value of the territory,* used Cabot's discoveries as a basis for a claim to the new territory.

_____ 33. The famous historians Charles A. and Mary R. Beard remarked *that the king opened for the English "the greatest real estate and investment opportunity in the history of Western civilization."*

_____ 34. *Though many years passed before the English developed the territory,* the land proved to be a great asset.

_____ 35. *That North Americans are English-speaking people today* is the result of historic coincidences and accidents.

_____ 36. Few people realize *how English became the dominant language in North America.*

C. ANALYZING WORD GROUPS AND SENTENCES

Examine each of the word groups below. If the word group is a full sentence, correctly written and punctuated, mark the letter a. If not, mark the letter b.

_____ 37. The panda, an animal frequently mistaken for a bear is a mammal found in China and Tibet.

_____ 38. Two giant pandas, Ling-Ling and Hsing-Hsing, were given to the United States in 1972 by the People's Republic of China.

_____ 39. Eating bamboo in great quantity, the zoo staff must constantly seek additional supplies.

_____ 40. Supplying the two pandas, fifty pounds a day is needed.

_____ 41. The pandas live in the National Zoological Park in Washington, D.C., an area where ornamental bamboo grows in abundance.

_____ 42. Luckily, the people of the area, offer bamboo from their yards knowing that the pandas need it.

_____ 43. The pandas eat a varied diet developed especially for them by the zoo staff.

_____ 44. To create a suitable environment for the pandas, was a challenge for the Zoological Park staff.

_____ 45. Knowing that their native habitat, was the forests of the Chinese Himalayan Mountains the staff provided cool housing, offering a constant sixty-degree temperature.

_____ 46. Playing outside in temperatures of seventy degrees or less, the pandas remain comfortable indoors or outdoors.

_____ 47. Another member of the panda family is called, the lesser panda, distinguishing it from the giant panda.

_____ 48. Having reddish fur and a long, ringed tail, northeastern Asia is its home.

_____ 49. To distinguish the lesser panda from the raccoon is sometimes difficult because of the resemblance.

_____ 50. The giant pandas, unlike the more common lesser pandas, had not been seen in the Western Hemisphere for many years before their arrival in Washington, D.C., in 1972.

Part 2 (50 POINTS)

Change the italicized sentences here into the kinds of units indicated in parentheses at the end of each line. Write the complete new sentence, punctuating correctly. Your new sentence should preserve the meaning of the original. Select any ten of the following twelve problems. (5 points each)

1. Gilbert Stuart was an American portraitist who lived from 1755 to 1828. *He is best known for his portraits of George Washington.* (participial phrase)

   _____

   _____

   _____

2. Gilbert Stuart is best known for his portraits of George Washington. *He was an American painter.* (appositive phrase)

   _____

   _____

3. *George Washington retired from public life in 1797.* He returned to his home at Mount Vernon and remained there the rest of his life. (adverb clause)

   _____

   _____

   _____

4. In 1775, Washington was a delegate to the Second Continental Congress. *The group met in Philadelphia.* (adjective clause)

   _____

   _____

5. The Second Continental Congress made a decision about Washington. *They decided he should be commander-in-chief of the Continental Army.* (noun clause as a direct object)

_____

_____

_____

6. *He commanded the army until 1783.* That work kept him away from his home except for very brief visits. (gerund phrase used as a subject)

_____

_____

7. The earth is a comfortable distance from the sun. *It is located about 93 million miles from the sun.* (participial phrase)

_____

_____

8. The planets closer to the sun are too hot for life. *They are Venus and Mercury.* (appositive phrase)

_____

_____

9. *Pluto is a slow-moving planet.* It has an eccentric orbit with an average distance of about 3.6 billion miles from the sun. (adjective clause)

_____

_____

_____

10. *Completing one orbit of the sun takes Pluto about 248 years.* Pluto is a slow-moving planet. (infinitive phrase)

_____

_____

11. Scientists believe that Mercury has a core of iron. *The core extends four-fifths of the way to its surface.* (participial phrase)

_____

_____

_____

12. Astronomers believe there can be no life on Saturn and Jupiter. *Those planets are so far from the sun that they are too cold for life.* (adverb clause)

_____

_____

_____

CREATING EFFECTIVE SENTENCES

OBJECTIVES

Grammar and Sentence Structure

To review the handling of modifiers

To turn fragments and run-ons into well-written sentences

To develop parallelism and sentence variety

Writing

To refine wording in sentences and paragraphs

To write paragraphs for work-related situations

To write job application letters tailored to students' needs

To revise paragraphs within letters, memos, and reports

10

Modifying the Meaning

Reviewing Modifiers

Modifiers range in length from single words to groups of words; those groups range in complexity from simple prepositional phrases to more complicated verbal phrases and subordinate clauses. Whatever their length or complexity, modifiers change and enrich the meaning of other words.

In early chapters, we removed modifiers to find subjects, verbs, objects, and complements more easily. Here we will look at the modifiers themselves, consider their value, review their proper uses, and examine problems related to their use.

Modifiers fall into two familiar categories: adjectives and adverbs.

Adjectives modify nouns and pronouns, telling us whose, which one(s), what kind(s), or how many. Usually adjectives are near the words they modify. The main exception is the subject complement; there the adjective follows the linking verb and refers to the subject at the other end of the sentence.

Individual words, phrases, and clauses can be adjectives. In the sentences below, the adjectives are italicized, disregarding the articles *a, an,* and *the.* Arrows point to the words being modified.

The pianist, *who is a music major,* accompanied the *soprano* soloist.

The pianist, a *talented college* student, is *popular* with *local* audiences.

The usher *near the back door* turned up the lights *on the concert stage.*

The singer *to appear first that evening* sang *fewer* songs

than Marilyn.

PRACTICE 1 —

In the following sentences, underline the adjectives, and draw arrows to the words being modified, as shown in the examples above. (Disregard the articles a, an, *and* the.*)*

1. The rain, falling heavily, slowed traffic near the concert hall.

2. The German folk songs that Marilyn sang were poignant and sad.

3. The audience, young and old alike, were attentive and appreciative.

4. The young artists easily won their applause, singing and playing beauti-

fully.

You should have found various kinds of adjectives, including single words, phrases, and adjective clauses. You can find examples of many kinds of adjectives in your own writing as well.

Adverbs modify verbs, adverbs, and adjectives, telling us when, where, how, how well, under what circumstances, to what extent, and why. Although single-word adverbs often end with *ly*, many common adverbs do not. There is no standard visual signal to identify adverbs.

Individual words, phrases, and clauses can be adverbs, just as they can be adjectives. In the passage below, the adverbs are italicized, and arrows are drawn to the words being modified.

Though Joan sings *well*, Sue performs *more artistically*.

Joan sings *only* for her family and her friends.

Sue *often* performs *on the concert stage*.

Usually Joan sings *to please herself*, and Sue sings

to inspire an audience.

PRACTICE 2 —

In the following sentences, underline the adverbs, and draw arrows to the words being modified, as shown in the examples above.

1. When we want to see a new musical comedy, we usually go to New York City's famous theater district.

2. Musical comedy is generally entertaining because it features a light-hearted plot interspersed with songs and dances.

3. An operetta closely resembles a musical comedy, but operetta plots are somewhat more substantial.

4. Conductors look carefully at the orchestra scores before performances.

In your own writing, you should be able to find various kinds of adverbs, including single words, phrases of several types, and adverb clauses, just as you can find many kinds of adjectives.

Modifiers are important and useful. They can refine and enrich the meaning of our statements, provided they are chosen well. Nonetheless, they should be used sparingly, not excessively, and they must add, not detract. Modifiers that add little or no meaning detract in that they create unnecessary clutter in our sentences.

In these examples, the modifiers add nothing to the meaning of the words to which they refer:

loud crash	heartfelt sorrow
prejudiced bigot	racing fast

Can a crash be quiet or a bigot be unprejudiced? If someone is racing, isn't speed implied? The modifiers on the words above appear to be useless. When we see examples like these, standing in isolation on the page of a textbook, their uselessness is obvious.

At the early stages of our writing, we should write down every detail, just as it occurs to us. Ideally, in the first draft, we want more details than we need. Then, as we go back and examine what we have written, we rethink the topic and our statements. As we revise, we should watch for unnecessary modifiers. At the same time, we should replace weaker words with stronger ones.

The goal in our writing is to choose exact nouns and powerful verbs. Those words should convey the meaning; adjectives and adverbs merely heighten the effect.

Consider what happens when we try to prop up weak nouns and verbs with modifiers. We must use many words, and the statements limp along, eventually making the point but weakly:

Poor: Grandmother's best knitting material became looped around, back and forth, many different ways.

Better: Grandmother's knitting yarn became twisted.

"Knitting material" is yarn. When yarn becomes looped around, back and forth, many different ways, it is twisted. By using exact words, *yarn* and *twisted,* we can express the same idea in fewer words. Consider this example:

Poor: The dieter thought longingly about chocolate candy and wanted it very much.

Better: The dieter yearned for chocolate candy.

When the dieter "thought longingly about and wanted," the dieter yearned. The verb *yearned* conveys the meaning of two verbs, *thought* and *wanted,* even when one of them is propped up with the adverb *longingly.*

PRACTICE 3

Revise the following sentences, using stronger nouns and verbs and eliminating unnecessary modifiers. Preserve the original meaning as much as possible, but add details if you need them.

1. Standing in the wet rain with the bitter, biting chill of the strong wind, we became quite uncomfortably cold and completely soaked.

   _____

   _____

   _____

2. During the fourth inning of the baseball game, the ball went through the air with much speed after the batter had succeeded in hitting it.

   _____

   _____

   _____

3. After my uncle took a lot of his money and put it into investments like stocks and bonds, the financial markets did not do so well as he had half hoped and half expected.

   _____

   _____

   _____

4. The person who was in charge of preparing our food put the egg into the grease and let it cook, and meanwhile he took the slice of the bread and put it into the toaster.

_____

_____

_____

5. By making careful choices of modifiers, those of us who write can probably cut back on the number of words we use.

_____

_____

_____

Avoiding Problems with Modifiers

Assuming we choose modifiers carefully, we should have relatively few problems with them. Those problems that do arise generally fall into one of these three categories:

- Improper word choice, usually involving a single word
- Misplaced modifier, involving a word or a phrase
- Dangling modifier, usually involving a verbal phrase

IMPROPER WORD CHOICE

One problem with word choice can come from carelessness with this familiar pattern: S + LV + SC (subject + linking verb + subject complement). The part that can cause confusion is the subject complement. Adjectives, not adverbs, are properly used as subject complements. The meaning of a sentence may depend on the part of speech used as the subject complement. For instance, consider the meanings of these sentences:

I feel badly. (*badly* is an adverb)
(This sentence uses *feel* as an action verb. In making this statement, I am referring to the poor use of my hands, perhaps because I have a faulty sense of touch.)

I feel bad. (*bad* is an adjective)

> (This statement is more probable than the statement above. Here, *feel* is a linking verb. The statement refers to my health or my emotions.)

In the sample sentences below, the subject complements are adjectives, not adverbs, and properly so. As we know, complements follow linking verbs, and they describe the subjects (nouns or pronouns). Therefore, adjectives are the proper choice:

Marilyn, the singer, is *gifted*.

Her pianist looks *attentive*.

They sound *beautiful* together, and they look *calm* on the stage.

I feel *bad* that I missed their earlier performances.

The nature of the verb is important. Notice that in the sentences below, the verbs are action verbs, making adverbs, not adjectives, the appropriate modifiers.

The pianist looks *eagerly* at Marilyn before beginning.

She *gently* feels the piano keys under her fingers.

PRACTICE 4

Underline the correct choices in the following sentences.

1. Patrons of rock concerts feel (glad, gladly) when their favorite stars perform locally.

2. Rumors about the stars' private lives attract (eager, eagerly) magazine readers.

3. The magazines are purchased (eager, eagerly) by curious fans.

4. Unflattering publicity may sell magazines (easy, easily), but it makes the stars feel (bad, badly).

Improper word choice can also occur when **degrees of comparison** are confused or mishandled. Comparison involves changes in modifiers, such as these:

good→better→best
tall→taller→tallest

The modifiers themselves change to show degrees of the qualities expressed. The three degrees of comparison are positive (the regular form), comparative, and superlative. Here are the distinctions:

The comparative degree is used when two persons or entities are being compared. Usually the *er* ending is used.

One basketball player is *taller* than another.

The superlative degree is used when three or more persons or entities are being compared. Usually the *est* ending is used.

Paul is the *tallest* player on the team.

PRACTICE 5

Underline the correct choices in the following sentences.

1. The cucumber grows (fast, faster, fastest) of all the many plants in the garden.

2. The cucumbers are planted (early, earlier) than the green beans.

3. This new variety of zucchini produces (good, better, best) squash than the variety I tried last year.

4. Zucchini is a (long, longer) and (slim, slimmer) squash than butternut squash.

The degrees of comparison usually are formed according to these guidelines:

1. Most one-syllable modifiers take *er* or *est* endings:

long	longer	longest
big	bigger	biggest

2. Most two-syllable modifiers take *er* or *est* endings or use the additional words *more* or *most, less* or *least*:

happy	happier	happiest
gifted	more gifted	most gifted
pleasant	less pleasant	least pleasant

3. Modifiers with three or more syllables use the additional words *more* or *most, less* or *least*:

intelligent	more intelligent	most intelligent
willingly	less willingly	least willingly

4. A few common modifiers do not follow the standard patterns; that is, they change their spelling rather than adding *er* or *est*, *more* or *most*, *less* or *least*:

good	better	best
well	better	best
bad	worse	worst
many	more	most
much	more	most
less	less	least

PRACTICE 6

Underline the correct choices in the following sentences.

1. Health-conscious Americans are tending to eat (many, more, most) fish than red meat these days.

2. How (much, more, most) cholesterol is in the body depends on several factors.

3. Restricting one's fat intake brings (good, better, best) cholesterol control than does ignoring one's diet.

4. Those Americans who are (less willing, least willing) to modify their diets may be among the (more threatened, most threatened) with health problems.

A few other details about word choice should be noted here. First, when comparing one entity with others in a group of which it is a part, do not omit the word *other*.

> *Poor:* Minnesota has more lakes than *any* state in the United States.
> *Better:* Minnesota has more lakes than *any other* state in the United States.

Second, use one means of comparison, not two. In other words, avoid double comparisons.

> *Poor:* Marilyn is *more happier* than most artists.
> *Better:* Marilyn is *happier* than most artists.

Third, use *good* as an adjective, but *well* as either an adjective or an adverb, depending on its use in context.

Poor:	Marilyn sings *good*.

Better:	Marilyn sings *well*. (*well* is an adverb here, modifying *sings*)

Better:	Marilyn feels *well*. (here, *well* is an adjective, a subject complement)

PRACTICE 7

Underline the correct choices in the following sentences.

1. Dutch elm disease killed more trees than (any, any other) disease in recent times.

2. We feel (sad, sadly) as we see a mature tree wilt with the disease.

3. Sometimes chemical treatment in the early stages produces (good, well) results.

4. Showing brown leaves in mid-summer indicates that the tree is not doing (good, well).

MISPLACED MODIFIERS

A modifier is misplaced if it is too far away from the word it modifies. Modifiers typically attach to the words nearby. If too many words intervene between the modifier and its reference, the meaning may be lost or distorted.

The sentences below show what can happen when modifiers are misplaced. The modifiers are italicized, and arrows point to the words to which they are apparently attached. Note that the connections between the modifiers and these references make no sense.

Poor:	Marilyn wore a diamond pendant around her neck *that she had bought on a trip to Europe.*
	(Did she buy her neck in Europe?)

Poor:	During intermission, I saw a friend whom I hadn't seen for ten years *in the lobby.*
	(Was that friend in the lobby for ten years? Had I been in the lobby for ten years? Had we both spent ten years in the lobby without seeing each other? The statement is so confused that it can be interpreted in various ways.)

By contrast, notice the connections in these revised sentences:

Better: Around her neck, Marilyn wore a diamond pendant *that she had bought on a trip to Europe.*

Better: During intermission, I saw *in the lobby* a friend whom I hadn't seen for ten years.

PRACTICE 8

Revise the following sentences, placing the modifiers near the words to which they refer. Reword and drop some of the modifiers if you wish.

1. The governor's wife appeared at a fund raiser for his presidential campaign 1,500 miles from her home.

_____

_____

2. Only eight people turned out to hear her speak at a Saturday breakfast for her husband in one small town.

_____

_____

3. The governor also traveled thousands of miles in his quest for votes from his home across the country.

_____

_____

4. The prolonged presidential campaigns tire the candidates, their supporters, and the press, lasting almost two years.

_____

_____

A special type of misplaced modifier is called a **squinting modifier.** This strange name fits in that the modifier seems to look two or more ways at once as though trying to discern which way to look. Readers are confused because the modifier could refer to either of two words or groups of words:

Unclear:	Marilyn *only* has been singing for six years.
Clear:	Marilyn has been singing for *only* six years.

                  (Apparently Marilyn has less experience than her competitors or associates.)

Clear: Only Marilyn has been singing for six years.

                  (Apparently other singers have less experience than Marilyn.)

Clear: For six years, Marilyn has *only* been singing.

                  (Marilyn has been singing, not singing and dancing.)

A particularly common error of this type concerns the powerful adverb *not*. Careless placement of *not* can drastically change the meaning of a sentence. Compare the meanings of these two statements, noticing that either one could be accurate, depending on what the writer intends:

All the students are *not* here today.

Not all the students are here today.

In the first sentence, all the students are gone; no one is here today. In the second sentence, some of the students are here; some are not here.

PRACTICE 9 _____

Revise the following sentences to make the meanings clear.

    Example: All the busy intersections do not have stop signs.

      Not all the busy intersections have stop signs.

1. All the states are not holding caucuses; some of them only have primary elections.

2. The governor of your state only traveled to our city for a campaign speech.

3. This political rally only featured invited speakers who supported the sixty-five-mile-per-hour speed limit on interstate highways.

_____

_____

4. The governor talked an hour almost, persuading us to vote for him.

_____

_____

As the sentences in this practice show, where we place modifiers in a sentence can make a big difference in our meaning. We want modifiers to clarify and enrich our intended meaning, not to distort or confuse it. To produce these desired effects, modifiers must be selected carefully and then positioned carefully in sentences.

DANGLING MODIFIERS

A modifier "dangles" if it has no logical reference within the sentence. As noted in Chapter 8, verbal phrases can create dangling modifiers if they are not handled carefully. Dangling modifiers are most likely to occur in this pattern:

opening phrase, subject + verb

The opening phrase attaches to the subject, whether or not the reference makes sense. This example is familiar:

Running for the train, the suitcase was lost.

To repair dangling modifier sentences, either reword the phrase or reword the main part of the sentence. Using the active voice often helps avoid dangling modifiers altogether. These versions of the sample sentence all eliminate the dangling modifier; for the most part, they use the active voice:

Running for the train, I lost my suitcase.   (ACTIVE VOICE)

While I was running for the train, I lost my suitcase.

(ACTIVE VOICE)

While I was running for the train, my suitcase was lost.

(PASSIVE VOICE)

Reword the following sentences to eliminate the dangling modifiers. Use the active voice. Invent a doer if none is present. There may be more than one correct answer. In your revised sentences, underline subjects once and verbs twice.

> **Example:** Hurrying to the concert, the car was left unlocked.
>
> *Because we were hurrying to the concert, we forgot to lock our car.*
>
> *Hurrying to the concert, I left the car unlocked.*

1. Listening to the music, a fire truck raced by the concert hall.

   _____

   _____

2. Wearing only a light sweater, the air conditioning seemed too cold.

   _____

   _____

3. To get a better view, our seats had to be changed.

   _____

4. Attending the concert during the holidays, the Christmas decorations obstructed our view of the stage.

   _____

   _____

In the sentences in the practice above, the dangling modifiers are verbal phrases (as is often the case). Another type of word group, however, might be added to the list of possible dangling modifiers—namely, the ***elliptical adverb clause.***

Elliptical means that something has been left out. The parts left out of an elliptical adverb clause are the subject and the helping verb. In fact, these parts are implied and are sufficiently clear to the reader, even though they have not been written or spoken, as in these examples:

While listening to the music, a fire truck raced by.
    (implying while <u>we</u> <u>were</u> <u>listening</u> or while <u>someone</u> <u>was listening</u>)

When wearing only a light sweater, the air conditioning seemed too cold.
    (implying when <u>I</u> <u>was wearing</u> or when <u>someone</u> <u>was wearing</u>)

Sometimes elliptical clauses can be confusing because it is not clear which subject is implied. Usually, however, the implied subject is clearly the writer himself or herself. For instance, consider this sentence:

After suffering continuous asthma attacks, my doctor suggested a change in climate.

Apparently the writer meant this:

After <u>I</u> <u>had suffered</u> continuous asthma attacks, my doctor suggested a change in climate.

However, it is possible that the writer meant this:

After my <u>doctor</u> <u>had suffered</u> continuous asthma attacks, she suggested a change in climate.

With elliptical clauses, as with verbal phrases, the main point to remember is that the opening word group must connect logically with the subject that follows.

PRACTICE 11

Revise the following sentences to eliminate the dangling modifiers.

1. While speaking at the political rally, the loudspeakers quit working.

_____

_____

2. The campaign travel was extensive, being the candidate's press agent.

_____

_____

3. When rushing to the airport, briefing papers had to be prepared for the next appearance.

_____

_____

4. Since facing the reporters this morning, a position paper on tax increases has been drafted.

_____

_____

_____

Points to Use

- Use adjectives and adverbs to change and refine meaning, selecting the most precise modifiers possible.
- Use well-chosen nouns and strong verbs, preferably action verbs, to convey the meaning.
- Choose subject-form pronouns or adjectives for subject complements.
- Use comparative and superlative degrees with care, noting whether two or more than two persons or entities are being compared.
- Phrase comparisons carefully so that the critical word *other* is included when needed and so that you have no double comparisons.
- Know where the modifiers are and which words they modify; then be sure to keep the modifiers close to their references.
- Make sure that modifiers have only one possible reference within a sentence, avoiding the squinting modifier problem.
- Pay special attention to opening phrases, especially verbal phrases, because they can so easily become dangling modifiers.

Points to Remember

- Modifiers can be adjectives or adverbs. They may be single words, phrases, or clauses. Their purpose is to change and refine the meaning of other words in the sentence.
- Adjectives modify nouns and pronouns. Adjectives typically are found beside the words they refer to, though the adjectives used as subject complements depart from this pattern.
- Adverbs modify the meaning of verbs, adjectives, and other adverbs. They also appear near the words they modify.
- Positive (regular), comparative, and superlative degrees are used to express degrees or gradations of comparison. Modifiers change form to show the comparative and superlative degrees, or the words *more, most, less,* or *least* are used with the regular forms.

- The comparative degree is used when two persons or entities are compared; the superlative degree is used when three or more are involved.
- A misplaced modifier is too far removed from the word to which it refers. It attaches to whatever is nearby, often distorting the meaning or creating a ridiculous statement.
- A squinting modifier is ambiguous because it can be interpreted as referring to more than one word.
- A dangling modifier has no logical word to which it refers. In the most common cases, dangling modifiers involve verbal phrases at the beginnings of sentences. Immediately after these phrases, the logical reference must be provided.

EXERCISE 1. Selecting the Correct Modifiers

Underline the correct choices in the following sentences. Check your answers with those at the back of the book.

1. Animal lovers feel (bad, badly) about abandoned pets.

2. Some pet owners feel their animals will be (happier, more happier) in the country than in the city.

3. In a class of thirty students, one of the (better, best) writers wrote about pets abandoned in the country.

4. She began by describing a vacation that sounded (good, well) and (restful, restfully) to the reader.

5. She and her family had traveled (quick, quickly) to the rural home of her brother-in-law and his family.

6. On the day of their arrival, Uncle Paul found a handsome Irish setter along the road, a dog (more handsome, most handsome) than their pet collie.

7. The children were excited and cried (eager, eagerly), "Can we keep that wonderful dog?"

8. The adults (reluctant, reluctantly) replied, "No, we must take him to the pound tomorrow."

9. Later that (calm, calmly) day, a terrible noise arose (sudden, suddenly) in the front yard.

10. Everyone rushed (quick, quickly) to the yard, where they saw the Irish setter chasing (wild, wildly) around the visitors' car.

11. Barking and meowing sounded (loud, loudly) in the yard.

12. Uncle Paul traced the meowing to the car engine, where a terrified cat appeared (anxious, anxiously) and cried (pitiful, pitifully).

13. Looking closely at their car, the visitors found scratch marks gouging (deep, deeply) into the surface.

14. The Irish setter, (less excited, least excited) by now than the cat, looked (sleepy, sleepily) at the people.

15. The next morning, while the children watched (sad, sadly), the men loaded the Irish setter into the truck.

16. On the way to the pound, the dog bolted from the truck (sudden, sud-

denly), raced (rash, rashly) into an intersection, and caused three vehicles to screech (abrupt, abruptly) to a stop, narrowly avoiding a collision.

17. The dog was hit and injured so (bad, badly) that he nearly died on the spot.

18. The men loaded him into the truck, returned to the farm, and got out the hunting rifle, (reluctant, reluctantly) resolved to do their grim duty.

19. The children were the (sadder, saddest) people in the family, but no one felt (good, well) about the dog's fate.

20. Having put the dog out of its misery, Uncle Paul commented (sad, sadly), "If only those irresponsible owners had found a home for their pet, this ending could have been avoided."

21. He added later, "We have seen many (brave, bravely) animals left out here, and it is one of the (worse, worst) choices a pet owner can make."

22. This episode and others like it illustrate the (heavy, heavily) burden (thoughtless, thoughtlessly) placed on society by some people.

23. People who have (real, really) concern about animals should (active, actively) support humane societies.

24. Members of the Animal Humane Society of Hennepin County, Minnesota, (proud, proudly) display a (small, smallest) card that reads, "I'm a voice for those who cannot speak."

25. Human society is (richer, more rich) because of the work of humane societies.

EXERCISE 2. *Revising Sentences*

Correct any problems with modifiers in the following sentences. Reword as you wish, but write a clear, complete sentence. There may be more than one correct answer.

Example: I heard a good song coming home on the radio.

Coming home, I heard a good song on the radio.

I heard a good song on the radio while I was coming home.

1. I met a man who had a wooden leg named Mike Allison.

   _____

   _____

2. After working hard in the field all day, the abandoned pets are unwelcome
   so far as the farmers are concerned.

   _____

   _____

3. The German shepherd is better than any breed of dog.

   _____

   _____

4. All the breeds are not so intelligent as the German shepherd.

   _____

   _____

5. Chasing the insolent cat over the back fence, exhaustion and disgust filled
   the dog's face.

   _____

   _____

6. If completely untamed, Peter thinks the animals are unmanageable.

   _____

   _____

7. The robin looked helplessly after the baby robin had fallen to the ground,
   unable to lift the baby back into the nest.

   _____

   _____

   _____

8. Lying on the ground for two days, the neighbor's cat finally killed the unfortunate little bird.

_____

_____

9. All animals are not that helpless when their young stray from home.

_____

_____

10. Watching our pet cat, the mother cat grasps her kittens by the skin of their necks and moves them with her mouth.

_____

_____

_____

EXERCISE 3.   *Evaluating Modifiers in Context*

Read the story below twice. The first time, ignore the italicized modifiers. The second time, consider which of those modifiers help and which hinder the story. In some instances, the value of the modifier is debatable.

Put an × through the modifiers that you believe should be eliminated and a ? over the ones about which you have doubt.

The bright September sun was moving *swiftly* toward the *western* horizon. Officer Evans glanced *down briefly* at his watch, *hoping to discover that his shift was about over.* Instead, he had another forty-five minutes left before 5 P.M., time to go home from an *uneventful* day as a police officer in a *quiet* Minneapolis suburb.

He couldn't help hearing another officer on the phone. "Yes, we've found the address. We'll drive over and talk to the people." A *long, heavy* pause, *full of hesitance,* hung in the air. "Sure, we'll go right away. We *always* prefer going in person in cases like this." The officer hung up, then looked down at his *desk* blotter *solemnly, looking as though he wished the job belonged to someone else. Finally* his *firm, resonant bass* voice filled the room, "Come on, Evans. We have a call to make."

When they arrived at the house, they walked up the front steps *silently, side by side, unhurried, dreading their duty.* A man answered the doorbell *at once.* He looked *as though he wanted to speak,* but before uttering a word, he appeared *stricken.* The officers had no way to know that when he glanced at two *uniformed* policemen, the man *instantly* thought of his *teenage* son, *who was out with the family car that afternoon.*

"Is this the Pembertons?" asked the officer, *firmly but gently.* The man turned ashen, *full of dread as he imagined his son, the car, and possible accidents.*

"Yes." He was *frantically* searching his mind for other reasons why these *strong, dignified young* men *in their sharp blue uniforms* were standing on *his front* step.

"Is your wife's name Carol?" was the next question. When the man nodded, the officer went on. "May we come in?"

The *weakening* rays of the *autumn* sun came in *through the front door* with the officers. Now words came *quickly, but softly, so softly that only those* men *in the front hall* could hear what was being said.

"We've just heard from the police in your wife's hometown in Iowa. Her father was found dead *earlier this afternoon.* In the shock and confusion *down there,* no one could find her phone number, so they called us. May we see her?"

EXERCISE 4. *Using Modifiers in Original Paragraphs*

On a separate piece of paper, describe a moment in which you felt panic, fear, embarrassment, indecision, or another powerful emotion. The moment must be brief, limited to minutes, not hours or days. Be as exact as you can in relating the circumstances and your reactions, but rely on strong nouns and verbs to convey the meaning.

When you finish, underline your modifiers (disregarding the articles a, an, and the). Bring copies of your paper to class to share in peer group evaluation, or prepare a copy to turn in to the teacher. You will be graded partly on how wisely you select modifiers.

Note: Divide your material into paragraphs. Generally a new paragraph begins with a change of time or place or focus. If you use direct quotes, use quotation marks. With each change of speaker in dialogue, begin a new paragraph.

EXERCISE 5.   *Evaluating Modifiers in Context*

The paragraphs below were written by a college freshman in response to Exercise 4 above. Read the paragraphs for their content. Then read them a second time, slowly and critically, evaluating the modifiers and, more generally, the writer's choice of supporting details.

Which modifiers add worthwhile detail? Many of them do. Underline the modifiers that help you understand what the writer means and how the writer felt in that situation.

Which modifiers need revision? In the margin, put an × beside passages that you think need improvement.

In class, compare your responses to this writing with those of your classmates. Be sure to consider what is good about the passage as well as what could be improved.

Last March, I had a disappointing and slightly embarrassing experience. I attended an Andrés Segovia concert at Orchestra Hall. It really should have been a wonderful experience, but as it happened, it did not turn out the way I had hoped and expected.

Segovia is the man who pioneered the art of classical guitar. He single-handedly turned a Spanish peasant folk instrument into a miniature orchestra capable of performing complicated two- and three-part music written by masters such as Bach, Vivaldi, and Mozart. At the same time, he was able to keep in the music all the fire and passion of rebellious gypsy-blooded players before him, such guitar masters as Villa-Lobos and Tárrega.

In his prime, Segovia was the best guitarist in the world, and many of his guitar techniques will be studied far and wide and used by other guitarists forever. But the important word there is "prime." In March of 1987, the man was 91 years old.

I thought that 91 was a very extreme old age for anyone to be giving a concert on any instrument. But my reasoning was that this great, world-famous musician, probably a proud man at that, would not be touring and giving concerts if he was truly not physically able to do it. I was wrong.

Weeks in advance, I bought a twenty-dollar, second-row, front-center seat.

I also talked four of my guitar-playing friends, all students, into accompanying me. So they also paid for tickets that were very expensive for our limited budgets as students. It turned out that the concert was so terrible we had to leave at intermission.

Besides being disappointed, I actually felt sad, but mostly embarrassed watching the poor, fumbling old man. He was not even able to complete a simple musical idea to a sold-out Orchestra Hall audience. He played out of tune and had no sense of tempo and didn't seem to realize it. He had terrible fret-buzzed notes because of lack of strength in his left hand. He had a weak right hand that was unable to produce an even phrase with a distinct beginning and end. He simply could not complete a single musical phrase without major errors.

In my opinion, he had no right to be on that stage performing in front of paying people. I could not believe that the man who was once such a great soloist would even want the public to see him making so many pitiful, obvious, and very elementary mistakes like that.

About two months ago, Andrés Segovia died. Now I am left with all these mixed feelings. Partly I have to respect him for what he was and for all he did for guitar music and musicians. But I am also still trying to erase the unpleasant memories of that last concert because I don't want that to be my last impression.

EXERCISE 6. *Using Modifiers in Work-Related Writing*

On a separate piece of paper, write a one-page memo to your supervisor at work. Describe an unusual or difficult episode that you dealt with recently. Explain what happened and how you handled it.

If you are a supervisor, write a one-page memo to your employees, either directing them in a critical step of their work or helping them resolve a difficult problem.

If you are not currently employed, use an episode you recall from previous work experience, military service, or participation in community organizations.

Here, as in Exercise 4, use strong nouns and verbs to convey your meaning. (The memo format to use is shown in Exercise 4, Chapter 4, p. 96.)

The memo below is based on a student's response to Exercise 6 above. In this memo, you will find both misplaced and dangling modifiers. You will also find examples of vague words where specific words are needed. You will also see the passive voice used in places where the active voice would be more direct and appropriate.

On a separate piece of paper, revise this memo to make it clearer and more concise. Repair the modifier problems. Replace vague words with more precise ones, particularly strong nouns and verbs. Use active-voice statements when you can. In short, rewrite freely, adding details, changing the arrangement of ideas, and rewording the sentences.

Cross-the-Continent Trucking Company

To: All Truck Employees   Date: November 3, 1990
From: George Genius, Manager
Subject: Truck Fueling and Maintenance

Preparing for truck fueling, the following items have to be checked: the oil level, the water level, and the tires. If the little marks showing the level of the oil on the dipstick should read below normal level, add oil. As you all know, except for the ones who are newer employees, the oil barrel is kept along the wall at the east end of the garage along with the funnels.

Remember that the long-range forecast for the expected weather this winter sounded pretty bad. Approaching cold weather, the correct amount of anti-freeze for each truck's radiator is important. Water and antifreeze mixture can be found along with a gauge for checking the mixture on a shelf above the oil barrel in the garage.

The truck tires should be visually inspected for baldness, uneven wear, tears, and recaps starting to come loose. Checking the inside tires, a club has to be used. With a firm swing of the arm, you hit that tire and watch for the results. If the club bounces off the tire rapidly, the tire has the proper amount of air in it. A club that will work just right for you for this job is located next to the mechanic's desk.

Fueling the truck in the yard, the motor can be left running. However, there can be no smoking. When finished, write down the number of gallons of fuel you used that day on your daily maintenance report.

At the end of the day, file your fuel report along with any truck problems with the mechanic. If you have any questions, feel free to ask the mechanic or me.

11

Writing Stronger Sentences

Reviewing Fragments and Run-ons

In the previous ten chapters, you have worked to write strong sentences by learning the standard patterns, selecting correct verbs and pronouns, and handling phrases and clauses. One goal has been consistent from the start: creating strong, well-worded sentences that convey their meaning clearly. The purpose of this chapter is to review and consolidate all that has gone before and then expand on it to build even stronger sentences.

The importance of good sentences cannot be overemphasized. Complete, correct sentences are the foundation on which all writers build. Readers generally need a complete sentence to get a complete idea. Moreover, readers are taught to expect complete sentences. Just as we expect drivers to follow standard practice on the highway, we expect writers to follow standard practice in their writing. Drivers who behave unpredictably on the highway cause confusion and panic; similarly, writers who handle word groups unpredictably cause confusion and uneasiness for readers who feel they must be missing the meaning.

The writer who fails to produce complete, correct sentences is like a drunk driver whose car swerves all over the road. The expected—and required—control is missing in both cases. Readers suspect that such a writer is ignorant or careless or both, and readers quickly lose patience and respect for the writer, just as other drivers lose patience and respect for the drunk driver.

By definition, each sentence is a vehicle for delivering a full thought. If a word group is not complete, something essential is missing. That essential element may be the subject or the verb or the completeness of the thought itself. When incomplete word groups are treated like sentences, they are called *sentence fragments,* or simply *fragments.*

AVOIDING FRAGMENTS

When fragments were introduced in Chapter 3, we emphasized the incompleteness of the unit. Fragments do not stand alone; they do not make sense alone. At that time, little attention was paid to the reasons why fragments occur. Now, using the knowledge you have gathered since then, you can analyze fragments in more depth.

Most sentence fragments, like most car accidents, are caused by carelessness. But unlike car accidents, fragments happen in fairly predictable times and places:

- When phrases are mistaken for full sentences
- When appositives or other word groups are added to sentences as afterthoughts
- When dependent clauses are mistaken for full sentences

Mistaking phrases for full sentences is most likely to occur when those phrases contain some form of verb. Verbal phrases are potential traps for the unwary because verbals look like verbs, even though they do not act like verbs.

Participles, for instance, look like verbs but act like adjectives. Sometimes word groups containing participial phrases look much like full sentences, especially when a noun (a potential subject) comes right before the participle:

> The car, getting a fresh coat of paint over the rust spots.
> The garage, seeking more business during the slack time of the year.

These fragments can become complete sentences if we add helping verbs. Now the *ing* word is the main verb, not a participle:

> The car is getting a fresh coat of paint over the rust spots.
> The garage is seeking more business during the slack time of the year.

PRACTICE 1

Revise the following fragments to make them independent sentences.

1. The mechanic, wanting to help his regular customers.

_____

2. A receptionist, taking phone messages for the garage.

_____

3. Taking phone messages for the garage, the busy receptionist, trying to help walk-in customers as well.

_____

_____

Adding afterthoughts to full sentences comes naturally because we all have afterthoughts, often worthwhile ones that add meaning. But afterthoughts must be added properly to existing sentences or made to stand apart in separate sentences. Any kind of unit can be an afterthought—a prepositional phrase, a verbal phrase, an appositive, or a dependent clause.

Consider the italicized word group examples in this passage:

> One of our cars needs a new starter. *Not a rebuilt starter this time.* Getting the right parts for that ten-year-old car can take a lot of time. *Maybe eight or ten days.* Meanwhile, I have to arrange rides with friends. *Working the same hours as I do.*

PRACTICE 2

Underline the fragments in this paragraph. Then, on a separate piece of paper, revise the paragraph to eliminate the fragments.

The car, needing a fresh coat of paint over the rust spots, stood on the lot next to the garage. Waiting for the work to begin. The garage, wanting more business during the slack time of the year, offered a reduced price on engine overhauling. Partly to get new customers. Partly to please regular customers. The paint job on my car had to wait until the men finished two other cars. A 1983 Camaro and a 1984 Mustang. I was eager to have the work done. Because I wanted to take a trip.

Mistaking dependent clauses for full sentences is the most understandable of the fragment-producing accidents. Because these units have subjects and verbs, they are structurally closer to being full sentences than any of the phrases. Nonetheless, these word groups cannot stand alone because they do not express a complete thought. Consider the italicized examples in this passage:

We are upset when rust eats away the metal on our cars. Some damage is almost impossible to avoid. *Because salt is thrown on the highways during the winter.* Clearing the highways is necessary in the winter, and salt is one possible treatment. *Which does melt ice.* The damage to cars may not be apparent at first. *Simply because the car rusts on the underside first.* Later we discover what has happened. *When the car is examined closely.*

Dependent clauses can be turned into sentences in at least two ways. First, in adverb clauses, the subordinating conjunction can be dropped so that there is no sense of the clause leaning on another clause:

Frag: Because salt is thrown on the highways during the winter.

Sentence: Salt is thrown on the highways during the winter.

Second, the clause can be left alone, with a main clause added:

Sentence: Some damage is almost impossible to avoid because salt is thrown on the highways during the winter.

Sentence: Because salt is thrown on the highways during the winter, some damage is almost impossible to avoid.

PRACTICE 3

Revise the following fragments into sentences by making them into complete thoughts. Do not add words; just drop the subordinating conjunction.

Example: If the car is well maintained.

The car is well maintained.

1. Because the car rusts on the underside.

_____

2. When the car is examined closely.

_____

PRACTICE 4

Revise these same fragments into sentences by adding a main clause.

Example: If the car is well maintained.

If the car is well maintained, it will run better.

1. Because the car rusts on the underside.

_____

_____

2. When the car is examined closely.

_____

_____

Fragments can be turned into full sentences easily by adding words or adding meaning. With rare exceptions, writers who can spot fragments in their work can fix them.

If you have a problem with fragments, read your writing slowly, out loud. Start at the end, and read sentence by sentence backward. In this way, you can think about each word group separately. Listen to every word group to see whether it stands alone. Use your knowledge of sentence structure to examine word groups, paying special attention to the situations in which fragments commonly occur.

AVOIDING RUN-ON SENTENCES

Full, independent thoughts must be correctly separated or correctly joined. If they are joined correctly, they create compound sentences, as described in Chapter 3. If two or more separate, independent thoughts are not properly separated or joined, a special kind of accident occurs: the **run-on sentence.** The term *run-on sentence* covers two separate problems:

- The comma splice (CS) or comma fault (CF) sentence
- The run-together or fused sentence

Like the fragment, the run-on sentence is regarded as a mark of the writer's ignorance or carelessness or both.

The run-on sentence derives its name from the fact that one sentence runs right into the next, causing a collision between the two. Just as vehicles on a highway must have space between them to avoid a collision, sentences must have the proper space between them to avoid a collision.

The most common way to avoid collisions between sentences is to end the first one with a period and to begin the second one with a capital letter. This conventional use of punctuation and capitalization signals a distinct space between the two thoughts.

SENTENCE 1   SENTENCE 2

Subject + verb . . . . Subject + verb . . . .

The most common run-on occurs when writers use only a comma between two complete thoughts. When this type of sentence error was introduced in Chapter 3, you learned that a comma can be used between sentences, *provided a coordinating conjunction is used with it.* A semicolon between the two sentences also serves to separate them properly.

When the comma is used alone at the critical point between independent thoughts, it is so deeply implicated in the sentence error that the error is called a **comma splice** (CS) or **comma fault** (CF).

SENTENCE 1   SENTENCE 2

Subject + verb . . . , subject + verb . . . .

Notice how the independent thoughts have collided in these examples:

> The mechanic who checked my car was pleased, he said it was in good shape.
> I was glad to hear that good news, I hate big repair bills.
> Last month I bought a new battery, it helped a lot.
> He checks my car every six months, he should know if any problems have developed.
> Regular checkups usually uncover any problems, however, I watch for signs of trouble all the time.
> Driving an old car has its advantages, it saves me money, then sometimes I have big repair bills.

In some cases, personal pronouns are subjects of the second independent thought. Because comma splice sentences often begin the second idea with personal pronouns, writers should be especially careful with sentences that follow this pattern.

PRACTICE 5 ─────────────────────────────

Correctly punctuate the comma splice sentences in the examples above. Rewrite the correct sentences below.

1. _____

   _____

2. _____

   _____

3. _____

_____

4. _____

_____

5. _____

_____

6. _____

_____

Here is a summary of the various ways in which comma splice sentences can be corrected:

- Put a period at the end of the first sentence and begin the second sentence with a capital letter.
- Revise the thoughts, subordinating one or the other by using the phrases and clauses studied in Chapters 8 and 9.
- Leave the statements as they are, but join them with one of the coordinating conjunctions plus a comma:

  for   and   nor   but   or   yet   so   (FANBOYS)

- Leave the statements as they are, but join them with a semicolon.

When the ideas are closely related, the last two techniques are appropriate. For instance, if the second sentence explains the first or elaborates upon the meaning of the first, these methods are appropriate. In the following examples, notice the connection between the ideas:

The mechanic who checked my car was pleased; in fact, he said that it was in good shape.
He checks my car every six months; therefore, he should know whether any problems have developed.

Use a semicolon plus a transitional word or phrase if that word or phrase will smooth the readers' way into the second sentence. Typical transitional devices are these:

however	therefore
moreover	consequently
nevertheless	furthermore
in addition	on the other hand
in fact	for example

Rewording the statements so that the comma splice disappears is often the best solution. The two independent ideas can then become one independent thought with subordinate clauses or phrases expressing the other, lesser thoughts. For instance, consider these alternate versions of the same basic thoughts:

> I was glad to hear that good news; I hate big repair bills.
> (separate independent thoughts)

> Hating big repair bills, I was glad to hear that good news.
> (participial phrase)

> I was glad to hear that good news because I hate big repair bills.
> (adverb clause)

PRACTICE 6

Combine the following independent thoughts three different ways, as shown in the example above. (Note: You may use any of the punctuation devices listed above or any kind of phrase or clause.)

> I was preparing for a 500-mile trip. My car needed routine servicing and a careful checkup before I began.

1. _____

_____

_____

2. _____

_____

_____

3. _____

_____

_____

Another collision, less common but more confusing than the comma splice, is called the **run-together** or *fused sentence.* The term *run-together* is descriptive because it refers to an outright collision in which no mark of punctuation separates the sentences. The term *fused* is also descriptive because it refers to the sentences running together nonstop, or fusing.

SENTENCE 1   SENTENCE 2
Subject + verb . . . subject + verb . . . .

A fused sentence may have punctuation at various spots, but at the critical point—between the two complete thoughts—there is no punctuation. The fused sentence is particularly troublesome because it forces readers to sort out the ideas for themselves.

When confronted with a fused sentence, most readers assume that they have misread a line or two. They stop to reread the passage, thus breaking the flow of thoughts and disrupting the pace, to try to unravel what the writer meant. Most readers will tolerate very little of this inconvenience; instead, they will soon dismiss the writing (and the writer) altogether.

Fused sentences require the same remedies as comma splice sentences: division into separate sentences or proper joining either with semicolons or with commas plus coordinating conjunctions. Rewording these sentences into new independent statements with subordination is again a possibility and often is preferable.

PRACTICE 7

Separate the independent thoughts in this passage by inserting the necessary punctuation. Then, on a separate piece of paper, rewrite the paragraph using subordination techniques (see Chapter 9 for review if necessary).

The owner of the Camaro wanted a light blue for the new paint on his car the owner of the Mustang chose a bright, red-orange color for his car which of the two is more attractive is hard to say in my opinion, the red is gaudy. The body shop ordered enough paint for both paint jobs the work can begin as soon as the owners leave their cars. The work takes at least a week, however, it can take two weeks the amount of time depends on the condition of the car.

You should have found nine separate, independent thoughts in Practice 7. In that respect, the passage was an extreme example of fused sentences. Writers usually make some attempt to separate their thoughts. Even when they do so incorrectly and create comma splices, they are trying to separate their thoughts for the readers' convenience.

Fused sentences generally are easy to spot in proofreading, particularly when passages are read aloud. The sense of the passage comes across not just through the words but also from the groupings of words. In reading words aloud, we find the groupings and make sense of meanings.

Working for Variety and Balance

Monotonous repetition of sentence patterns, even correct ones, can undermine the otherwise good effects of a piece of writing. The previous chapters about sentence patterns have given you many effective ways of putting words together. By using the many types of word groupings discussed in this book, you can vary your sentences and make them more interesting to your readers. As a quick summary of a few possibilities, consider these two main ways to vary basic sentences: by using introductory elements and by using all the various sentence types.

Use introductory elements to vary the openings of some of your sentences. We have examined many such elements, from single words to various phrases to clauses. You should recognize the various types illustrated here:

Hurriedly, Janet finished her homework.
Breathing a sigh of relief, Janet finished her homework.
To earn a good grade, Janet finished her homework.
In time for class, Janet finished her homework.
Her head aching, Janet finished her homework.
After she had heard the early evening news, Janet finished her homework.
While listening to her favorite radio station, Janet finished her homework.

PRACTICE 8

Write three versions of the following sentence, varying them by adding different introductory elements.

We noticed a crack in the plaster above the door.

1. _____

_____

2. _____

_____

3. _____

_____

The elements used as introductions could appear elsewhere in the sentences, too, adding variety. Phrases and clauses contribute variety, a bonus added to the advantages of subordination (discussed in Chapter 9).

Use all the sentence types for variety as well as for their own special effects. Through the use of the four sentence types—simple, compound, complex, and compound/complex—a basic sentence can be varied:

Simple:	Janet finished her homework for this class.
Compound:	Janet finished her homework for this class, and then she worked on her math.
Complex:	After Janet had finished her homework for this class, she worked on her math.
Compound/complex:	After Janet had finished her homework for this class, she did her math, and then she watched the late evening news on television.

PRACTICE 9

Revise this simple sentence, adding details as necessary to create examples of the other sentence types, as shown in the examples above.

Simple: We found cracks in the basement wall.

Compound: _____

_____

Complex: _____

_____

Compound/complex: _____

_____

Just as variety is important to readers, so is the smooth, rhythmic flow of words and word groups, sentence by sentence. Achieving this effect involves *parallelism*—that is, using parallel structures where appropriate.

Parallel structure means the deliberate repetition of patterns: items of equal importance are cast into the same grammatical forms. For instance, a series of adjectives will be cast into single-word adjectives or prepositional phrases or verbal phrases or adjective clauses. Consider this example:

Nonparallel: He is tall, with a slim build, and having a
                graceful manner.
Parallel: He is tall, slim, and graceful.

PRACTICE 10 ⎯⎯⎯⎯⎯⎯⎯⎯⎯⎯⎯⎯⎯⎯⎯⎯

Fill in a revised, parallel version.

Nonparallel: The climate is hot, often having high humidity, and it is dis-
                agreeable.

Parallel: ⎯⎯⎯⎯⎯⎯⎯⎯⎯⎯⎯⎯⎯⎯⎯⎯⎯

                ⎯⎯⎯⎯⎯⎯⎯⎯⎯⎯⎯⎯⎯⎯⎯⎯⎯

Balance comes from repetition in form. Balance, not variety, is the goal when items are equal. In this context, the word *equal* means doing the same thing in the sentence: for instance, all subjects, all objects, all modifiers, all subject complements. Consider this example:

Nonparallel subjects: My two brothers, my three uncles,
                         and five nephews of ours went to the
                         family reunion.
Parallel subjects: My two brothers, three uncles, and
                         five nephews went to the family
                         reunion.

PRACTICE 11 ⎯⎯⎯⎯⎯⎯⎯⎯⎯⎯⎯⎯⎯⎯⎯⎯

Fill in a revised, parallel version.

Nonparallel subjects: Finishing the ten-mile marathon, coming in second,
                         and then to be awarded a fifty-dollar prize made
                         Michelle very happy.

Parallel subjects: ⎯⎯⎯⎯⎯⎯⎯⎯⎯⎯⎯⎯

                         ⎯⎯⎯⎯⎯⎯⎯⎯⎯⎯⎯⎯

Deliberate repetition is involved in parallelism. Sometimes words are repeated in a rhythmic pattern for special effect. Consider, for example, these stirring words from the Gettysburg Address:

"government of the people, by the people, and for the people."

President Lincoln knew that parallelism could turn humble material—prepositional phrases—into powerful, memorable words. Many other writers and speakers have used repetition of patterns for powerful effect. Consider President Kennedy's famous statement:

> "Ask not what your country can do for you; ask what you can do for your country."

In short, parallelism makes words flow rhythmically. If you have a good musical ear, you can hear a rhythm in word patterns just as you can hear a rhythmic beat in music. But a sense of parallelism can also be seen when we look for patterns in sentences.

Although parallelism makes our sentences more pleasing and more concise, its chief advantage is its rhetorical power: it makes statements more attractive, more memorable, more compelling. These qualities make sentences that contain parallelism good for emphasis: good as topic sentences, thesis statements, beginning and ending sentences, and other sentences that deserve emphasis.

Contrast the following examples of nonparallel and parallel structures, noting the differences in rhythmic flow, conciseness versus wordiness, and rhetorical effect:

Nonparallel: Ken came late because his alarm clock had stopped, his car wouldn't start, and because of icy roads.

Parallel: Ken came late because is alarm clock had stopped, his car wouldn't start, and the roads were icy.

Nonparallel: He prefers driving his own car, running his own errands, and to make his own decisions.

Parallel: He prefers driving his own car, running his own errands, and making his own decisions.

    or

He prefers to drive his own car, run his own errands, and make his own decisions.

Nonparallel: To run her own business and making a profit are Sandra's goals.

Parallel: To run her own business and to make a profit are Sandra's goals.

    or

Running her own business and making a profit are Sandra's goals.

Nonparallel: Going hunting is more pleasant for Pete than to go fishing.

Parallel: Going hunting is more pleasant for Pete than going fishing.

    or

To go hunting is more pleasant for Pete than to go fishing.

Nonparallel: Grocery shopping takes time, energy, and the willingness to stand in long lines behind impatient customers.

Parallel: Grocery shopping takes time, energy, and patience.
or
Grocery shopping takes time and energy. It also takes the willingness to stand in long lines with impatient customers.

We do not want to use parallelism for every series of items. To call attention to a particular item, we might choose to set it apart, as shown in the second version of the last example above.

PRACTICE 12

Create parallel versions of these nonparallel sentences.

1. The current interest in fitness may be a fad; maybe the interest is serious enough to be a permanent change in lifestyle.

   _____

   _____

   _____

2. The best ways to lose weight and to keep it off permanently are eating moderately and to continue exercising regularly.

   _____

   _____

   _____

3. Dave likes to jog on the weekends, but during the week he prefers swimming.

   _____

   _____

4. How far he jogs depends on the weather; the distance that he swims depends on the amount of time he has.

   _____

   _____

5. Katie plays tennis for fun and as a means of controlling her weight.

_____

_____

6. Bowling on the company league gave Penny some light exercise, a sense of accomplishment, and provided her with a chance to meet new people.

_____

_____

_____

Points to Use

- Make every sentence complete with at least a subject and a verb; be sure that each sentence expresses a complete thought.
- Pay particular attention to three potential pitfalls that can lead to fragments:

  Mistaking a verbal phrase for a sentence
  Adding appositives or other word groups as afterthoughts
  Mistaking a dependent clause for a sentence

- Watch for comma splices, the most common forms of collision between sentences.
- Use either a coordinating conjunction with a comma or a semicolon between separate independent thoughts. Join separate independent thoughts in these ways if the thoughts are related. If the thoughts are not related, separate them completely with a period and a new sentence.
- Use transitional words or phrases with semicolons when they will ease readers into the new thought or establish the connection between the two thoughts.
- Use subordination to express relationships between ideas.
- Read your writing aloud to check for breaks in thought. Try reading backward, sentence by sentence, through your paper. Check sentences individually to be sure that each sentence is complete.
- Work for variety in sentence patterns, using phrases and clauses in varied ways within sentences.
- Use all four sentence types for their distinctive advantages and for variety in writing.
- Put grammatically equal items into grammatically equal forms for parallelism.

- Use sentences with parallel structure for important ideas, such as topic sentences, beginning and ending sentences, and main points.

Points to Remember

- Complete, correct sentences are basic to good writing. Readers expect complete thoughts in each word group that is written as a sentence.
- A sentence fragment is less than a sentence. Phrases and clauses can easily be mistaken for full sentences, particularly ones that are added to complete sentences as afterthoughts.
- A run-on sentence is one in which two or more complete thoughts have collided without the proper space or the proper joining devices between them. The most common type of run-on sentence is the comma splice or comma fault.
- A comma splice (comma fault) sentence consists of two or more independent thoughts that have been put together (spliced) with only a comma.
- To repair a comma splice, the writer can either separate the thoughts into separate sentences or join them with a semicolon or a comma plus a coordinating conjunction. In some cases, re-wording the ideas is preferable.
- The semicolon by itself can join separate independent thoughts. Transitional devices can be used with the semicolon if they are helpful in connecting the ideas.
- A fused sentence is one in which two or more separate independent thoughts have collided with no mark of punctuation between them. Marks of punctuation may appear elsewhere in the fused sentence, but at the critical point between sentences, readers have no clues marking the end of one idea and the beginning of the next.
- Sentence variety can be achieved by using phrases and dependent clauses at various points within sentences. Subordinating with phrases and dependent clauses also expresses relationships between ideas.
- The four sentence types (simple, compound, complex, and compound/complex) are useful for variety and for their own special effects.
- Parallelism is the deliberate repetition of patterns for grammatically equal parts of sentences. Parallelism makes sentences concise, rhythmic, and powerful.

EXERCISE 1.   Identifying Fragments and Run-ons

Match the following sentences with the appropriate choice. Check your answers with those at the back of the book.

a. correct   c. comma splice
b. fragment   d. fused

_____ 1. Americans, taking up crafts and hobbies these days.

_____ 2. Some hobbies are creative, others are merely time-killers.

_____ 3. Philatelists are stamp collectors, their hobby has been popular for decades.

_____ 4. Numismatists, coin collectors, often buy, sell, and trade coins with other collectors that way they can improve their own collections.

_____ 5. Civil War buffs form clubs and stage mock battles, often with carefully collected, historically authentic props and costumes.

_____ 6. Macramé, creating objects by knotting strands of materials into various shapes.

_____ 7. Macramé objects, plant holders and wall hangings, for instance, decorate many homes.

_____ 8. According to *The Wall Street Journal*, July 14, 1978, calligraphy was the "macramé of the 70s" it was a very popular hobby at that time.

_____ 9. The article said that about thirty-five societies of calligraphers were formed in the mid-1970s.

_____ 10. Beginners starting with italic letters and going on to Gothic lettering, forming lovely writing.

_____ 11. Gothic lettering from the late Middle Ages, from northern European scribes and early printers.

_____ 12. Originally, the term *Gothic* was used scornfully, Italians used the term to scoff at works done north of the Alps.

_____ 13. The tall, pointed Gothic letters parallel tall, pointed Gothic arches small letters, not fancy capitals, are the great glory of Gothic style.

_____ 14. A universal art, dating back as far as history reaches, is embroidery, in fact, authorities think ancient women used pierced fishbones as needles.

_____ 15. American Indians from Maine to Mexico had beautiful embroidery; each tribe had distinctive patterns.

_____ 16. The women, embroidering on doeskin with quills, creating designs full of meaning for their tribes.

_____ 17. Needlepoint, the favorite handwork of Elizabeth I, was already thousands of years old by the time of her reign, she ruled from 1558–1603.

_____ 18. Archaeologists have found needlepoint pieces in Egyptian tombs, pieces of knitting were found also.

_____ 19. Patchwork, an American folk art, unique to the pioneers, dating back to pre-Revolutionary days.

_____ 20. Crazy quilts, bits of fabric put together randomly, are not patchwork. Which is carefully planned.

EXERCISE 2. _Revising Fragments and Run-ons_

Change the following word groups into complete, correct sentences. You may reword or divide these ideas into separate sentences if you get better results that way.

1. Americans, taking up crafts and hobbies these days.

   _____

   _____

2. Some hobbies are creative, others are merely time-killers.

   _____

   _____

3. Numismatists, coin collectors, often buy, sell, and trade coins with other collectors that way they can improve their own collections.

   _____

   _____

4. Beginning calligraphers, starting with italic lettering and going on to Gothic lettering, forming lovely handwriting.

_____

_____

5. Gothic lettering from the late Middle Ages, from northern European scribes and early printers.

_____

_____

6. Originally, the term *Gothic* was used scornfully, Italians used the term to scoff at works done north of the Alps.

_____

_____

_____

7. The tall, pointed Gothic letters parallel tall, pointed Gothic arches small letters, not fancy capitals, are the great glory of Gothic style.

_____

_____

_____

8. A universal art, dating back as far as history reaches, is embroidery, in fact, authorities think ancient women used pierced fishbones as needles.

_____

_____

_____

9. Indian women, embroidering on doeskin with quills, creating designs full of meaning for their tribes.

_____

_____

10. Needlepoint, the favorite handwork of Elizabeth I, was already thousands of years old by the time of her reign, she ruled from 1558–1603.

_____

_____

_____

11. Archaeologists have found needlepoint pieces in Egyptian tombs, pieces of knitting were found also.

_____

_____

12. Patchwork, an American folk art, unique to the pioneers, dating back to pre-Revolutionary days.

_____

_____

13. Crazy quilts, bits of fabric put together randomly, are not patchwork. Which is carefully planned.

_____

_____

14. Making quilts to use scraps of fabric and creating unusual designs, showing imagination.

_____

_____

15. Grandmother Mathews won prizes at the fair for her afghans, Aunt Jessie also entered needlework, she specialized in tatting.

_____

_____

16. Collecting baseball cards as children, a way of beginning a lifelong interest in the sport.

_____

_____

17. One student wrote a detailed account of Babe Ruth's career, he needed no notes but wrote from memory, he had studied Babe Ruth for many years.

_____

_____

_____

18. Some fishermen have learned what to expect in each of the nearby lakes they rely on memories of their fishing experiences over the years.

_____

_____

_____

19. Deer hunters look forward to fall, they may even count the days until hunting season opens.

_____

_____

20. Venison, prepared well, rewarding for the hunters and their families it makes a delicious meal.

_____

_____

EXERCISE 3.   Putting Revised Sentences into Paragraphs

Use the factual information in Exercises 1 and 2 as a basis for paragraphs. Select sentences that pertain to a central idea. On a separate piece of paper, arrange those sentences logically to form a paragraph. You may reword sentences. You may also add details and examples of your own in support of the topic idea.

EXERCISE 4.   Revising Sentences in Student Paragraphs

On a separate piece of paper, revise the sentences in the following paragraphs, eliminating fragments and run-ons. Combine the ideas as appropriate, using subordination techniques. You may rearrange sentences, putting them into more logical order. Some details may be dropped and others expanded.

These examples were written by college freshmen.

Paragraph 1

Students interested in a career in forestry must meet certain requirements in college. Their first two years in college are very important. Because they lead into specialized courses later on. Students should take freshman and sophomore classes in English, math, public speaking, and science. Most importantly, biology and chemistry. Forming a foundation for advanced work in botany in the junior year. Math is also emphasized. Student programs including calculus, analysis, and trigonometry. Some courses in economics, business, sociology, and psychology are also suggested, some are even required. Giving the student a basis for a broader understanding.

Paragraph 2

Last summer my family and I went on vacation with my grandma and grandpa. We rented a van, then we drove to the Black Hills in South Dakota. My grandma had been there before. She enjoyed it the first time, so she wanted to go back again. We all decided we would go along, it was a place the rest of us had not seen before. When we arrived, my dad parked the van. It was evening, but still light. Everyone got out except me. I was fooling around with the controls in the van. I knew how to drive, but I had never driven a van before. All of a sudden, the gears slipped from park to drive. It started moving. My father was standing by the window. Which was lucky for me. He started yelling at me. "Hit the brake pedal!" I did, and the van stopped. Fortunately no one was hurt.

Paragraph 3

After work one day I was driving down the road, then without warning, the car lost power. It coughed and gasped, it acted like it was choking. Finally quitting completely. I managed to pull over to the side of the road. With the shoulder very wet, the car started to sink into the gravel, I knew I would be stuck. Especially when I got out and saw the tires sunk a couple inches into the gravel. I started walking, if I could find a phone, I could call for help. A house was up ahead. When I got there, I rang the doorbell, there was no answer. After trying the bell several times, still no answer. By then I was really discouraged it seemed like I was so alone. Also with everything going wrong. I started to walk again, then I saw a familiar car coming toward me. It slowed up, I thought maybe I can hitch a ride. But it was a friend of mine, he was surprised to see me. As for me, you can't imagine how glad I was to see him.

EXERCISE 5. *Revising Sentences for Parallelism*

On a separate piece of paper, write improved versions of the following sentences, using parallelism and subordination techniques. You may divide sentences into two or more sentences if that creates a better arrangement of the ideas.

1. Good health depends on proper nutrition, adequate rest, and getting plenty of vigorous exercise regularly.

2. To play racquetball on weekends and biking in the summer are not sufficient exercise.

3. Mike thinks that he will improve his grades this term, that his boss will give him a raise, and hoping for a good ski season.

4. Students should come to class ready for listening, to take good notes, and participating in class discussion.

5. Jill works two days a week, three weeks a month, and of the twelve month year, she works about eight months.

6. Many people think that it is easier to listen to the news on television than reading the newspaper.

7. It is wise to shop for Christmas gifts in the summer and storing them away for later.

8. Exercise is fun, makes us feel good, sleep better, and it burns off calories while toning the muscles.

9. To get the most benefit from exercise, be moderate, and we have to continue exercising all our lives.

10. People who exercise regularly are likely to be the most fit to begin with, and they are not likely to be people burdened with eating disorders, drug abuse, nor do they smoke a lot.

11. For many people, the word *diet* refers to a plan to "go on" for a while, limiting food eaten in order to lose weight, and then people "go off" their diets and gain the weight back.

12. Nutrition experts and medical experts warn of the dangers of yo-yo dieting, meaning losing weight, and then in a comparatively short time, to gain it back, perhaps gaining back more than was lost.

EXERCISE 6. *Revising a Job Application Letter*

Correct all the errors in the following job application letter. The writer has problems in every sentence, some of them covered in previous chapters and others discussed in this chapter. Rewrite the letter on a separate piece of paper.

4590 West 198th Street
West Town, MN 55555
January 29, 1989

Mr. Ralph J. Theisenable
Personal Director
Roberts Insurance Agency
1876 East Avenue
Minneapolis, MN 55400

Dear Mr. Theisinible,

I read your ad in the West Town Sun for a secretary. Having secretarial training, my background fits the job very good.

I want to work part-time during school, it will last until June 9. After which I'll be free the entire summer when I can work full-time.

I am well qualified for the position. I won the Gregg Typting Award in High School. I type 60 words a minute, I take dictation at 83 words a minute, I do that steadily. Which my teacher thinks is pretty good.

I am enclosing a Data Sheet that provides detailed information about me. Ending school at 3 P.M. every day, an interview after that time would be fine. Or call 555–1823.

Cordially,

Kennan Michols

Kennan Michols

Enclosure

EXERCISE 7. Using Sentence and Paragraph Skills in a Job Application Letter

Create a job application letter that you might send. Use plain paper and the business letter form shown in Exercise 8, Chapter 5 (p. 118).

If you are currently job hunting, use a real-life situation. If you are not currently job hunting, respond to an advertisement for a job that might interest you at some point, or create an entirely fictitious situation.

__Note:__ The prospective employer will form an impression of you on the basis of your writing. Make every sentence not only complete and correct, but also an accurate expression of your thoughts. Each paragraph needs detail so that the main points are developed with solid support.

This general pattern, paragraph by paragraph, is a guide to organizing your letter. You may vary the arrangement of material, but cover these points in some orderly way. More details are included in a résumé, but in the letter, be specific enough to make a favorable impression.

Paragraph 1

State that you are applying for the job.
Be specific about what that job is.
Mention where you learned about this opening.

Paragraph 2

Describe your qualifications, stressing the most desirable qualifications:
 —your recent education, including school and on-the-job training, or
 —your work experience, including volunteer work, military service, and regular paid employment.
Be specific. Promote yourself honestly and fully.

Paragraph 3

Continue selling your qualifications.
 —If you stressed education in paragraph 2, cover work experience in paragraph 3, or vice versa.
 —If you have taken part in extracurricular activities in school or in volunteer work in the community, your participation could be included.
Stress evidence of your leadership, initiative, creativity, or on-the-job advancement.

Paragraph 4

Mention that your résumé is enclosed.
Tell the employer exactly how to reach you, including phone number and hours you are available for an interview.
Ask for an interview.

EXERCISE 8. *Analysis of Sentences and Paragraphs in Students' Letters*

In response to Exercise 7, students wrote letters containing the following paragraphs. Pretend that you are the employer. What is your impression of each applicant? Discuss your reactions to each example in class. Revise these letters if your teacher so directs.

Example 1

I am applying for the position of Living Skills Instructor advertised in Sunday's newspaper. I believe I am qualified to fill the position that you offer.

I have had previous experience working with autistic individuals. Last summer, I received an internship to work with thirty autistic children. I worked for the Children's Medical Center and held the position of Assistant

Developmental Therapist. I have also worked, for three years, in the service industry. My duties included the following: overseeing transactions, training new hires, and handling customer complaints.

I am currently enrolled in college and have taken courses in sociology and psychology. My field of study is closely related to the position that you offer. I have enclosed a résumé, and I am looking forward to our interview. I am available after 1 P.M. You can reach me at 555–8951.

Example 2

I heard of a flight instructor's position available. As I understand it, this job is instructing new students at the flight school to help them obtain their licenses. Through this I am able to log the hours I spend in flight with my students. It was through other instructors that I became aware of this opening.

I have attended college and while there, obtained an associates degree in Mass Communication. I maintained a 3.0 average. I was also a member of the student newspaper. In the last eighteen months I have obtained my private pilot, IFR, and multi-engine license.

I am a motivated person. Who is very social oriented. Because of this, I find it very easy to get along with people. I am patient and all of my past jobs I have dealt with people. Because of my past experience, I find it easy to handle situations under pressure. My motivation has helped me advance in past jobs rapidly from part-time employee to assistant manager. I feel with my motivation I can help the flight school stay in the top five for this region and even make it higher!

Enclosed you will find a data sheet . . . .

Example 3

I am offering my services to complete fine grooming and manicuring of the golf course. These tasks would include trimming, weeding, spraying, keeping water in ball washers, and attending general maintenance around the clubhouse.

As a member and golfer of Central City Golf Club, I have noticed that manicuring is one of the steps toward maintaining a beautiful golf course. I feel that I can accomplish this job over a summer.

I am a freshman at Normandale Community College. During the spring, I will be a member of the college golf team. I try to be and do the best I can. I believe in maximum performance on and off the golf course.

I am enclosing a data sheet . . . .

Example 4

This morning I read your ad, saying you need help unloading trucks at night. I'm interested in a job of that kind and have been looking for a couple of weeks.

I used to work at K-Mart, unloading trucks and putting the orders away. I am also able to do paper work of different sorts, and I work in a quick and organized manner.

I rarely ever call in sick, and I am never late for work. I attend college, so the night time hours will fit my schedule perfectly. I have never quit a job, before a year's time of working there. I have also never been fired from a job or written up for any reason. The reason I would like to work for your company is because you offer the best salary, and it is a large company, so there is room for advancement.

To reach me for an interview or if you want to ask me some questions, just call me at home anytime in the late afternoon or in the evening. My phone number is 555-7682.

Example 5

I am interested in the position of pediatric nursing which I read about in the Sunday paper.

I am currently a nursing student at Normandale Community College. I will be graduated in June 1990. My course work has involved clinical and hospital work as well as specific areas in pediatrics. Being in the top third of my class, I believe I am well qualified for this position.

During my school years, I have held many supervisory positions in the restaurant field. These positions ranged from assistant manager to manager with job duties including scheduling, money managing, and food purchasing. I have also worked as a hospital volunteer working with the elderly and very small children.

I have enclosed my résumé . . . .

12

Writing Graceful Sentences

The understanding of grammar and sentence structure that you have gained in the previous chapters is basic for all your writing. But strong, graceful writing requires more than knowledge of grammar and structure; it also requires the art of putting words together effectively.

Although the word *art* is appropriate here, it does not mean that only the gifted can succeed. Instead it means that graceful writing requires skill so that words are used together to their best advantage. We can all develop this skill through patient, careful practice.

This chapter cannot cover every principle of artistry or style useful in writing, but it will point out common stumbling blocks to avoid and common techniques to use. These points take us beyond mere freedom from error to the strength and grace—the artistic side—of writing.

Creating Concise Sentences

Wordiness is the first stumbling block to graceful sentences. Here is an extreme example:

> In speaking with my friends and acquaintances at home and with my co-workers at the office on my job, I am told over and over that I need more training and education for my job if I am ever going to advance much in the business world. I myself have found that it is rather difficult and hard to get ahead and advance on my job or within the company at all without a college degree. Therefore, I decided to go back to school and take some college classes. My supervisor allows me time off the job so that I can be on campus regularly for three classes. The classes are economics, history, and English.

The paragraph is boring, partly because the content is dull. In addition, however, the reader becomes too bogged down in useless words to care what the writer is saying.

PRACTICE 1

State in a few sentences the central ideas in the paragraph above.

_____

_____

_____

_____

_____

_____

The extra words in the paragraph above are the result of certain bad habits, including needless compounding, redundancy, wordy expressions, and wordy constructions. The following sections will discuss these bad habits.

Needless Compounding. Imagine that two items—X and Y—are joined with a coordinating conjunction. With this structure the reader has two items to consider, and the meaning is enriched or clarified:

> slow and steady
> clean and sharp
> dark and damp

Sometimes, however, writers join two elements that have the same meaning (X and X) or elements that are so similar that their distinction is unimportant. Consider these examples:

> tired and exhausted
> difficult and hard
> go to school and take some classes
> training and education

In such cases one word or the other would be enough.

PRACTICE 2

Draw a line through the extra words in the needless compounds in the following sentences.

1. On that 98-degree day, a dip in the pool was refreshing and invigorating.

2. The water was clear and cool, even though many young people and teen-agers had been swimming there.

3. Water skiing and water sports fill many happy hours during the warm days of spring and summer.

4. Most restaurants offer cool or iced beverages during the hot months of the year.

Redundancy.   The word *redundancy* means needless repetition. Redundancy is very much like needless compounding, except that there is not as predictable a pattern. The repetition is just as boring, and it clutters the writing with unnecessary words. Consider these examples from the passage we examined earlier:

> co-workers at the office on my job (meaning: co-workers)
> allows me time off the job (meaning: allows me time off)

Here are some other typical examples:

> circular in shape (circular)   red in color (red)
> 7 A.M. in the morning (7 A.M.)   most perfect (perfect)

PRACTICE 3

Draw a line through each redundant expression in the following sentences.

1. Draw a line through redundant words, phrases, word groups, and expressions that you find here in this exercise.

2. Textbook writers are every bit as redundant as anyone else, or at least they can be, or perhaps they are worse than other writers.

3. Useful repetition can serve a useful purpose, reinforcing main or significant points.

4. Too much repetition of main points tends to lull students into inattention because excessive repetition is easily tuned out of their minds.

Wordy Expressions.   Many common expressions involve more words than necessary. Using these expressions can become routine, like any other bad habit. Consider such common expressions as these and their concise equivalents:

> as in the case of (as)
> at this point in time (now)
> due to the fact that (because)

Write one-word equivalents of these expressions:

1. in the event of ——————————————————

2. by means of ——————————————————

3. during the time that ——————————————————

4. each and every one ——————————————————

Wordy Constructions. In this category, we have several separate problems, some of which have already been discussed in other chapters. Passive voice, for instance, requires more words than does active voice. Active voice is preferred for many reasons, including the fact that it results in a shorter statement. (See Chapter 6, pp. 131–132, for a review of active and passive voice.)

Revise the following passive-voice statements, expressing the same idea in the active voice:

Example: Information on filing tax returns was received by the taxpayers in December.

In December, taxpayers received information on filing tax returns.

1. The completed form must be mailed by the taxpayer by April 15.

   ——————————————————————————————————

   ——————————————————————————————————

2. Signatures of the preparer and the taxpayer must be included at the bottom of pages 1 and 5.

   ——————————————————————————————————

   ——————————————————————————————————

3. Completed registration forms for next term should be filed with your adviser before January 1.

_____

_____

4. Registration forms signed by your adviser should be received by you no later than January 15.

_____

_____

Another problem is beginning a main clause with *there is, there are, it is,* or *it was,* all of which require more words than subject-first openings. Contrast these examples:

> There are more students enrolling today than yesterday.
> More students are enrolling today than yesterday.

> It is time-consuming for students to wait through the long lines.
> Waiting through the long lines takes a lot of time.
> *or*
> Students spend a lot of time waiting in long lines.

In other words, try to avoid roundabout beginnings and delayed subjects when possible.

Using a complicated grammatical unit as opposed to a simpler one also requires more words. Try to reduce units from clauses to phrases and from phrases to words when possible. Consider, for instance, the last two ideas in the sample paragraph at the beginning of this chapter:

> I can be on campus regularly for three classes. The classes are economics, history, and English.

Revising with an appositive saves words:

> I can be on campus regularly for three classes, economics, history, and English.

So does revising with a prepositional phrase:

> I can be on campus regularly for classes in economics, history, and English.

Write shorter versions of the following sentences.

Example: There are many excellent courses for students to select in college.

College students can select excellent courses.

1. There are many students waiting to enroll for Advanced French.

   _____

   _____

2. The most popular classes in computer science and computer technology are quickest to fill, and they are Problem Solving and Computer Design I and II.

   _____

   _____

   _____

3. After registration time ends and registration is complete, there are sometimes additional openings because students change their minds and withdraw for some reason.

   _____

   _____

   _____

4. The various algebra and precalculus sections in the math curriculum are among the first to fill during each of the registration periods.

   _____

   _____

   _____

Your goal should be direct, straightforward language that is as concise as possible. Every word must add to the meaning. One idea is that we should think of words as costing money; just as we cannot afford to waste money, we as writers cannot afford to waste words.

Improving Word Choice

Poor word choice is the second stumbling block to graceful sentences. Five blemishes we can readily remove from our writing are these:

- Slang
- Clichés
- Euphemisms
- Jargon
- Faulty *is when/is where* constructions

Slang. Generally, slang has no place in college or career writing. The only likely exceptions are direct quotes or special effects. Slang does not usually help us communicate in school or at work because it is faddish; the meanings of slang terms may be clear only to those who keep current with its ever-changing vocabulary.

PRACTICE 7 _____

Write a few current slang expressions here.

_____

_____

_____

Putting quotation marks around slang expressions does not validate their use. Most of us recognize slang easily. When in doubt, avoid questionable words or expressions.

Clichés. These dull, overworked expressions may have been fresh and appealing once, but now they are trite and wearisome to readers. Their careless use suggests that writers are too lazy to think of their own wording.

Many clichés are similes—that is, comparisons using *like* or *as:*

pretty as a picture	strong as an ox
quiet as a mouse	dead as a doornail
run like the wind	sly as a fox

Not all clichés are similes, however. Some of them began as slang expressions or metaphors, but they now share with overworked similes the dreariness of overuse:

last but not least	put the squeeze on
kicking up his heels	to the bitter end
off his rocker	a hollow leg

Proverbs can also become clichés through overuse:

He is a jack of all trades, master of none.
A bird in the hand is worth two in the bush.
It is the pot of gold at the end of the rainbow.

PRACTICE 8

List four clichés not mentioned above.

1. _____

2. _____

3. _____

4. _____

Clichés should be avoided unless they contribute to a deliberate effect, and that is rarely the case. In casual speech, they may be useful as verbal short cuts, yet, even there, they are better avoided.

Euphemisms. The word *euphemism* has a Greek root meaning the use of "good words." Our English word makes sense in light of that derivation; by *euphemism*, we mean the substitution of a good word for a potentially offensive one. Euphemisms are appropriate when they protect the feelings of others, but when they are stilted or obscure meaning, they are inappropriate.

Many common euphemisms pertain to death: the departed, the mortal remains, the slumber room (a special room in a funeral parlor). Euphemisms can be used for anything that might be disagreeable: the golden years (old age); maturing skin (wrinkling or aging skin); substandard housing (slums); furloughed (laid off).

Sometimes euphemisms change our language permanently. For example, the terms *white meat* and *dark meat* grew out of the Victorian dread of the words *breast* and *leg*, even when referring to poultry. Their "good word" substitutions remain with us as part of our everyday language.

Euphemisms are effective when they protect the feelings of others. But at times, euphemisms conceal the truth: political leaders speak of *revenue enhancement*, not *increased taxes*. The truth about revenue enhancement is concealed from taxpayers until they face their tax bills. In government documents, killing was glossed over by the seemingly positive word *pacification* and the more neutral word *elimination* during at least one American war.

Careful readers and writers recognize euphemisms for what they are. Careful writers use them thoughtfully, with taste and judgment.

Jargon. The term *jargon* has two separate definitions. By its first definition, jargon means the specialized vocabulary of a particular vocational or avocational group. Used within the group, this jargon is understood; it may even be essential.

Sometimes this kind of jargon is adopted by persons outside the group (or misused by people in the group) to impress others. Far from being impressive, such usage reveals the writer's or speaker's arrogance and insecurity. Readers are not impressed with obscure words (even if they have many syllables); instead, readers are annoyed by such inappropriate and pompous word choice. If we must use words that are unfamiliar to readers, we should define those words for our readers.

By its second definition, jargon means confused, unintelligible, and contrived language—or gibberish. For various reasons, again including a misguided attempt to impress readers with fancy words, some writers and speakers contrive words, often by adding suffixes or converting verbs into nouns. Here are some modern monstrosities:

> People aren't *incentivized* to conserve energy.
> The clergyman asked his people to *actionize* the word of God.
> We will *signalize* traffic by installing lights.
> We will hear the television reporter give us the news *weather-wise* or *government-wise* or *science-wise*.

PRACTICE 9

Revise any three of the four sentences above, using simple, direct language.

1. _____

2. _____

3. _____

Students do not ordinarily devise their own original jargon. At worst, students occasionally pick up some of these terms. The goal for writers is not to use big, obscure, or "fancy" words, but to use words that convey the exact meaning intended.

Faulty *is when*/*is where* Constructions. The words *when* and *where* refer to time and place, respectively. When we use these words to refer to time or place, we have logical statements:

> The end of October *is when* Daylight Savings Time ends.
> The skating rink *is where* the Halloween party will be held.

But sometimes these expressions are used incorrectly as part of a definition, producing illogical statements:

> Democracy *is when* people elect their leaders.
> Democracy *is where* people elect their leaders.

Democracy is neither a time nor a place, but rather a system of government. Therefore, a logical definition of democracy might begin like this:

> Democracy is a system of government in which . . .

Generally, if we are simply aware of the *is when/is where* pitfall, we can keep from making this error.

In conclusion, the goal in writing is to select the most effective words possible. But how do we find effective words? Most of our vocabulary comes from listening and reading, at times when we are paying little attention to vocabulary. Here are a few suggestions that might help you with effective word choice.

- *Consider your readers.* Use familiar words when possible. Your goal is to communicate with your readers. Use words that readers will know. If you use specialized words that may be unfamiliar to your readers, provide brief, clear definitions.
- *Be sensitive to word connotations,* that is, the emotional overtones that accompany words. *Denotation,* the strictly literal meaning of a word, is only part of a word's power. Compare these words, for example: *home, house, shack, bungalow, mansion, hut, palace, domicile.* As a writer, you must select words with sensitivity to their various meanings and senses to readers.
- *Use words precisely, following their exact meanings.* Rely on your dictionary and thesaurus for help in getting the exact word you want.
- *Listen to the sounds of the words you use.* The words should sound smooth, natural, and rhythmic; they should reflect your natural speech patterns. If your writing sounds stiff and formal when read aloud, or if it sounds like someone else is speaking, try to listen more closely to yourself and allow your writing to reflect your natural voice.

Points to Use

- Work for concise wording, making every word count.
- Look at compound units to be sure that both (or all) parts are necessary.
- Eliminate redundancy by watching for common redundant expressions and by checking modifiers to see whether they add meaning.

- Reduce wordy expressions to brief equivalent expressions.
- Whenever possible, use subject-first sentence patterns rather than *there is* or *there are* openings.
- Select the most effective words possible, being particularly careful about slang, clichés, euphemisms, jargon, and *is when/is where* constructions.
- Avoid slang and clichés in college and career writing, except for special effects.
- Use euphemisms to protect the feelings of others when appropriate, but not to obscure the truth from others.
- Use jargon in the sense of specialized vocabulary, but only when you are communicating with people who understand that vocabulary. When you are unsure of the readers' comprehension, define unfamiliar terms or simplify the vocabulary.
- Avoid the *is when/is where* construction unless you are referring to a time or place.
- Refine your choice of words by using the resources freely available; read and listen for new words and new ways to use familiar words.
- Develop sensitivity to connotations and denotations of words.
- Refer to your dictionary and thesaurus for alternative terms.
- Read your writing aloud, listening to its sound. Listen for the natural patterns of your own speech.

Points to Remember

- The best language is direct and precise. Writers must work to eliminate needless repetition and wordiness.
- In college and career writing, slang, clichés, euphemisms, jargon, and *is when/is where* constructions are generally inappropriate.
- Clichés are dull, worn-out expressions. Euphemisms are expressions used as substitutes for terms that might be offensive, but sometimes they can be stilted and misleading.
- Jargon has two meanings: (a) the specialized vocabulary of a particular group; (b) contrived, unintelligible language. The former usage is appropriate when it has meaning to the persons involved. The latter should always be avoided.
- The phrases *is when* and *is where* can be used in reference to time or place, but they should not be used carelessly as the beginning of a definition.
- Effective words can be found in resources near at hand: in our reading, in listening to ourselves and others, and in consulting the dictionary and thesaurus.
- Denotation is the literal definition of a word, the dictionary definition. Connotation is the emotional meaning attached to a word. Writers must be aware of both.

EXERCISE 1. Identifying Poor Word Choice and Lack of Parallelism

Match the following sentences to one of the choices below. Sometimes more than one answer can be used for each statement. Check your answers with those at the back of the book.

a. wordiness	e. jargon
b. slang	f. faulty *is when* or *is where* construction
c. cliché	g. lack of parallelism
d. euphemism	h. correct parallelism

_____ 1. "Food prices are a real rip-off!" cry the angry consumers.

_____ 2. Farmers who have been on their land for decades and having seen many changes are sympathetic to them.

_____ 3. "We ourselves have been, are, and always will be consumers too because we are part of the consuming public," the farmer leaders say.

_____ 4. They add, "Let's tell it like it is about farming."

_____ 5. "Inflation and having to pay tremendous taxes are crippling farmers," they point out.

_____ 6. Very few people realize the physical dangers, the financial hazards, and the psychological strains of farming.

_____ 7. Many people trivialize the conundrum posed by contemporary agribusiness posturing, wishing to finalize solutions to complex societywide issues.

_____ 8. A typical example tells the story and proves the point about the dangers of modern farming.

_____ 9. Harvest time is when more accidents happen than any other single time of the entire year.

_____ 10. On a clear-as-a-bell October day, a young farmer and his brother, both of them up at the crack of dawn, started combining soybeans.

_____ 11. Combining is where the beans are picked from the plant and put into the combine.

_____ 12. At noon, the men were sweaty, hungry, and they were impatient to finish that particular field.

_____ 13. "Empty this load of beans; take the truck to the end of the field, and wait for me there," said the older brother to the younger brother.

_____ 14. The younger man, who had for years followed his brother's directions without question or hesitation, did so now, just as he was told.

_____ 15. Later, while waiting for his brother, the young man thought to himself, "He's slower than molasses in January today. Where can he be all this time?"

_____ 16. Panic is when an early snowstorm comes before the crops are harvested.

_____ 17. It never occurred to the young man that his brother might have been hurt or injured in some way even though during the harvest season, many farmers experience accidents with the farm machinery.

_____ 18. Nothing could have prepared the young man for seeing a combine upside down near an embankment and watching a neighbor trying to free his brother.

_____ 19. The farmer had gone to his eternal reward.

_____ 20. In his haste to finish the field, he turned a corner too sharply, causing the machine to overturn and to crush him instantaneously.

EXERCISE 2.   Revising Sentences and Forming Paragraphs

On a separate piece of paper, revise the twenty sentences in Exercise 1 to improve their wording. Organize the sentences into paragraphs. You may add or delete details as you wish. You may change the wording, the order of ideas, or the focus of the story.

EXERCISE 3.   Revising Sentences for Conciseness

In the following sentences, change the italicized words to the kind of word group indicated in parentheses. Write your new, revised sentences in the space provided. Check your answers with those at the back of the book.

1. The writing assignments _that we were given on Monday_ are due Friday. (participial phrase)

_____

_____

2. Students must finish their assignments *when they are due.* (prepositional phrase)

_____

_____

3. Lisa should take more time to proofread her job application letter. *She wants to be an underwriter for an insurance agency.* (adjective clause)

_____

_____

_____

4. *Monica wanted to be a claims adjuster for that insurance company.* She wrote her letter and included her résumé. (adverb clause)

_____

_____

_____

5. Secretaries *who work for that company* must learn a standard letter format. (prepositional phrase)

_____

_____

6. That company uses one letter format. *It is the semiblock format.* (one word)

_____

_____

7. The room *that is the largest room* in the White House is called the East Room. (one word)

_____

_____

8. The East Room has been used for receptions, weddings, concerts, and funerals. *Many times press conferences have been held there as well.* (two words)

_____

_____

_____

9. The White House contains many art objects, antiques, paintings, and valuable pieces of china and silver. *Many of these valuable pieces of china and silver have been donated by individuals or organizations.* (participial phrase)

_____

_____

_____

_____

10. The funerals of three presidents were held in the East Room of the White House. *They were Presidents Harrison, Lincoln, and Harding.* (appositive phrase)

_____

_____

_____

EXERCISE 4. *Reducing Wordy Expressions*

Write short replacements for the following wordy expressions. Check your answers with those at the back of the book.

1. actual truth   _____

2. ask the question   _____

3. at this point in time _____

4. honest truth   _____

5. enclosed you will find _____

6. open up _____

7. refer back to _____

8. surrounded on all sides _____

9. very unique _____

10. personal opinion _____

11. first and foremost _____

12. absolutely necessary _____

13. in the event that _____

14. during the time that _____

15. for the purpose of _____

16. fair and just _____

17. due to the fact that _____

18. reason is because _____

19. in accordance with _____

20. by means of _____

Write the familiar equivalents for the following terms.

1. remuneration _____

2. multitudinous _____

3. bestow upon _____

4. facilitate _____

5. optimum _____

6. terminate _____

7. utilize _____

8. implement _____

9. wherewithal _____

10. cognizant _____

Write equivalents for the following clichés.

1. busy as a bee _____

2. method in his madness _____

3. sadder but wiser _____

4. nip it in the bud _____

5. last but not least _____

6. move at a snail's pace _____

7. better late than never _____

8. slow but sure _____

9. Keep up the good work. _____

10. Have a nice day. _____

EXERCISE 5. *Revising Sentences for Conciseness and Precision*

Revise the following sentences to eliminate faulty wording.

1. The students, most of them anyway, know that turning in their assignments later than the deadlines will result in penalties of some kind.

   _____

   _____

2. The optimal plan is feasible engineering-wise, but the practicalities of the
   endeavor and the expertise of the designers are questionable.

   _____

   _____

   _____

3. Looking out over the sea of faces, the architect made his presentation so that each and every one of the members of the audience present that day could see precisely and exactly what he meant.

_____

_____

_____

_____

4. Knowing that his plans might not be accepted, the architect spoke as persuasively as he could, feeling that the polite reaction of the audience might be the calm before the storm.

_____

_____

_____

_____

5. One listener who had lived to a ripe old age looked at the young speaker, green with envy over the opportunities as opposed to the trials and tribulations of his own life.

_____

_____

_____

_____

6. The speech ended. The audience applauded, and the speaker smiled. But the audience might not have been convinced. The speaker was left in doubt.

_____

_____

_____

EXERCISE 6. Translating Jargon, Passive Voice Constructions, and Wordiness into Clear Prose

Read the following excerpt from a state bulletin on weed control; then answer the questions about what you have read.

Preplant herbicides are applied before the crop is planted and may be soil-incorporated. Early preplant herbicides are applied if planting in no-tillage crop culture.

Preplant herbicide treatments are most effective when applied just ahead of crop planting and incorporated immediately. Optimum herbicide efficacy is achieved when treatments are incorporated twice. . . .

Cultivation to control weeds missed by herbicides is an effective and popular weed control as evidenced by the fact that about 97 percent of the corn and soybeans in Iowa are cultivated at least once. . . . Reduced tillage may not allow the use of a rotary hoe or conventional cultivator depending upon the amount of crop residue. Special cultivators are needed for till-planted crops and normally available cultivation equipment may not be acceptable if no-till production has been used in a sod.

Postemergence herbicides are applied after the crop and weeds have emerged. To be effective, most postemergence herbicides should be applied when weeds are small and actively growing. . . . Foliar-applied herbicides or postemergence treatments are often used as a standard component of a full-spectrum weed control program or to control weed escapes from soil-applied treatments. . . .

1. How many sentences are in active voice? _____
   If you find any, put an × in the margin beside it.

2. List two examples of jargon:

   _____

   _____

3. State in your own words the central ideas of these paragraphs.

   _____

   _____

   _____

   _____

4. If you find question 3 difficult, skip it, but answer these questions instead:
   a. What specific features of the paragraphs above make the reading so hard?

   _____

   _____

   _____

   b. What advice would you give the writer of those paragraphs so that the writer would communicate better with readers?

   _____

   _____

   _____

EXERCISE 7.   *Analyzing and Revising a Business Letter*

You are the office manager at Travel Right travel agency. Today you are helping a new employee learn his job. He has just written a letter to his first customer, and he has brought the letter to you for approval. It is printed on page 304. Though you are pleased with his enthusiasm, you are unhappy about his letter. Take the steps listed below.

1. Mark passages that should be changed. Consider the following points, among others:
   Where can you eliminate wordiness?
   Which sentences can be improved?
   Is any necessary information missing?
   Is the order logical?
2. Bring your marked copy and comments to class for discussion. (You are a college student as well as office manager of the travel agency.)
3. After class discussion, compose a good letter to this customer. Make your letter a model for all employees, not just the newcomer. Though your letter will be somewhat shorter, you want it to be friendly, well organized, and informative.

   Use the style shown in the example, and make a letterhead. Using the draft below as a starting point, you may add, subtract, or rearrange details as you think appropriate. Your goals are simple: you are to provide necessary information about the trip and to reinforce the customer's faith in your travel agency.
4. Write a brief memo to your employee, suggesting ways to improve future correspondence with customers. Naturally you want to compliment him for the good features of his letter, but you also want to see him improve. (If he does not improve, just think how much time you will have to spend cleaning up his writing.)

TRAVEL RIGHT

938 North Jefferson Avenue
Centerville, Arkansas XXXXX

March 4, 1989

Ms. Shannon Mathews, President
Business and Professional Women's Club
112 West Fairview Avenue
Centerville, Arkansas XXXXX

Dear Ms. Mathews:

I am so pleased and happy to know that you and your group are now or soon will be planning a trip this spring to the Cherry Blossom Festival in Washington, D.C. It's pretty as a picture there, I know, I was there last spring. I am sure that you will enjoy each and every minute of the tour, and I know you will be thrilled and delighted with all the details we can arrange for you and your friends.

We can arrange a charter bus, just as you requested, leaving Centerville at 7 A.M. on Friday, March 25. There will be seats on the bus for about 35 people, surely that will be enough space for your group. If not, another bus goes that direction, but it takes longer because it goes via Jacksonville, Florida, so maybe we shouldn't use it after all. The bus is air-conditioned and rides well, you will be pleased.

We can arrange for all of you to stay in one hotel in Washington. Let me know what price range you have in mind, then I'll see what I can find. You said you wanted three nights there, that should be no problem.

Just to confirm things. You wanted to be there Saturday, Sunday, and Monday, March 26, 27, 28. You wanted to come back Tuesday. Arriving late that evening, the trip won't interfere with your returning to your jobs Wednesday. Or Thursday at the lastest.

You can phone me to firm up these plans. I'm in the office by 8 every morning, staying until about 4:30 in the afternoon. Call 555–9245 and ask for me. Remember: You'll travel right with TRAVEL RIGHT!

Yours for happier travels,

Stanley J. Runell

Stanley J. Runell

UNIT IV PRACTICE TEST
Chapters 10, 11, 12

Part 1 (50 POINTS)

Read each question carefully. Identify each statement as one of the four choices. Mark your answer on the line to the left of each question. Check your answers with those at the back of the book.

      a. correct sentence   c. comma splice
      b. fragment   d. fused sentence

_____ 1. Agates, one of many varieties of quartz used today.

_____ 2. Topaz, the birthstone for November, is related to quartz.

_____ 3. Hold topaz up to the light to see the clarity of that amber-colored stone.

_____ 4. Quartz, a hard crystalline substance, is found worldwide, its pure crystals include varieties of opal, flint, agate, and rock crystal.

_____ 5. Topaz contrasts beautifully with emerald, a brilliant green stone, the emerald, like the topaz, is a birthstone.

_____ 6. The emerald is the birthstone for May, the amethyst is the birthstone for February.

_____ 7. Supernatural powers attributed to inanimate objects, including gem stones related to birth dates.

_____ 8. Long before scientists analyzed stones chemically, powers were ascribed to them some stones were supposed to be able to ward off evil others were supposed to have healing powers.

_____ 9. Emerald and topaz stones were supposedly effective in healing eyesight, as were some other gems as well.

_____ 10. Ruby, the birthstone for July, is well-known garnet, the birthstone for January, is less well known.

_____ 11. That handsome dog is a malamute, a breed developed as a sled dog, sometimes it is called an Alaskan malamute.

_____ 12. The word *finicky* reminds Sara of her cat and his taste in food, since babyhood that cat has refused to eat any dry food.

_____ 13. Demanding canned food and turning up his nose at all but the most expensive brands.

_____ 14. "You are just an alley cat," Sara exclaimed one day, while the cat looked condescendingly at the food dish, "How fussy would a pure-bred cat be?"

_____ 15. John James Audubon, a French-born American naturalist best known for his paintings of birds.

_____ 16. Birds are distinguished from reptiles, their nearest relatives, by certain features, without exception, all the 10,000 or more species are clothed in feathers.

_____ 17. Birds are also distinguished by keen vision and by their reproduction by means of hard-shelled eggs, also they are warm-blooded animals.

_____ 18. Many people think that a cold, wet nose is a mark of a healthy dog, but some dogs with hot noses are healthy while some dogs with cold noses have high fevers.

_____ 19. Puppies usually are born with their eyelids tightly shut, just as kittens are, this protects the babies' eyes during their early days.

_____ 20. Relying more on the sense of smell and hearing than on their eyesight.

_____ 21. Because they are carnivorous and don't like vegetables.

_____ 22. Easily frightened by loud noises, many dogs will run from firecrackers, thunder, blowouts, and other noises.

_____ 23. Although it is commonly believed that lightning will never strike twice in the same place.

_____ 24. Scientists have proved that lightning can strike repeatedly in the same place.

_____ 25. Another common belief is that bats are blind, but they have very keen eyesight that serves them well.

_____ 26. Some people believe that elephants are afraid of mice perhaps they recall an old story that tells of a mouse trying to frighten an elephant by running up its trunk.

_____ 27. Authorities say that elephants are unafraid of all animals except for man, a mouse running up the trunk of an elephant would be blown into the next county.

_____ 28. The old belief that a rattlesnake shakes its rattles before striking to warn its victim is wrong the snake is tensing itself for a strike and cares nothing about its victim.

_____ 29. It is believed that the age of a rattlesnake can be told by the number of rattles on its tail, but this idea is also incorrect.

_____ 30. The various rings or rattles, appearing with no particular regularity, several being added in a season.

Read each question carefully. Select the correct word or words, given the choices in parentheses. Mark a for the first choice, b for the second choice, and c for the third choice. (Most of these questions have only two parenthetical choices.)

_____ 31. Melissa feels (happier, happiest) of the three sisters.

_____ 32. She earned (more money, the most money) of the three.

_____ 33. Mona looked (sad, sadly) as she studied her net pay.

_____ 34. Donna looked (intent, intently) at her paycheck stub, examining the many deductions.

_____ 35. Kristina typed (well, good), though she was nervous.

_____ 36. (Smooth, smoothly) typing requires rhythmic motions.

_____ 37. The employer seemed (happy, happily) about Joe's work.

_____ 38. Joe smiled (happy, happily) about his raise.

_____ 39. Paula finished (fast, faster, fastest) than Jennie.

_____ 40. Tamara felt (well, good) about her day's work.

For the following sentences, circle a *or* b *to indicate the correct sentence in each pair.*

41. a. Spattered with grease, that coat must go to the dry cleaners.

    b. Spattered with grease, the dry cleaners must work on that coat.

42. a. The cleaners can take the grease stains from Bill's coat using a powerful spot remover.

    b. Using a powerful spot remover, the cleaners can take the grease stains from Bill's coat.

43. a. Jack uses a dry cleaner who has a store near his house called ABC Dry Cleaning.

    b. Jack uses a dry cleaner called ABC Dry Cleaning that has a store near his house.

44. a. Taking his jacket to the cleaner and picking it up later will take only a few minutes.

    b. Taking his jacket to the cleaner and then to pick it up later will take only a few minutes.

45. a. Unless completely removed, the spot of grease will still show on Don's trousers.

    b. Unless completely removed, Don's trousers will still show the spot of grease.

46. a. The dessert looked delicious, but we were too full to want any. Which sometimes happens.

    b. As sometimes happens, we were too full to want any dessert even though it looked delicious.

47. a. That apple pie was more tastier than most, some are rather dry.

    b. That apple pie was tastier than most; some are rather dry.

48. a. Kim felt bad about eating quickly and leaving immediately.

    b. Kim felt badly about eating quickly and the fact that she had to leave immediately.

49. a. After eating dinner, the apple pie was all gone.

    b. After eating dinner, we saw that the apple pie was all gone.

50. a. Eating dessert early in the evening is better than to snack off and on throughout the evening.

    b. Eating dessert early in the evening is better than snacking off and on throughout the evening.

Part 2 (50 POINTS)

Rewrite any ten of the following sentences to eliminate faulty wording or phrasing. You may omit some details and invent others, but preserve the original meaning as much as possible.

1. In choosing to attend college, these considerations were the most important.

    _____

    _____

2. The disadvantages of being the oldest child are more responsibility and always having to set a good example.

    _____

    _____

    _____

3. There are also disadvantages for a younger child, they have to do some of the chores when older children have left home.

    _____

    _____

    _____

4. Attending the university, classes were very large.

    _____

    _____

5. While your parents focus their attention on the oldest because he or she is their firstborn or on the baby because he or she is their last.

    _____

    _____

    _____

6. The pay is good, starting at $5.35 per hour and can go as high as $6.85 per hour.

_____

_____

7. Backing that truck, which moves at a snail's pace, up to a dock that was made for horse-and-buggy times, not for a 21,000 pound gross weight vehicle.

_____

_____

_____

8. Being an airline pilot takes responsibility, courage, and the ability to keep your cool under stress.

_____

_____

_____

9. Upon passing this test, the bus must be driven on a state driving range.

_____

_____

10. Instead of waking up around noon and then to take a few classes after noon, at this point in time too hard for me.

_____

_____

_____

11. I'm working a construction job, roofing houses, my day begins before sunrise, after working all morning, I manage to squeeze in a math class.

_____

_____

_____

12. When you are in the mood of being sad, a good friend will take time to come and cheer you up and making you laugh by telling you a joke or a funny story.

_____

_____

_____

HANDLING PUNCTUATION, CAPITALIZATION, AND SPELLING

OBJECTIVES

Grammar and Sentence Structure

To edit with effective punctuation

To review capitalization

To handle abbreviations and numbers

To avoid common spelling problems

Writing

To write letters, memos, and reports directly related to employment or college work

To practice editing skills on papers written earlier in the term

13

Signaling Pauses

Using Commas

The comma is one of the most commonly used marks of punctuation. It is probably also the most *misused* mark.

The purpose of commas and other punctuation marks is easy to understand. Speakers punctuate their words by using vocal inflections, pauses, altered pacing, gestures, and facial expressions. Writers need marks to indicate the pauses, breaks, and points of emphasis that speakers show through nonverbal devices. Punctuation helps readers move through writing smoothly, in step with the pace and emphasis that writers intend. We have seen many uses of the comma in previous chapters. In this chapter, we will review those uses and add others.

First, we use commas with coordinate conjunctions to join independent clauses. These seven conjunctions, preceded by a comma, can be used between independent clauses:

for   and   nor   but   or   yet   so

If the comma is used alone, without the coordinate conjunction, we have the comma splice, a serious error. When two or more independent clauses are related in thought, it is appropriate to connect them with a comma plus a coordinate conjunction. In fact, the proper conjunction will highlight that relationship. The word *and* connects and emphasizes similarities; the word *but* separates and emphasizes differences. Contrast these sample sentences:

The highway was winding, *and* the curves were sharp.
The trucker knew the road, *but* the bus driver did not.

Second, we use commas to set off introductory parts of sentences. Introductory elements range from single words to phrases and dependent clauses. In any case, they point toward the main clause. The comma after the introduction calls attention to the subject and to the idea that follows in the main clause. (Examples are shown in Chapter 11, p. 266.)

PRACTICE 1 _____

Create two original sentences using introductory elements set off by commas.

1. _____

_____

2. _____

_____

We can also use commas to set off nouns of direct address. Nouns of direct address are names or titles of persons spoken to or persons addressed in writing. The noun of direct address is set off by commas regardless of where it appears in a sentence:

> *Mr. Adams,* did you mail my letter this morning?
> As you know, *Mr. Adams,* the letter must be mailed.
> In fact, the letter must be sent today, *Mr. Adams.*
> *Professor,* can you explain this rule more clearly?

PRACTICE 2 _____

Create a sentence with a noun of direct address set off by a comma.

_____

_____

_____

In addition, commas are used to set off nonessential modifiers in sentences. Among the nonessential modifiers, we often find modifiers referring to the subject. If those or any modifiers are **nonessential** (also called **nonrestrictive**), they are set apart with commas. *Nonessential* means that although these modifiers add information, the basic sentence pattern is complete without them. These modifiers are not essential in pointing out or limiting; they are *nonrestrictive* because they do not restrict the meaning. (For further discussion, see Chapter 9, pp. 200–202.) Here are some examples of nonessential modifiers:

> That tossed salad, *which I put together just now,* contains fresh lettuce from the garden.

The iced tea, *made by pouring hot water over tea leaves,* tastes good on this hot day.

Notice that the same sentences would make sense without the italicized modifiers:

That tossed salad contains fresh lettuce from the garden.
The iced tea tastes good on this hot day.

By contrast, when modifiers are essential, they limit or restrict meaning, or they identify nouns or pronouns. If the modifiers are essential, no commas are used. Here are some examples of essential modifiers:

The salad *that I put together just now* differs from the salad *that we had for lunch.*
The iced tea *made by pouring hot water over the tea leaves* tastes better than the iced tea *made from instant tea.*

When the modifiers are removed from the last two sentences, the sentences make no sense:

The salad differs from the salad.
The iced tea tastes better than the iced tea.

We can also use commas to set off sentence interrupters, including appositives, parenthetical expressions, and transitional words. Sentence interrupters are words, phrases, or clauses that interrupt between essential parts of the sentence, such as between the subject and verb or between the verb and object. Common interrupters are appositives and other transitional words, phrases, and abbreviations like the following:

however	consequently	moreover
on the other hand	namely	in fact
on the contrary	therefore	in short
in conclusion	i.e. (*id est,* meaning	
e.g. (*exempli gratia,*	"that is")	
meaning "for example")	for example	

Note: When these interrupters are used in the middle of a sentence, be sure to use commas on both sides of them.

Parenthetical expressions involve extra information. They could be set aside, just like the extra material inside parentheses. Sometimes parenthetical expressions look like separate subjects and verbs, particularly with such expressions as *I think, he says, we assume.* But we treat these expressions just like other interrupters, setting them aside with commas:

A fresh cup of hot tea is refreshing, *I think,* especially after a busy morning.
Spiced tea, *for instance,* is a treat after hours of typing.
Instant tea, *on the other hand,* is quicker to prepare.

Put commas around the parenthetical expressions and nonessential modifiers in the following sentences.

1. I think that herbal tea is weak, but on the other hand it is flavorful and pleasant.

2. Herbal tea which is recommended by some authorities is supposed to be better for us than other beverages.

3. Beverages containing caffeine for example are regarded as less wholesome, but coffee suits my tastes perfectly.

4. Diet soft drinks which are popular with Americans of all ages are available with and without caffeine.

Appositives are generally set off with commas, as in this example:

> The teapot, *a blue-and-gold porcelain heirloom*, was a gift from my grandmother.

However, if the appositive is very short and closely related to the word that precedes it, no comma is needed. How short is "very short" and how related is "closely related"? There is no precise answer, although "very short" suggests a word or two. You will develop a sense of what is right by watching for appositives and noticing how they are handled. Here are some examples:

> The poem "*Trees*" is a well-known work by the poet *Joyce Kilmer.*
> My Uncle *Ted* prefers tea, but my Aunt *Martha* likes coffee better.
>> (Note that the names are appositives in a way, but the entire unit, such as "Uncle Ted," can also be considered a title plus a name.)

Before you decide whether short appositives need commas, consider whether the appositives are restrictive or nonrestrictive. Appositives can restrict meaning, as in the first example above, where the names of the poet and the poem restrict the meaning of the sentence to that poet and that poem. Appositives, like other units, are not set off by commas when they are restrictive.

Before you interrupt a sentence with commas, make sure you have a good reason to do so. The presence of a sentence interrupter is one such reason. Notice that the interrupter is set off entirely, with a comma on each side. Typically, we do not separate the essential parts of sentences: subject from verb or verb from object or complement.

Look at these examples of what not to do, and on the lines, indicate which essential sentence parts are interrupted.

Example: That recipe makes, three loaves of bread. *verb/direct object*

1. Three loaves, last only two days. _____

2. The bread in the oven, bakes in twenty minutes. _____

3. The pans are full, and ready for the oven. _____

As the examples in Practice 4 show, incorrectly placed commas disturb the normal flow of words and ideas.

Another point to remember is to use commas between items in a series. A series consists of three or more items listed consecutively. These items should appear in grammatically the same form, provided the writer has followed the principle of parallelism. The items will all be words or phrases or clauses, not a mixture.

The last two items in a series are usually joined by *and*. Whether to put a comma before that *and* is often a matter of opinion and personal preference. One argument for using the comma is that it guarantees a separation between the last two items, ruling out the possibility that a reader might take the last two items to be a unit.

Right: For breakfast, Sue had toast, juice, coffee, ham and eggs.

Right: For breakfast, Sue had toast, juice, coffee, ham, and eggs.

> (Do we consider "ham and eggs" one unit, or do we consider the two separate items? Using a comma definitely separates them.)

The last comma in the series clearly separates the last two items. In the case of Sue's breakfast, either interpretation is acceptable.

Sometimes the presence or absence of a comma alters the meaning. For instance, consider this listing on a menu:

cod or scrod with potato salad and toast

A restaurant customer who was fond of potato salad might be disappointed if this is what the menu meant:

cod or scrod with potato, salad, and toast
        or
cod or scrod with potato, salad and toast

Therefore, it is important to use punctuation to make the meaning clear.

PRACTICE 5 _____

How you punctuate the following sentence may depend on where you live. Put in the appropriate commas.

Each month we pay these utility bills: gas telephone electricity water and sewer.

_____

Your answer to Practice 5 will vary depending on how your city bills for utilities. In some municipalities, one bill covers water and sewer; in others, separate bills are sent for these two items. Your punctuated sentence can end one of two ways, depending on whether you receive five bills or four:

Right: . . . gas, telephone, electricity, water, and sewer.
Right: . . . gas, telephone, electricity, water and sewer.

Occasionally, for special effect, a writer will put conjunctions between all items in the series. Then no commas are used to separate the items. This special effect deliberately slows the reader down and calls attention to each item. For instance, in "The War Prayer," Mark Twain deliberately sets apart each item in this series:

. . . daily the young volunteers marched down the wide avenue . . . , the proud fathers and mothers and sisters and sweethearts cheering them with voices choked with happy emotion as they swung by . . . .

The author calls our attention to fathers and to mothers and to sisters and to sweethearts by separating them with *and*'s rather than with commas in a list like this: fathers, mothers, sisters, and sweethearts. Unless we are working for some special effect, however, items in a series are set off with commas.

In addition, we use commas to set off coordinate adjectives. If adjectives are coordinate, they are equal in value. To see whether adjectives are in fact coordinate, reverse their order. If the new word order works as well as the original word order, the adjectives can be separated by commas.

This stove has a strong, reliable, and efficient oven.
This stove has a reliable, strong, and efficient oven.

If the reversed order does not work, the adjectives should not be separated by commas, as in this example:

The five large loaves of bread are cooling on the counter.
The large five loaves of bread are cooling on the counter.

Another test is this: put *and* between the adjectives. If the meaning is not disturbed, the adjectives are coordinate and can be separated by commas.

This stove has a strong, reliable, and efficient oven.
This stove has a strong and reliable and efficient oven.
(Either statement makes sense.)

The five large loaves of bread are cooling on the counter.
The five and large loaves of bread are cooling on the counter.
(The second sentence makes no sense.)

PRACTICE 6

Put in commas as needed in the following sentences.

1. Nutrition experts urge us to eat breakfast lunch and dinner every day.

2. Skipping meals they believe leads to overeating or eating unbalanced diets, yet many Americans particularly those who are dieting skip meals.

3. Those rich sweet breakfast rolls which are covered with thick white frosting provide too many calories and too little nutrition.

4. The salad bar may be a poor choice for a dieter because it offers many calories in the salad dressings potato salad macaroni salad fresh rolls and blueberry muffins.

We also use commas to set off short quotations unless they are part of the core sentence. Direct quotations are the exact words of a speaker or writer, words we can borrow and repeat, provided we show that we are borrowing. For quotes of fewer than five lines or fifty words, use quotation marks, unless the quoted words are the subject or subject complement in your sentence.

In the following examples, notice that commas do not interrupt the subject–linking verb–subject complement pattern:

"Are you ready to go?" he asked, "or should I go alone?"
"Are you ready?" was his main question.
(The quoted words in the second sentence are the subject of that sentence; no comma should separate the subject from the verb *was*.)

Joan replied, "I will be ready soon."
Her answer was "I will be ready soon."
(The quoted words in the second sentence are the subject complement; no comma should separate the subject complement from the verb *was*.)

Put in commas as needed in these sentences.

1. "When will you be ready for lunch?" was his first question.

2. "In a few minutes" she answered "after I finish this letter."

3. "We must remember to lock the back door before we go" he said thinking aloud.

4. The nearest restaurant posted a sign that said simply "Lunch served 11–2."

Use a comma to set off contrasting words or phrases or short questions added after a statement. Contrasting words or phrases are usually negatives reflecting upon the original statements and are italicized in these sentences:

> You can miss a quiz once, *but never again.*
> The teacher accepted Jane's paper, *but not Harry's.*
> You understand the rules about late papers, *don't you?*
> Mitchell has missed a lot of classes, *hasn't he?*

In addition, use commas to separate other units, such as separate parts of dates and addresses:

> The letter arrived on June 19, 1989, in Seattle, Washington, at the company's headquarters.

You can also separate the title or degree from a person's name:

> Carla Jackson, M.D., opened her new office on the first of last month.

Or separate the salutation of a friendly letter from the body of the letter, or the complimentary closing of a letter from the signature:

> Dear George,
> Yours truly,

Using Semicolons and Dashes

First, we use a semicolon between related independent clauses that are not joined by a comma plus a conjunction. This use of the semicolon was discussed in previous chapters, for joining the two or more separate clauses of a compound sentence and for avoiding comma splices. The semicolon provides a pause between ideas yet pulls them together as related in thought. By contrast, using separate sentences separates ideas.

In these sentences, notice that the two independent thoughts are related in that the second either supplements or contrasts with the first:

> Yeast, an essential ingredient in bread, cannot be rushed; a living organism, yeast grows at its own pace.
> White bread is easier to make than rye or wheat bread; whole wheat bread is the hardest to make.

The semicolons join separate main clauses. When transitional words follow semicolons, they ease the readers' way into the new idea, but they do not join words in the sense that coordinating conjunctions do. The transitional words are set off with commas, as in these examples:

> Yeast can sometimes act slowly; on the other hand, it can grow amazingly fast on hot days.
> White bread is easy to make; however, whole wheat bread is more nutritious.

PRACTICE 8

Add semicolons and commas as needed in these sentences.

1. Diabetics must limit their fat sugar and starch intake however they can enjoy a nutritious and tasty diet.

2. Unless they have other health problems diabetics need not restrict their use of salt and other seasonings consequently their food can be flavorful.

3. Diabetes is dangerous because of its possible long-term damage to the circulatory system kidneys and eyes however by controlling their disease, many diabetics limit or avoid such damage.

4. Diabetes is one of the risk factors for heart disease other factors are overweight sedentary lifestyle hypertension and family history of heart disease.

In addition, we use semicolons to signal pauses in sentences that contain many commas. Sometimes a semicolon is useful as a dividing mark with less power than a period but more power than a comma; in other words, we sometimes need a "super comma." This use is rather rare, but upon occasion, the semicolon helps clarify divisions for the reader. Here are two examples:

> Yeast, an essential ingredient in bread, cannot be pushed, prodded, or rushed; but, if conditions are right, it will grow quickly enough.
> You can order reliable road maps through the ABC Publishing Co., 197 E. Main, Morristown, Tennessee; EFG Pub-

lishing Co., 783 W. Sixth Street, Ute, Idaho; and XYZ
Publishing Co., 9241 First Avenue, Jonset, Missouri.

PRACTICE 9

*Create an original example of using a semicolon in a sentence containing
many commas.*

_____

_____

_____

Use a dash or a pair of dashes to set off dramatic sentence interrupters, including a sentence within a sentence. The dash is a straight
horizontal line about twice the length of a hyphen mark. In printed
matter, the dash looks like this—. Typists use two hyphen marks consecutively to create a dash, like this--. No additional spaces are left
before or after the dash.

Because dashes look a lot like hyphens, it can be easy to confuse
the two marks. Keep in mind that dashes are used less often than
hyphens, and they are used for completely different purposes. A dash
is a dramatic mark. It is also considered casual and, in the opinion of
some authorities, generally inappropriate in formal writing. It should
be used sparingly, but if it is used properly, it adds emphasis.

The dash signals abrupt changes in mood or thought, as shown by
these sentences:

> There I stood by the cash register—panicky at the sign of the
> gunman.
> I took a deep breath—and he shot. But he missed me!
> The bread will soon be—oh, I forgot to turn on the oven!
> Pass the butter and jelly—don't reach across the table—so I
> can spread them on the bread.
> > (Note that the main sentence is interrupted by a second full
> > sentence in this example.)

PRACTICE 10

Create an original example of a sentence with a dash.

_____

_____

_____

_____

In casual conversation, speakers sometimes break off one thought and insert another. When you write dialogue, you may need dashes to reflect this feature of conversation.

We also can use a dash or dashes to set off units that contain several commas. Appositives that contain several commas can be set apart clearly by a single dash or a pair of dashes, as in these examples:

> The necessary ingredients—water, yeast, sugar, and flour— are all here for baking bread.
>
> Water, yeast, sugar, and flour—these are the ingredients needed for bread.

A dash sometimes sets off a concluding unit, one that provides examples or a list that supplements the previous statement. The dash signals a pause between the statement and the list that follows:

> The ingredients we need are all here—water, yeast, sugar, and flour.
>
> Certain other ingredients can be added if they are desired— salt, shortening, wheat flour, rye flour, and raisins.

In formal English, the two examples above would use a colon rather than a dash. In general, the colon is formal; the dash is informal. As writers, we must judge which marks are appropriate in given situations.

PRACTICE 11

Create two examples using the dash to set off units that contain commas.

1. _____

_____

2. _____

_____

Points to Use

- Use punctuation marks purposefully, not haphazardly.
- Let the punctuation follow the structure of sentences, setting nonessential elements apart and highlighting core sentences.
- Set off introductory elements and sentence interrupters, thereby signaling to the reader that these "extras" can be moved out of the way of the main ideas.
- Select conjunctions and transitional words to tie parts of com-

pound sentences together smoothly and logically, but use compound sentences only when the independent clauses are related in thought.

- Use commas to set off words and units that interrupt the basic sentence: nouns of direct address, appositives (unless they are very short), parenthetical expressions, nonessential modifiers.
- Use commas to set off individual items in a series, making clear by the commas that individual items are separate.
- Use semicolons within compound sentences when the independent thoughts are related.
- Let semicolons serve as "super commas" to provide breaks in sentences that have many commas.
- Use dashes to show abrupt and dramatic changes in thought or to set aside units that contain main internal commas, such as appositives that contain a series.
- Be sparing with dashes, knowing that they are informal, but use them when they are needed for special effects.

Points to Remember

- Commas are used in the following ways:

  To join two or more independent clauses with coordinating conjunctions: *for, and, nor, but, or, yet, so*
  To separate introductory elements and main clauses
  To set off nouns of direct address
  To set off nonessential elements
  To set off sentence interrupters, such as appositives, parenthetical expressions, and transitional words and phrases
  To separate items in a series
  To separate coordinate adjectives
  To set off direct quotations from the rest of the sentence, unless the quotes are subjects or subject complements
  To set off contrasting phrases or concluding questions from the rest of the sentence
  To separate parts of dates or addresses
  To separate names from titles and degrees that follow them
  To set off salutation of friendly letters and complimentary closings of business and friendly letters

- Semicolons are used in these ways:

  To join two independent clauses
  To set apart units in sentences that contain many commas

- Dashes are used in these ways:

  To signal dramatic changes in mood or thought
  To separate units that have many commas

EXERCISE 1. Using Commas

Put in commas as needed in the following sentences. On the lines to the left of the sentences, write the number of commas you added. (You should use from zero to six per sentence.) Check your answers with those at the back of the book.

_____ 1. One clear starry evening Mary my younger sister and I were walking in our neighborhood when we came upon a frightening scene.

_____ 2. When the old house on the corner of First Street and Alden Avenue was torn down last spring a big hole remained where the basement had been and a tree having been struck by lightning fell into the hole.

_____ 3. Set against the night sky the tree roots torn branches and twisted trunk made a grotesque form.

_____ 4. The owner of the property lives at 8397 North Street Detroit Michigan having left our city after the scare with the lightning.

_____ 5. He owns houses and office buildings and parking lots in this city and he manages all of them.

_____ 6. Once you have lived in the country you will be reluctant to go back to the noisy congested city.

_____ 7. When you are in the city you can see many things of interest such as skyscrapers museums airports ethnic restaurants and shopping malls.

_____ 8. Randy's trip to the city began December 28 1989 and ended January 9 1990 when he returned home.

_____ 9. When he saw his friend Chris he said "You should have been with us because we had a great time."

_____ 10. "Time was too short" he added "for all we had to see and do while we were in the city."

_____ 11. To write a book one needs time experience training and determination.

_____ 12. A book that sells well can make an author famous.

_____ 13. That new novel which is already a best seller has made its author a lot of money hasn't it?

_____ 14. The main difference between high school and college is that in college a student has more free time and more responsibility for efficient use of his or her time.

_____ 15. Dan you do agree with that statement don't you?

_____ 16. The important thing is wise use of one's time not the abundance of time a college schedule allows.

_____ 17. Looking forward to the next vacation Jim smiled happily.

_____ 18. Looking forward to the next vacation is a popular mental pastime when class is boring difficult or overly repetitive.

_____ 19. The third Monday in February will be Presidents' Day a welcome holiday for college students staff and faculty.

_____ 20. Faculty members on the other hand might welcome three four five or more holidays per term.

EXERCISE 2. Creating Sentences with Commas, Semicolons, and Dashes

In the space provided, write and punctuate statements that fit the following sentence patterns. Examples are provided with each exercise.

1. A sentence that uses a series of three subject complements:

   Example: He is tall, dark, and handsome.

   _____

   _____

2. A sentence that begins with a series set off with a dash:

   Example: Bouncing the ball, laughing, and screaming—the children made lots of noise.

   _____

   _____

3. A compound sentence joined with a comma plus a conjunction:

   Example: The wind blew hard all night, and it scattered leaves all over our yard.

   _____

   _____

4. A compound sentence joined with a semicolon followed by a transitional phrase:

    Example: The wind blew hard all night; consequently, we found leaves scattered all over the yard this morning.

_____

_____

5. A sentence in which a pair of dashes encloses the sentence "I could hardly believe my eyes":

    Example: Our oak tree was almost bare—I could hardly believe my eyes—though yesterday it was beautiful, with its yellow and orange leaves.

_____

_____

6. A sentence in which a pair of dashes encloses an interrupting element:

    Example: The wind was so strong—didn't you hear it during the night?—that the trash cans blew down the street.

_____

_____

7. A sentence in which a nonessential modifier is set off by commas:

    Example: The remaining oak tree, which miraculously escaped oak wilt, shades the back of the house.

_____

_____

8. A sentence that begins with an introductory element set off with a comma:

    Example: When oak wilt invaded our yard, we lost three beautiful oak trees.

_____

_____

EXERCISE 3. Revising a Report

On a separate piece of paper, write a revised version of the police report below. Punctuation, sentence structure, handling of tense and modifiers—all these elements need revision.

Divide the material into short paragraphs, grouping ideas logically. You may change the order of the details, but do not change the content.

At 3 A.M. on January 30, 1989 I was called to a domestic situation. At 386 Fourth Ave No. Maintown. A Mr. Jake Galoot, age fifty-two 392 Fourth Ave No Maintown had heard screams, in the house next to his, and called police. When I arrived at the scene I saw a man sitting on the front steps, he was crying. Had blood on his shirt. He said his name was Thomas Minks, he was thirty-nine. He said, "I didnt mean to hit her that hard." I handcuffed him to the porch railing. Then ran inside. I followed a pool of blood from the living room into the kitchen. There was blood on the stove refrigerator and cabinets. I saw a woman lying in the snow behind Galoots house. Calling for an ambulance, she was taken to North Side Hospital. To close the wound on her head it took fifteen stitches, she was Rosabelle Minks, age thirty-five. Thomas Minks was taken to the police station and charged with assault and battery. After he was read his rights he gave details of what happened. His wife returned home from her job at Leisure Lanes Bowling Emporium, she said she had an accident with the car. Struck a telephone pole with the front end of the car. After hearing of the accident Minks becomes angry. He picks up a marble chess board from the table and strikes his wife over the head. Later I talked to Rosabelle Minks. At the hospital. She confirmed the confession her husband had given. She said, "He weighs 240 lbs., I weigh 135 lbs, I'm tired of being beaten by him."

EXERCISE 4. Writing to Express an Opinion at Work

If you are currently employed, write a short letter or memo to express your opinion on a matter of concern to you on the job.* (See p. 96 for the memo format to use.) You might write to your employer about situations like those mentioned below or about some other issue.

Write a memo to the appropriate officer in your company, suggesting that the money spent on the annual company Christmas party be spent more sensibly some other way. You must specify how you would like to see the money spent; then support your ideas with reasons. You may refer to what you have seen of past parties as evidence to support your position.

Write a memo to the head of your department, asking for a change regarding scheduling work assignments, work hours, leave time, or vacations;

---

*If you are not presently employed, recall your past work experience, or contemplate what lies ahead. As another alternative, write to your representative on the city council, in the state legislature, or in Congress; to the editor of a local newspaper; or to some other community leader who might be able to help you.

training, supervising, or evaluating employees; offering on-site child care; changing the fringe benefits package; smoking in the work place; or some other issue. Be specific about the weaknesses of the current policy (as you see them) and your recommendations for change, well supported by reasons.

EXERCISE 5.   Writing to Address a Problem

Select one of the situations below and write a business letter. (See p. 118 for the business-letter format to use.) The letter will be more effective if you are courteous and reasonable, even though you are upset.

Situation 1

You are disappointed with the service you had at a bank, restaurant, hotel, or other business. At the time, you were as gracious as you could be, but now, after reflecting about the matter, you feel you should express your dissatisfaction. Describe what happened, and suggest any compensation you feel is appropriate.

Situation 2

You are disappointed with a product that you recently bought. Either it did not work at all, or it worked poorly. Include specific details about your purchase and your expectations; then specifically cite the reasons for your disappointment. Request a refund, replacement, or repair, as the circumstances warrant.

EXERCISE 6.   Organizing the Presentation of Specific Details

Your employer, an attorney, has asked you to write a summary of steps completed in the settling of a client's estate. The information is provided below.

Write your summary in two versions: (1) a standard paragraph and (2) an introductory sentence or two, followed by a listing of steps, set apart visually for quick reading. (See p. 103 for an example of such a list.)

In class, discuss the advantages of each version. In both versions, be careful to present the information in an organized manner and make your sentences parallel when parallelism is appropriate.

The items you need to include are listed below chronologically. Some of these items need to be combined because they belong together; some items are actually subdivisions of larger steps.

- Inventory of the safety deposit box
- Verification of the most recent will
- Reading of the will
- Application for the death certificate
- Court appointment of the executor named in the will (with waiver of bond because executor is next of kin)

- Issuance of letters of appointment to the executor
- Application for an identification number for reporting income of the estate to the Internal Revenue Service
- Notification to Social Security with request for death benefits for the surviving spouse
- Filing the marriage certificate to verify the claiming rights of the person identified as the surviving spouse
- Inventory of assets in the estate, drafted for approval and signature of executor and filed with the court
- Computation of the inheritance taxes due, preparation of the tax return, and payment of the inheritance taxes
- Receipt of clearance from the taxing agencies, acknowledging that inheritance taxes have been paid in full
- Preparation of fiduciary income tax returns, one for the state and another for the Internal Revenue Service
- Approval of the tax returns by the executor and payment of income taxes due
- Disbursement of assets to the heirs, change of titles to real estate, updating of abstracts for real estate
- Preparation of a final report
- Approval of the final report

14

Clarifying Meaning

Using Parentheses, Brackets, and Apostrophes

Besides the marks discussed in Chapter 13—commas, semicolons, and dashes—we have many other useful punctuation marks available to us in our writing. These other marks are not used as often as commas, nor do they have the impact of semicolons or dashes, but in their place, they are important and necessary for clarifying meaning.

PARENTHESES

Parentheses enclose nonessential details, such as page numbers, cross-references, dates, and incidental remarks, including full sentences. Remarks enclosed in parentheses are quiet, like asides in plays or whispers to the readers. Notice in the following sample sentences that the material in parentheses can be removed without affecting the core sentences:

> The first edition (1911) was a best seller, but the revised edition (1915) was a disappointment to the author (who had made a fortune by then anyway).
> The revised edition used one excellent illustration (Figure A, page 27) in place of two mediocre illustrations in the first edition (Figure A, page 25, and Figure B, page 29).

When a full sentence is enclosed in parentheses within another sentence, the enclosed sentence has neither the standard capital letter at the beginning nor the usual ending punctuation:

> The first book established the author's reputation (this development was a stroke of luck for her) before she tried to sell her more important works.

By contrast, when a full sentence is enclosed in parentheses outside other sentences, it has the regular capitalization and ending punctuation:

> The first edition established the author's reputation. (This development was a stroke of luck for her.) Later she was able to publish her more important works.

Commas that are needed in the sentence are placed outside the parentheses. Consider the following sentence:

> The first edition, published in 1989 by Scott, Foresman/ Little, Brown (Boston), was so well received that revisions began almost at once (1990), and that edition also sold well.

PRACTICE 1

Add parentheses as needed in these sentences.

1. The format for a business letter is shown earlier in this book Chapter 5, p. 118.

2. Memo form is also shown earlier Chapter 4, p. 96.

3. The original version of this book was written years ago 1978, gradually modified in subsequent years 1979–1985, and extensively revised in recent years 1986–1988.

4. During those years, the author was busy with other writing that writing was unrelated to grammar books and with other endeavors.

BRACKETS

Brackets also enclose extra detail, but only in specific, special circumstances. Brackets are not found on many typewriters, but they are found on word processors. If you need brackets and don't have them, draw them in with a pen.

You will seldom need brackets. They have only two purposes, both of which are most likely to occur in writing research papers:

- To enclose your own words within a direct quote.
- To enclose a secondary unit inside parentheses (within a complicated footnote [as can happen] or within another item enclosed, as in this example).

Although both uses are infrequent, of the two, the first is more common. You may need to insert your own words while you are in the midst of quoting someone else. When you are quoting someone, you must quote exactly, mistakes and all.

When you find a mistake in a source, quote it exactly as it appears, but insert the Latin term *sic* in brackets immediately after the mistake. *Sic* means "thus," or "as it was." By using [*sic*], you are telling the reader that you did the right thing: you quoted exactly but recognized that the quote had a mistake in it. Here is an example:

> *American History* reports, "Columbus discovered the New World in 1493 [*sic*], but he did not realize where he was."

When you quote the words of others, you should select the most significant ideas and leave out the rest. Omitting part of a passage economizes on words and emphasizes the parts quoted. But sometimes, when you omit a part of a passage, you lose the antecedents for pronouns or other information that the reader needs. That information should be inserted in brackets.

For example, suppose you came upon this paragraph while looking for evidence that book publishing grew rapidly in the United States during the mid-1800s:

> After music became part of the school curriculum in Boston, the demand for Mason's music books grew dramatically. At about the same time, book publishing was becoming a big business in America. This was virtually an overnight development. During the decade of the 1840s, the total books published more than doubled: from $2,850,000 in 1840 to $5,900,000 worth in 1850. Because of the advances in public education, the number of literate people nearly doubled during that same decade.

Let's say that you want to quote not the entire paragraph but just the part that supports the growth of book publishing. To make sense of selected portions, you may need to insert comments in brackets. To show that words were omitted, you would use the ellipsis, a mark consisting of three consecutive periods.

> At about the same time [1838], book publishing was becoming a big business in America. . . . During the decade of the 1840s, the total books published more than doubled: from $2,850,000 in 1840 to $5,900,000 worth in 1850. Because of the advances in public education, the number of literate people nearly doubled during that same decade.

Note that if the ellipsis comes at the end of a sentence, a fourth period is needed as the ending mark.

APOSTROPHES

Apostrophes show possession when nouns or indefinite pronouns do the possessing. Indefinite pronouns include such words as *someone, anyone, one, everybody, somebody*. (See p. 149 for other examples.)

Possessive pronouns (used as adjectives) do not take apostrophes; these words include *his, her, hers, their, theirs, whose,* and *its.* Note the following correct and incorrect uses of apostrophes:

Right: Tim's baseball cap	*Wrong:* hi's baseball cap
Right: Atlanta fans' baseball team	*Wrong:* thei'r baseball team
Right: the city's ballpark	*Wrong:* it's ballpark

PRACTICE 2

For the following phrases, write in the correct possessive pronouns that correspond to the possessive nouns on the left.

Tim's baseball cap _____ baseball cap

Atlanta fans' baseball team _____ baseball team

the city's ballpark _____ ballpark

the umpire's whistle _____ whistle

the whistle's shrill sound _____ shrill sound

The possessive pronouns *its* and *whose* are easily confused with the contractions pronounced the same way:

it is = it's   who's = who is

Do not use *it's* or *who's* unless you mean *it is* or *who is.* In the following examples, notice the difference between the contractions and the possessive words:

The squirrel seems unconcerned that *it's* raining on *its* nest. *Who's* going to *whose* party this weekend?

PRACTICE 3

Underline the correct words in the following sentences.

1. The game may be postponed because (its, it's) likely to rain.

2. (Whose, Who's) going to the game Friday night?

3. (Its, It's) likely to depend on (whose, who's) going to work the late shift that night.

4. The plant has (its, it's) own security system to monitor (whose, who's) going in and out.

Unlike possessive pronouns, nouns and indefinite pronouns must be changed to show possession. To make nouns and indefinite pronouns show possession, we use apostrophes and s endings. But first we must decide whether the apostrophe goes before or after the final s. Deciding requires a step-by-step process.

The first step is to make sure that possession or ownership is involved. If not, no apostrophe is necessary. Although possession or ownership can be obvious, at times we must test an expression to see whether ownership is present.

An easy way to test an expression is to turn it around, using *of* or *belonging to.* A possessive expression can be converted as shown in these examples:

> Jenny's coat = the coat belonging to Jenny
> the cars' engines = the engines of the cars
> a penny's worth = the worth of a penny
> three hours' delay = the delay of three hours
> Mr. Smith's vacation = the vacation belonging to Mr. Smith
>   (or the vacation of Mr. Smith)

If an expression can be turned into an *of* or *belonging to* construction without distorting the meaning, you have evidence that possession is involved. Notice that time and money amounts can be possessives; these expressions can easily be overlooked as possessives.

PRACTICE 4

Revise the following expressions into of *or* belonging to *constructions, as shown in the above examples.*

1. the day's end = _____

2. Grandpa's cane = _____

3. Pam's new watch = _____

4. ten dollars' worth = _____

The second step in determining where to put the apostrophe is to find out whether the owner is singular or plural. What is owned does not matter; only the owner matters. The word designating the owner is the word that is altered with a possessive ending, either *s'* or *'s.*

Now that you have established the presence of possession and ascertained whether the owner is singular or plural, the endings can be added according to the following rules.

For a singular noun or an indefinite pronoun, add an apostrophe plus an *s* unless the word already ends with *s:*

the girl's hat	anyone's picture
the man's gloves	the car's windshield
Mrs. Anderson's car	everybody's assignment

For a plural noun with an *s* or *es* ending, add an apostrophe after the ending that is already present:

the girls' hats	the boys' club
the classes' assignments	the cars' warranties
the Andersons' car	the houses' insulation

PRACTICE 5

Change the following expressions into singular or plural possessive forms.

Example: The preface of the book = *the book's preface*

1. the edges of the pages = _____

2. the colors of the rainbow = _____

3. the legs of the chairs = _____

4. the broken arm of the chair = _____

5. the oval frame of the picture = _____

6. a car belonging to Sandy = _____

For singular nouns ending in *s,* add an apostrophe or an apostrophe and *s:*

Lois' coat   or   Lois's coat
James' hat   or   James's hat

For plural nouns that do not end in *s* or *es,* add an apostrophe and *s* (just as you would treat singular nouns):

men's coats	women's hats
children's games	the people's choice

For joint ownership or ownership when a compound word is involved, add an apostrophe and *s* at the end:

Joe and Paul's mother
Ford and Chevrolet's new styles
my sister-in-law's car

Change the following expressions into possessives.

1. the votes of the people = _____

2. the keys belonging to Phyllis = _____

3. the nest belonging to the mice = _____

4. the leadership of Moses = _____

5. the shop belonging to Jack and Sam = _____

6. the three ties belonging to Francis = _____

There is one final small point about possessives: gerunds take possessive pronouns or possessive nouns. Notice the possessives used with the gerunds in these examples:

He was worried about *my* driving the car with the oil low.
We were all worried about *Don's* driving in the rainstorm.
He asked about *my* speaking with the teacher.
We wondered about the *teachers'* speaking with our parents.

Apostrophes are also used to form plurals of numbers and symbols. Here, too, the *s* is present, but there is no possession or ownership. The plural form uses an apostrophe with the *s* to avoid confusion:

Dot your *i*'s and cross your *t*'s.
There are two *9*'s in my street address.
In the 1980s, many companies merged and added &'s in
  their official company names.
> (Note: Decades can be written several ways: 1980's, 1980s,
> '80's, or '80s.)

PRACTICE 7

Add apostrophes or possessive forms where they are needed.

1. The word *Mississippi* has four *i*s and four *s*s.

2. Your phone number contains three *9*s.

3. The price tags use the printed $s with the amounts.

4. Bill water-skiing was good, but Paula handling of the boat was amazing.

Using Hyphens, Italics, and Other Marks

HYPHENS

The hyphen is a divider between parts of a word or between closely related words. The hyphen is best known as the short horizontal mark used to divide a word between lines. In such instances, we divide the word between syllables, insert the hyphen, and finish the word on the next line. When in doubt about correct word division, we check the dictionary.

The hyphen is also used to prevent misreadings of words in the following contexts.

- Between a prefix and a proper noun:

    post-Revolutionary War
    pre-Christian era
    ex-President Carter

- Between a prefix and a base word when the lack of a hyphen would make the word difficult to read:

    anti-inflation
    pre-existent

- Between a prefix and a base word to distinguish meanings:

    re-cover versus recover
    re-create versus recreate

We also use hyphens to separate parts of compound units:

- Compound numbers:

    twenty-one through ninety-nine

- Compound nouns:

    father-in-law
    jack-in-the-box

- Compound adjectives, which are units consisting of two or more words, but forming one concept about a noun:

    the tenth-floor window   the two-year-old boy
    the long-overdue book   a fifth-century pope
    a self-defeating attitude   a well-intentioned remark
    an I-don't-care-what-you-
        think attitude

(Note: Compound adjectives must precede a noun and must not include an *ly* word.)

Adjectives should be hyphenated when the two or more words form one unit. We can test the words by separating them and using each one as an adjective to the noun. For instance, consider the distinctions here:

> a small brown dog
>> (These words describe a dog in two ways: a *small* dog and a *brown* dog.)

> a light-brown dog
>> (These words describe a dog only one way; we are not describing a *light* dog that is *brown*, but only a light-brown dog.)

If you are not sure whether to hyphenate a compound adjective or number, it is better to leave out the hyphens. The handling of hyphens with numbers and the hyphenating of compound adjectives are erratic in modern usage.

PRACTICE 8

First, insert hyphens as needed in these sentences.

1. The check was written for forty seven dollars.

2. My first semester bill included a preenrollment charge of twenty one dollars.

3. An ammonia vinegar solution works well for washing windows.

4. A solution of ammonia and vinegar works well for washing windows.

Then, complete these statements:

5. To divide the word *birthright* between lines, I would write it like this:

_____.

6. A hyphenated noun that is familiar to me is _____.

COLONS

The colon divides statements, words, and numbers. It is used in several conventional ways, many of them probably familiar to you. Here is a list of the colon's uses:

- To separate a book's title from its subtitle, as in *Practical English: Using Grammar to Improve Writing*
- To separate the hour from the minutes, as in 6:15
- To separate chapter from verse in biblical references, as in Psalm 90:1

- To set off the salutation of a business letter, as in Dear Professor Wilson:
- To introduce a list, after the formal introduction that includes the words *as follows* or *the following*, as in these statements:

> The supplies you need are as follows: a pen, a tablet of lined paper, a dictionary, and a copy of the vocabulary list.
>
> We packed the following gear for our camping trip: a small stove, sleeping bags, a medium-sized tent, and food.

As the examples above show, the colon must follow a grammatically complete statement. Think of this mark like a stop sign. It brings readers to a complete stop and makes them look at what follows. Placing a colon between essential parts of a sentence is like putting a stop sign in the middle of a freeway; neither sign would make sense, but instead, would cause confusion and disrupt the flow of traffic or ideas.

You should note two additional points about this mark. First, use the colon between independent clauses when the second clause explains the first or introduces a formal quotation, as in these examples:

> A wise camper has good maps: he needs up-to-date maps with sufficient detail.
>
> Ronald is an unrealistic camper: he thinks that he could survive indefinitely if he could find enough food in the wilderness.
>
> The speaker stepped to the microphone and spoke distinctly: "Ladies and Gentlemen, today I am announcing my candidacy for the office of governor."
>
> The textbook was clear on the choice of pronouns: "Use objective-case pronouns as objects of verbs and objects of prepositions."

Second, do not let the colon interrupt essential elements of the core sentence—that is, between subject and verb, between verb and object, between verb and complement, or between preposition and object:

> *Wrong:* The news told of several tragedies, such as: floods, drownings, and traffic fatalities.
>
> *Right:* The news told of several tragedies, such as floods, drownings, and traffic fatalities.

PRACTICE 9

Correct the punctuation in these sentences.

1. The ingredients are: flour, sugar, salt, and yeast.

2. The experienced carpenter knew he had to carry the right tools and supplies, saws, hammers, drills, screwdrivers, files, nails, and other essential hardware.

3. In his toolbox, Andrew had screwdrivers of several sizes and kinds, such as: a square-bar standard, a Phillips, and a spiral ratchet.

4. A well-equipped kitchen has tools, too, such as: measuring cups and spoons, ladles, spatulas, cooking utensils, dishes, and silverware.

QUOTATION MARKS

Quotation marks set off titles of short published works: any pieces that form a part of a book, magazine, or newspaper. These short works might be poems, short stories, articles, essays, chapters, songs in song books, columns in newspapers, and any other individual portions of volumes. (See pp. 188–190 for some examples.)

Quotation marks also set off the exact words borrowed from a speaker or writer, if the borrowing is limited to a short passage. Short quotations are visually set apart from our own words by quotation marks at the start and the end of the quote.

Long quotations (five lines or fifty words or more) are visually set apart as single-spaced, indented blocks. When typeset, the print is often smaller. For long quotes, quotation marks are not needed because the spacing and placement show that the material is quoted. (See p. 335 for an example of a long quote.)

Short quotations are set off from the rest of the sentence with commas unless they are subjects or subject complements, as shown on page 321. Ending punctuation marks are combined with quotation marks according to these rules:

- Commas and periods go inside ending quotation marks:

  John greeted his friend, "Good morning, Jeff."
  Jeff said, "Hi, John," before he began work.

- Semicolons and colons go outside ending quotation marks:

  Pam said, "My watch must have stopped"; she had to take it to the jeweler for repair.
  The jeweler remarked, "This watch hasn't been cleaned for years": he recommends annual cleaning for all watches.

- Question marks and exclamation points go either inside or outside ending quotation marks, depending on which part of the statement forms the question or the exclamation:

  "What is the correct time?" Jean asked.
  Did Jean hear Jeff reply, "7:35"?
  Evidently she misunderstood, for she asked, "Isn't it later than 7 o'clock?"
  Soon Jeff became anxious. "Now it's nearly 7:45. We will be late for the party!"

How surprised Jean was to hear those words, "It's nearly 7:45"! She had lost track of the time.

Single quotation marks have only one use: they set off quotations within quotations. These marks look like apostrophes; typists use the apostrophe sign for single quotation marks. The ending punctuation rules listed above apply to single quotation marks just as they do to regular quotation marks. Notice how single quotation marks are used in these examples:

Lisa commented, "The best article in today's *Washington Post* is 'Jogging for Fun and Health.'"
Steve added, "Another good article on jogging is 'Pacing Yourself as a Jogger' in last Sunday's *New York Times*."
Lisa replied, "That's what I've heard. Yesterday Jack said to me, 'Read the *Times* article, and you will learn a lot.'"

ITALICS

It is increasingly common to use italics or underlining as a mark of punctuation. Generally, italicizing requires sophisticated office equipment or typesetting; underlining is substituted when italicizing is not possible, as in ordinary typing or handwriting.

Italicize or underline the full titles of books, magazines, and newspapers. Any volume of printed material, long or short, without respect to its contents, should be underlined, with these few exceptions:

the Scriptures of any religion: the Koran, the Bible
catalogues (such as mail-order catalogues)
directories (such as telephone directories)

Leaving aside those exceptions, underline complete titles, including the subtitles of volumes.

In these examples, contrast the use of italics and quotation marks:

The book *Moll Flanders* by Daniel DeFoe (1722) is considered by authorities to be one of the first English novels.
The anthology *Music for the Home* contains "Yankee Doodle" and other traditional pieces.

PRACTICE 10 _____

Add quotation marks or underlining in these sentences as appropriate.

1. The Chicago Tribune reprinted a story from Esquire magazine entitled Walking on Michigan Avenue.

2. The Baltimore Sun published an editorial with the heading Aid to Education: A High Cost.

3. Tracy's textbook, *American History*, contains an important chapter called The Pre—Civil War Era.

Italicize certain specific titles:

- Names of specific trains, ships, airplanes, and spacecraft:

    El Capitan; The Titanic; The Spirit of St. Louis; Voyager II

- Names of movies:

    Rocky IV; ET; Fatal Attraction

- Names of major works of art:

    da Vinci's *Mona Lisa*, a painting
    Michelangelo's *Pietà*, a statue
    Monet's *The Thames*, a painting

- Names of lengthy musical compositions:

    Handel's *Messiah*, an oratorio
    Mozart's *Don Giovanni*, an opera
    Tchaikovsky's *Nutcracker*, a ballet

Use italics to set off words or symbols under special circumstances:

- Foreign words and phrases:

    pièce de resistance
    femme fatale

- Words used as words and symbols used as symbols, including numbers and letters of the alphabet:

    The word *cat* is easy to spell; it begins with *c*.
    A careless writer makes his *7* look like a backward *F*.
    Use the *&* sign sparingly unless it is part of an official name.

Points to Use

- Use a wide range of punctuation marks to make your prose flexible and your meaning clear.
- Separate the essential sentence elements from the nonessential; punctuate to bring out the core pattern of the sentence: subject, verb, and completing elements.
- Pay attention to punctuation in reading material, watching especially for uses of marks that are new to you. Study punctuation in its context to develop a sense of how writers and editors handle these marks.

- Experiment with marks that are unfamiliar to you, and ask your teachers for guidance if you are unsure about usage.
- Try more than one version of a sentence, using different wording and punctuation. Make your writing capture and project your own natural pace and tone.

Points to Remember

- Parentheses enclose details such as dates, examples, cross-references, and incidental remarks, including sentences within sentences.
- Brackets enclose your own words inserted into a direct quotation or enclose a unit when it is inside parentheses.
- An ellipsis indicates that something has been omitted from a quotation.
- Apostrophes show possession when a noun or an indefinite pronoun does the possessing; form contractions; and form plurals of numerals, letters, and other symbols.
- Hyphens divide a word between syllables to carry part of a word to the following line; prevent misreading of words; and form compound numbers, compound nouns, and compound adjectives.
- Colons separate items for clarity, including titles from subtitles, minutes from hours in time designations, and verse from chapter in biblical references; appear after the salutation of a business letter; and introduce a formal list or a second independent clause that explains the first.
- Quotation marks set off titles of short printed works, works that are part of published volumes; enclose the exact words of another person, if the quote is short (fewer than five lines or fifty words); and set off a word used in a special sense (though italics can also be used for this purpose).
- Single quotation marks enclose a quote within a quote.
- Italics (underlining) set off titles of books, magazines, newspapers, and other volumes of printed material; set off names of certain things: specific trains, ships, airplanes, and spacecraft; movies; major works of art and music; and set off words borrowed from other languages and words used as words or symbols used as symbols.

EXERCISE 1. *Forming Possessives*

Using apostrophes, turn the following expressions into possessives. Check your answers with those at the back of the book.

1. The office of the president _____

2. The frustration of the moment _____

3. The leaves of the trees _____

4. The leaves of the tree _____

5. The porch of the Harrises _____

6. The suit of Mr. Thomas _____

7. The business of no one _____

8. The blades of their skates _____

9. The mothers of the babies _____

10. A vacation of a month _____

11. The end of its fiscal year _____

12. The consent of her parents _____

13. The scarf belonging to Doris _____

14. The house of the Willises _____

15. The son of the Millers _____

16. The tie belonging to Mr. Ross _____

17. The jackets of the men _____

18. The secretary of his boss _____

19. The secretaries of my bosses _____

20. The pencils of the children _____

21. The purchasing power of five dollars _____

22. The antlers of the reindeer _____

23. The suit belonging to Professor Thomas _____

24. A right belonging to everyone _____

EXERCISE 2. *Completing Statements for Review*

Complete the following statements.

1. Titles of certain printed works should be italicized, namely, titles of _____

   _____.

2. Titles of certain printed works should be enclosed in quotation marks,

   namely, titles of _____

   _____.

3. If writers cannot italicize, they should _____.

4. Single quotation marks have only one use. They are used to _____

   _____.

5. Parentheses enclose various details within a sentence, including _____

   _____.

6. Brackets would enclose the Latin word *sic* in this situation: _____

   _____.

7. In most cases, singular possessives are formed by _____

   _____.

8. In most cases, plural possessives are formed by _____

   _____.

9. To test a structure to see whether a possessive relationship is present, a

   writer should _____

   _____.

10. Two uses of the hyphen mark, besides dividing words between syllables at the ends of lines, are these:

a. _____

b. _____

11. To enclose a sentence within a sentence, use either _____ or

_____ .

EXERCISE 3.   Reviewing Punctuation

For the following sentences, mark T or F (for True or False) in the space at the left. Check your answers with those at the back of the book.

_____   1. Titles of movies are enclosed in quotation marks.

_____   2. Generally it is wrong to separate subject from verb with a comma.

_____   3. Most appositives are set off with commas.

_____   4. Parentheses and brackets are interchangeable.

_____   5. An ellipsis consists of three consecutive periods; it shows that words have been left out.

_____   6. Commas, periods, semicolons, and colons are always put inside ending quotation marks.

_____   7. The single quotation mark is used to set off titles of short printed works, such as poems and short stories.

_____   8. The most common use of the semicolon is to separate independent clauses within a compound sentence.

_____   9. When the semicolon is used, it must be used with a transitional word or phrase or a conjunction.

_____   10. Whenever items are joined with *and*, the writer must put in a comma just before *and*.

_____   11. Italicizing and underlining are often used interchangeably.

_____ 12. Quotation marks are used around direct quotes regardless of their length or their use.

_____ 13. A dash is relatively informal; a colon is formal.

_____ 14. After the salutation of a business letter, the writer may use either a comma or a colon.

_____ 15. Between the title and subtitle of a book, a writer should use a semicolon.

_____ 16. A series consists of three or more items.

_____ 17. Names of specific trains, ships, planes, and spacecraft are set in italics.

_____ 18. Quotation marks around slang expressions validate the use of those expressions in college writing.

_____ 19. A colon can be used to introduce a list or a second independent clause that explains the first.

_____ 20. A compound adjective can appear before or after a noun.

_____ 21. Compound numbers include two-word numbers through ninety-nine.

_____ 22. Hyphens can be used to separate prefixes from base words when their presence clarifies meaning or prevents confusion for the reader.

_____ 23. The question mark and the exclamation point are placed inside or outside ending quotation marks, depending on which part of the statement forms the question or the exclamation.

_____ 24. The title of a student's paper for English class is italicized.

_____ 25. Punctuation should make the readers' task easier by clarifying meaning and distinguishing between nonessential and essential elements.

EXERCISE 4. _Punctuating Sentences_

Punctuate these sentences, using any of the marks discussed in Chapters 13 and 14. You may adjust the tense as seems appropriate, but otherwise do not change the wording of the sentences.

1. Joan the blizzard swept across the Kansas/Oklahoma prairies and it closed down schools factories and shopping malls.

2. Everyones schedule is upset it just stands to reason by the storm, the severe cold alone is difficult to endure but the heavy wet snow and ice are even harder to handle.

3. My son building a model airplane on the family room floor made a big mess, he spread out the intricate parts and left the pungent smelling lacquer uncovered making a terrible stench in the room.

4. I asked Whose job is it to clean up after you Doug when you make such a mess.

5. The airplanes wings were attached easily but he had problems with the tight fitting propellor parts.

6. He was following directions in the Chicago Tribune in the February 10, 1988 issue in an article entitled Building Better Models.

7. Skiing, ice skating sledding these are some of the favored activities for the Wilsons children, they are your friends I believe.

8. The Swensons boys are building a snowfort, taking some concentration skill and attention to detail over several hours time.

9. Doug told his brother about the writers ideas in the newspaper article, "By their telling me how to put the parts together the job went faster" but his brother was not so sure, "That's a matter of opinion, just see how long it took you to make progress several hours I think before you got this far."

10. When this snow melts serious flooding could be the result, that is what happened in your area last year wasn't it.

11. Animals in the fields caught by the sudden raging winds and abrupt drop in temperature often freeze to death when they hear blizzard warnings ranchers work as fast as possible to get their animals to shelter.

EXERCISE 5.   Describing Your College Writing Experiences

Now that you have been a college student for several months, you have gained an understanding about the importance of good writing in college. Using essay, letter, or memo form (your choice), write to a high school student you know. Describe your own experience. Be specific about what you have learned.

Consider what you anticipated before entering college and what you now understand about writing in college. Offer advice, if you feel that is appropriate, but at least alert your reader to the writing requirements that lie ahead.

EXERCISE 6. Using Writing to Solve a Problem

Describe a problem in your community, at work, or at school, and recommend a remedy (or remedies) for that problem. Use business letter or essay format. The paper must be typed or word-processed. The minimum length is two pages.

You must specify your audience (the person or persons to whom this writing is addressed). If you are writing a letter, the audience will be the person addressed. If you are writing an essay, use a cover sheet, and briefly explain to whom you are writing. (Suggestions for topics were presented on pp. 192–193.)

This project requires your best grammar, sentence structure, paragraphing, and punctuating skills. This piece of writing should help you at work, in your community, or in college classes outside English. It is an opportunity for you to use writing as a powerful means of influencing change in some part of your life.

EXERCISE 7. Responding to a Writer's Viewpoint

Write a paragraph responding to the article below. Express your point of view in the topic sentence; then defend your position. These questions may stimulate your thinking:

- Did you experience any "warm fuzzies" in school? How can "hundreds of classroom hours of warm fuzzies and crossword puzzles mold a human being"? What does the author mean?
- Have you run into situations in which someone's ignorance of the language caused embarrassment for employers or customers?
- What is your reaction to this writer's experience? What point is the writer making? Do you agree or disagree?

Lucky It Wasn't An Umlaut
by Sandra Hoyt

My high school offered a course called English for Fun and Profit, an out for non–college-bound students who had to fulfill a language requirement and didn't want to waste their time with semicolons and the verses of Yeats because "they'd never use that stuff anyway."

I'm beginning to understand how hundreds of classroom hours of warm fuzzies and crossword puzzles can mold (literally) a human being. I recently called a restaurant and asked the person who answered the phone how to spell the name of the establishment. She proceeded with a list of letters, and when she got to what I presumed was an apostrophe, she said, "It's that funny little mark your typewriter makes."

"Do you mean an apostrophe?" I asked politely. Hearing no response, I offered more guesses. "A hyphen? A dash?"

"You know," she insisted (and suddenly I was feeling dumb because I didn't), "that funny little mark your typewriter makes."

Exasperated, I asked, "Is it vertical or horizontal?"

She took a few moments to mull it over. "Vertical."

An answer, at last. I asked her to mail a business card from the restaurant so I could verify the spelling once more (it wasn't that I didn't trust her), and I discovered that the funny little thing my typewriter makes was an apostrophe, just as I had suspected.

15

Capitalizing Correctly

Using Capital Letters for Proper Nouns

Capitalization follows conventional rules, many of them already familiar to you. Some of those rules are easily understood, while others are confusing. In this chapter, the rules are organized around central principles in an attempt to clear up the confusion.

The first principle is an extension of our knowledge of proper nouns. Capitalize names of specific persons, places, or things. Wherever those names appear, they should be capitalized. This rule is sometimes misused because of misunderstanding over which nouns are **proper** and which are **common**. The most obvious proper nouns are names like these:

> Lexington, Kentucky (a certain city, a certain state)
> Peter Jennings (a certain television newscaster)
> Guthrie Theater (a certain theater)
> Northeast Louisiana University (a certain school)

Contrast the common and proper nouns here:

> My best friend went to Lake Park High School, where the student body was about half that of my high school.
> Sheri lives on Walnut Street, a block away from our street.

In addition, the names of specific geographic locations, groups, organizations, religions, historical events and periods, and historical documents are capitalized. The days of the week, the months of the year, and holidays are also capitalized, but the seasons generally are not capitalized.

In the three sentences below, all the nouns are italicized, including those that work as adjectives. Contrast the capitalization of proper and common nouns, noting that capitals are used when the proper noun works as an adjective, as, for instance, *Lutheran* in the third sentence:

My *neighbors* decided to form a new *club* when they met in
our *town hall* yesterday.

The *Morristown Garden Club* met *Wednesday* at the *Morris-town City Center* because their regular monthly *meeting*
would have been on *Labor Day.*

The *pioneers* built the first *Lutheran church* in this *state*
during the *summer* of their *arrival.*

PRACTICE 1

Add capital letters as needed to the italicized words.

1. The *swedish immigrants* founded *st. paul's lutheran church* in *wright county.*

2. The *senior class* at our *high school* invited the *seniors* at *west high school*
to the *halloween dance.*

3. This *school year, fall semester* had begun before *fall* arrived on the *cal-endar.*

4. After Thomas Wolfe finished *high school,* he went to the *university* of *north carolina* at *chapel hill.*

Capitalize the names of specific courses of study. Use capitals for
any word derived from the name of a country, such as the names of all
languages: English, French, Italian, Chinese, among others:

Janeen studied French and Latin in high school, but she
majored in American history in college because she was
fascinated with the Civil War.

Use capitals for specific titles of courses:

Henry enrolled in Modern Economics 128, Music Literature
143, and Basic Algebra 103.

Do not capitalize general areas of study unless they derive from the
name of a country:

Most freshmen study math, history, and English.

PRACTICE 2

In the following sentences, add capital letters as needed, and remove incor-rect capital letters.

1. Computer science majors at the University must complete four years of
Math, three years of Physics, plus Computer Design I, II, and III.

2. Liberal Arts Majors must pass foreign language requirements by completing two years of french, german, latin, or russian.

3. Some colleges allow students to substitute a Computer Language for the foreign language requirement.

4. Education students must finish introduction to education, a course identified in the University Catalogue as education 110.

Capitalize all references to a deity and sacred writings. This application of the proper-noun principle covers nouns such as these: the Lord, God, Allah, Jehovah, Yahweh, the Messiah, the Bible, Biblical, the Koran, the Scriptures. Other dieties—such as Pan, Diana, Zeus, and others—are also capitalized. By extension, the principle is also applied to pronouns referring to the deity:

They shall worship Him Who gave the Sermon on the Mount.

Capitalize words used as proper nouns to designate regions of the country, such as North, South, East, West, and Midwest. These words need capitalization only when they are used in this specific way, to designate certain regions. When used to indicate directions or points on the compass, these words are not capitalized. Note in the examples below that words such as *southern* and *northern*, used as adjectives, are not capitalized:

We travel south to get to the heart of the Midwest.
We spent the winter in the South, then drove back to the
    North by way of the southern and eastern United States.
The east side of the city reminds me of the Northeast, partic-
    ularly of Boston.

PRACTICE 3

In the following sentences, add capital letters as needed, and remove incorrect capital letters.

1. Thomas Wolfe traveled East from his hometown of Asheville, North Carolina, to attend the University.

2. One of Wolfe's biographers says that the young man had "dreamed and hungered for the proud unknown North," but his family persuaded him to begin College at the State University.

3. He absorbed Math, English, History, and other basic courses as thoroughly there as he could have in any College in the north, west, midwest, or anywhere in the country.

4. Among the treasures to be examined in english literature classes is the King James version of the scriptures.

Using Other Capital Letters

Capitalize the first word of a sentence and the first word of each line of poetry. Although a few poets (e.e. cummings, for instance) deliberately set aside this convention, most poets use capital letters at the beginning of each line of poetry. Here, for instance, is Robert Frost's poem "The Road Not Taken." Notice that capital letters are at the beginning of lines, not necessarily at the beginning of sentences:

Two roads diverged in a yellow wood,
And sorry I could not travel both
And be one traveler, long I stood
And looked down one as far as I could
To where it bent in the undergrowth;

Then took the other, as just as fair,
And having perhaps the better claim,
Because it was grassy and wanted wear,
Though as for that the passing there
Had worn them really about the same,

And both that morning equally lay
In leaves no step had trodden black.
Oh, I kept the first for another day!
Yet knowing how way leads on to way,
I doubted if I should ever come back.

I shall be telling this with a sigh
Somewhere ages and ages hence;
Two roads diverged in a wood, and I—
I took the one less traveled by,
And that has made all the difference.

In addition, capital letters can be used for special effects and personification. Personification is the treatment of an entity as though it were a person with human form or qualities. Here is a well-known example:

"O Death, where is thy sting? O Grave, where is thy victory?"
(1 Corinthians 15:55)

Capitalize the first word of a direct quotation. Typically, we capitalize the first word in a quotation whether it is a complete sentence or not:

Norman asked, "Is it time to go home yet?"
Sheila answered, "No, not yet."
He grumbled, "O.K."
Not hearing him, Sheila said, "Huh?"

Exceptions to this practice arise when quoted words are incorporated into a sentence as an integral part of the sentence, as, for instance, when the quotes are subject complements:

> Patrick Henry's most famous words were "give me liberty or give me death."
> A common response to Patrick Henry was "and I agree."

PRACTICE 4

In these sentences, add capital letters as needed, and remove incorrect capital letters.

1. Frost's speaker realized that he would probably never get back to the road not taken; he said, "yet knowing how way leads on to way, I doubted if I should ever come back."

2. But he knew he could not forget the road not taken, saying that he would be telling the story with a sigh, "somewhere ages and ages hence."

3. Perhaps Frost's most famous lines come from "Stopping by the Woods on a Snowy Evening"; in that poem he concluded by saying, "but I have promises to keep, And miles to go before I sleep."

4. The professor said, "read the rest of Frost's poetry for tomorrow and write a critique of three poems by Monday."

Capitalize the first word, the last word, and all important words in titles, including the second part of a hyphenated word. Short words such as prepositions, conjunctions, and articles within the title need no capitalization. As these examples show, the rule also applies to subtitles.

> *The Last of the Mohicans*
> "After Part-Time Work, What Does the Future Hold?"
> *Lowell Mason: His Life and Work*

PRACTICE 5

Fill in the name of a book with a subtitle.

Example: <u>The Making of a Bibliography: Problems, Strategies and Insights</u>

_____

_____

_____

Capitalize common nouns used in place of relatives' names unless possessive words are present. Use capital letters when the words refer to specific individuals, but no capitals when the words refer to relationships in general:

> The clerk asked Mother if she wanted to buy that purse.
> Ideally, mothers and fathers agree on child-rearing practices.

Do not use capital letters when possessive words are used with the nouns:

> The PTA committee included Sally's mother, Mike's father, and my mother.

PRACTICE 6

In the following sentences, add capital letters as needed, and remove incorrect capital letters.

1. On mother's day last year, my dad and I bought roses for mother and grandmother peterson.

2. Jill's dad and Tony's grandmother are running for the school board position vacated last spring when mother resigned.

3. My mother attended the State University in Florida, but Paul's mother attended a liberal arts college, Rollins college, in Winter Park, Florida.

Capitalize titles used with names. When a title is used with a relative's name, capitalize the title even if a possessive word is present:

> On his way home, my Uncle Ted bought roses for Aunt Edith.
> She showed my mother and my Grandpa Williams the flowers the next day.

The same principle applies to other words used as titles, such as *mayor, governor, dean, lieutenant, captain,* and so forth:

> The dean spoke to the college president, asking if Mayor Sanderson could be the commencement speaker.
> That plan was not possible because Governor Truesome had already been invited.

One exception should be noted: capitalize the title of the head of a nation even without the person's name, as in the President of the United States.

In the following sentences, add capital letters as needed, and remove incorrect capital letters.

1. My uncle Roy met the governor of Texas during his trip to Austin.

2. My aunt Ellen went with him on that trip to the south last Winter.

3. Although their stay in Austin was brief, they visited a long-time friend, professor Carla Jurgens, now teaching at the university of Texas.

Capitalize the first word of the salutation of a letter and all the words if you are using titles. Ideally, business letters should begin like this, addressing the recipient by name:

> Dear Ms. Kingman:
> Dear Professor Thompson:

If you do not know the name of the person you are addressing, you may use the person's job description:

> Dear Editor:
> Dear Customer Service Representative:

Or if you prefer, you can use one of these standard salutations:

> Ladies:
> Gentlemen:
> Dear Sir or Madam:

Capitalize the first word of a complimentary closing in a letter. Letters can close with one of many possible complimentary closings, such as these:

> Yours truly,
> Very truly yours,
> Sincerely yours,
> Sincerely,

Handling Numbers

Here are the two main principles to follow when using numbers in your writing:

- Consider your readers. Make their job easy.
- Be consistent. Make your paper attractive.

More specifically, follow these general guidelines:

- Use numerals for dates, addresses, percentages, formulas, measurements, statistics, times of day when used with A.M. or P.M., page references, and most fractions and dollar amounts:

On October 23, 1987, he moved into a co-op unit having a living room 13′ × 22′ and two bedrooms, one 12′ × 12′ and the other 11′ × 10.5′.

- Spell out numbers that can be expressed in one or two words, especially when the words are adjectives:

    He ordered three pancakes and two strips of bacon. Breakfast cost only four dollars, but dinner cost almost twenty-two dollars.

- Be consistent. If some of the numbers require more than two words, use numerals throughout:

    Breakfast cost only $4, but dinner cost $21.85.
    Meals cost only $35 per day, but the hotel cost $105 per day.

- Do not start a sentence with a number. Revise the wording to avoid that kind of opening:

    Poor: 1980, 1984, 1988, and 1992 are years for presidential elections.
    Better: Presidential elections occur in 1980, 1984, 1988, and 1992.

PRACTICE 8

Correct the handling of numbers in these sentences. Make your corrections between the lines.

1. The ticket cost about $158, but the airport added a two-dollar surcharge, meaning that I had to pay about one hundred sixty dollars.

2. 1987 was a year of bargain rates on airline tickets.

3. Gasoline costs about ninety-five cents a gallon, down from a dollar twenty-five cents or more in the early 1980s.

4. The gas tank on that new car holds about 13 gallons; older, larger cars had tanks that held about twenty-five gallons, roughly 50 percent more.

Points to Use

- Use the distinction between proper and common nouns as the basis for capitalizing or not capitalizing nouns and adjectives derived from nouns.
- Capitalize the names of specific courses of study; capitalize names of languages because they are derived from the proper names of countries.

- Capitalize words like *north, south, east,* and *west* when they refer to regions of the United States.
- Capitalize titles only when they appear with proper names or when they refer to heads of state.
- Capitalize words that refer to relatives, but only under certain circumstances.
- Handle numbers to accommodate readers and to follow conventional usage.

Points to Remember

- Capitalize proper nouns and adjectives derived from proper nouns.
- Capitalize words that designate a particular part of the country and words that refer to a deity or sacred writings.
- Capitalize the first words of lines of poetry, first words in sentences, and first words of direct quotations unless the quotation is built into the sentence as a subject complement or other essential element.
- Capitalize the first, last, and all important words in titles.
- Capitalize to designate a relative by title with or without the proper name, but do not capitalize if a possessive word appears with the title alone.
- Capitalize the first word of a letter's salutation and all the words if you are using titles.
- Capitalize only the first word of a letter's complimentary closing.
- Spell out numbers that can be expressed in one or two words, but use numerals for addresses, dates, formulas, measurements, statistics, and situations in which readers can more easily grasp the information with numerals.

EXERCISE 1. Reviewing Uses of Capital Letters, Quotation Marks, and Italics

Circle a or b to designate the correct answer in these sentences. Check your answers with those at the back of the book.

1. a. Dr. Pauline Watson, a Professor of botany, taught through last Spring, then retired to Arizona.
   b. Dr. Pauline Watson, a professor of botany, taught through last spring, then retired to Arizona.

2. a. Many sophomores study Biology 197 in Johnston Hall at the college.
   b. Many Sophomores study biology 197 in Johnston hall at the College.

3. a. We studied the Korean war in History class in High School and College.
   b. We studied the Korean War in history class in high school and college.

4. a. Bill's Mother drove South through Arkansas in June.
   b. Bill's mother drove south through Arkansas in June.

5. a. I attended my english class, meeting at 9:30 A.M.
   b. I attended my English class, meeting at 9:30 A.M.

6. a. Sue asked, "Have you been to the West?"
   b. Sue asked, "have you been to the West"?

7. a. Karl replied, "No, but I visited western Colorado."
   b. Karl replied, "no, but I visited Western Colorado."

8. a. She spoke of God in classes at the First Baptist Church.
   b. She spoke of God in classes at the first baptist church.

9. a. Are you going to the School picnic on Memorial Day at the Park or to the Cardinals game at the Stadium?
   b. Are you going to the school picnic on Memorial Day at the park or to the Cardinals game at the stadium?

10. a. The American Legion, an organization to which my Grandfather Daniels and my father belong, held its fall convention the weekend before Veterans' Day.
    b. The American Legion, an organization to which my grandfather Daniels and my Father belong, held its Fall convention the weekend before Veterans' Day.

11. a. Marian asked, "can mother and I buy designer jeans for under $60 a pair, are there such stores?"
    b. Marian asked, "Can Mother and I buy designer jeans for under sixty dollars a pair? Are there such stores?"

12. a. Tom replied; "if you look all over the midwest, you couldn't find such bargains."
    b. Tom replied, "If you look all over the Midwest, you couldn't find such bargains."

13. a. After you read that article in the magazine "Car and Driver," you will understand why I like Fords.
    b. After you read that article in the magazine *Car and Driver,* you will understand why I like Fords.

14. a. Looking for the word *blizzard* in my dictionary, my dad found information about its original use.
    b. Looking for the word 'blizzard' in my Dictionary, my Dad found information about it's original use.

15. a. After the Thompsons' had traveled North all day to their cabin, they found it had been attacked by vandals, who's destructiveness made them heartsick.
    b. After the Thompsons had traveled north all day to their cabin, they found it had been attacked by vandals whose destructiveness made them heartsick.

16. a. The word *vandal,* as it is used today comes from vandal, a member of tribes that ravaged Europe in the 5th century A.D.
    b. The word *vandal,* as it is used today, comes from *Vandal,* a member of tribes that ravaged Europe in the fifth century A.D.

17. a. "What," Kim asked, "are you going to do about our trip to the West this spring? Are we still going?"
    b. "What," Kim asked, "Are you going to do about our trip to the west this spring, are we still going?"

18. a. Peter answered, "its going to cost about four hundred twenty-five dollars just to get to Utah."
    b. Peter answered, "It's going to cost about $425 just to get to Utah."

19. a. When Kim heard that, she remembered that her dad had said it was "very expensive" to travel in the Midwest and West that fall.
    b. When Kim heard that, she remembered that her Dad had said it was "Very expensive" to travel in the Midwest and West that Fall.

20. a. If you read "Practical English" you should be ready for later english classes.
    b. If you read *Practical English,* you should be ready for later English classes.

21. a. The governor caught nine fish one weekend and twenty-one the next, but he said he was satisfied.
    b. The Governor caught nine fish one weekend and 21 the next, but he said "that he was satisfied."

22. a. "John, what did you say? My mind was wandering, I guess," his mother remarked.
    b. "John, what did you say?" "My mind was wandering I guess," his Mother remarked.

EXERCISE 2. Reviewing Grammar, Sentence Structure, Punctuation, and Capitalization

On a separate piece of paper, write a corrected version of this police report. Repair grammar, sentence structure, punctuation, and capitalization. You may reword and combine sentences.

The suspect was observed Northbound on Highway 20 at approximately 1:30 A.M. saturday July 7, 1989. The suspect appeared to be traveling at a speed above the posted fifty five mph limit. The suspect was observed meeting 4 oncoming cars without dimming his lights. The suspect passed the squad car, I began to follow him, he continued up the Highway. At about fifty feet south of International avenue, across from highview shopping mall, the suspect drove across the center line by approximately 2 feet. I attempted to stop him with my red lights and horn, he went right on, I turned on the siren. He turned right at the first corner, I followed, then he stopped in the 2200 block in front of Adams elementary school.

I approached the suspect, told him why he was being stopped and asked to see his drivers license. It took the suspect about 3 minutes to find and remove his license. I observed that the suspects eyes were bloodshot and there was a strong odor of alcohol on the suspects' breath. When I asked the suspect if he had been drinking he said, No, not me. I then asked the suspect to step out of the car to perform the field sobriety tests. When he was doing the heel-to-toe test the suspect had difficulty maintaining his balance. When he tried the finger-to-nose test the suspect completely missed, his arm hit his upper lip not his nose.

After I had completed the field sobriety tests I again asked the suspect if he had been drinking and he again stated No, I have not. I then asked him to come to the Station with me. The suspect got angry. He said you have no right to haul me in. Then he swung his arm around, I subdued him and he reluctantly got into the Squad car.

EXERCISE 3. Reviewing Grammar, Sentence Structure, Punctuation, and Capitalization

On a separate piece of paper, write corrected versions of the following student paragraphs. Repair grammar, sentence structure, punctuation, and capitalization. You may reword and combine sentences.

Example 1

Running the trap is one of the best ways to get a first down conversion. Our coach Fred Majors, said, that "this play is the most effective play in football." Traps work with a tackle or with a guard. The guard, big and strong usually, is the most-likely trapper. The object is to get a Defensive Player double-teamed by two Offensive Players. When the ball is snapped the guard pulls.

He turns down the line of scrimmage, then he turns up field and finds his man. The defensive player doesnt expect him because he is usually fighting off another Blocker. Hit by the charging guard, a knock down occurs. Creating a large hole for the running back. This back must be right behind the guard. Other defensive players fill the hole at the same time. When the play works right, you should get the first down. In the book "Fran Tarkenton," the trap is further explained from the eyes of a Quarterback.

Example 2

Hypertension (high blood pressure) is a silent mysterious disease that can be relieved if detected. Its silent because it has no characteristic symptoms, its mysterious because in ninety percent of the cases, the cause is unknown. My Doctor believes that blood pressure readings should be taken at home because it is as easy as reading a thermometer. For checking blood pressure at home, home kits are available with prices ranging from thirty-five to fifty dollars. Directions are included. The acceptable safe pressure levels are also included in the directions. If your pressure is about 120 over eighty, that is a normal reading. It helps to keep a chart, showing what your readings are and the time of day when you took the reading, then after 2 or 3 months, you will see a pattern of your pressure. Remember: only your Doctor can tell for sure what the readings mean, it depends on your medical history, but there are good medications available to help you lower the pressure.

Example 3

I have my two years associates degree from Normandale Community College. As I was going through the Dental Hygiene Program at Normandale, I worked at the University of Minnesota. Every Saturday I did volunteer work in the Dental Clinic there. The hands on experience improved my skills, also it helped others. I feel experience is so very important when learning a trade. I never knew how uneducated the general public was about proper oral hygiene. Thats why my job is so important; and hopefully it will serve it's purpose in educating the general public about oral hygiene.

Example 4

Besides my schooling at Vo-Tech in heavy duty diesel repair, I also have experience, working on diesel trucks out in the field. I have been a Shop Foreman for a small trucking company, its located in Brooklyn Park. At this job I was one hundred percent responsible for the maintenance of a fleet of 6 trucks and trailers. I also worked for a much larger company called Cross Country Express, its headquarters are in Rosemount. My main responsibilities there were to refuel and wash all trucks coming into the terminal, along with checking them for scheduled maintenance. This all fit in with my degree work, which includes major engine overhaul, repair of electrical systems, welding, and air conditioning maintenance.

Example 5

I have recently graduated from High School, as of June 1988. I have passed various classes that pertain to your secretarial position; such as word processing, typing, shorthand, and accounting. I also have 6 years of work related experience in various kinds of offices; for example, government, school and factory offices. I am fast and efficient. I type at 70 words per minute, take shorthand at 120 words per-minute, and type 55 words per minute using a Dictaphone. As you can see, I'd be a valuable worker for your company.

16

Spelling Correctly

Good spelling requires care and determination. Even good spellers need to watch out for certain troublesome words and to look up spellings when in doubt. This chapter offers several helpful strategies for improving your spelling, but none of them can replace that care and determination.

Experiment with various strategies and see what works best for you: applying spelling rules, examining commonly confused words, keeping a list of difficult words, and proofreading for misspellings in context. You may find that each of these strategies helps to some extent, and as you use them, you may discover other useful strategies of your own.

Following Guidelines

Spelling rules can help us avoid problems. Three potential problem areas are discussed here: adding suffixes, forming plurals, and handling *ie* or *ei* within words.

ADDING SUFFIXES

Spelling problems can arise in adding suffixes, such as *ing, ed, er, est, able, ness, ly, ence*. Some general rules can help. For words of one syllable, double the final consonant if the word ends with this pattern: consonant/vowel/consonant. Thus:

> *swim* (*w i m* is consonant/vowel/consonant) becomes
> *swimming*
> *plan* (*l a n* is consonant/vowel/consonant) becomes *planned*
>> (Note: The final consonant is doubled to keep the short vowel sound, as in the word *snipping* as opposed to *sniping*.)

Do not double the final consonant if the word ends with another pattern, such as vowel/vowel/consonant or vowel/consonant/consonant. Thus:

> boil (o i l is vowel/vowel/consonant) becomes *boiling*
> fast (a s t is vowel/consonant/consonant) becomes *faster*

PRACTICE 1

Add est *endings to these words. Put an* × *beside the words that end consonant/vowel/consonant.*

1. short _____   3. green _____

2. big _____   4. moist _____

Add ing *endings to these words.*

5. run _____   7. can _____

6. peel _____   8. brag _____

For words of more than one syllable, double the final consonant if the last three letters are consonant/vowel/consonant and the accent is on the last syllable. Thus:

> omit becomes *omitting, omitted*
> commit becomes *committing, committed*
> expel becomes *expelling, expelled*

Do not double the final consonant unless the accent is on the last syllable. Thus:

> pardon becomes *pardoning, pardoned*
> answer becomes *answering, answered*

PRACTICE 2

Add ed *endings to these words.*

1. prefer _____   4. listen _____

2. wrap _____   5. burn _____

3. admit _____   6. travel _____

For words ending with *e*, drop the final *e* if the suffix begins with a vowel (e.g., *ing, ed, able, ence*). Thus:

> *love* becomes *loving, lovable*
> *care* becomes *caring*

Do not drop the final *e* if the suffix begins with a consonant (e.g., *less, ment, ness, ly*). Thus:

> *care* becomes *careless*
> *love* becomes *lovely*

PRACTICE 3

Add able *endings to these words.*

1. desire   _____   3. pleasure _____

2. note   _____   4. dispense _____

Add ment *to these root words.*

5. arrange   _____   7. manage   _____

6. place   _____   8. commit   _____

Add ing *to these root words.*

9. write   _____   11. divide _____

10. travel   _____   12. pardon _____

For words that end with *y*, change the *y* to *i* if the letter before the *y* is a consonant. Thus:

> *bury* becomes *buried*
> *happy* becomes *happiness*

Leave the final *y* if the letter before the *y* is a vowel. Thus:

> *enjoy* becomes *enjoyed*
> *delay* becomes *delayed*

Leave the final *y* if the suffix is *ing:*

> *bury* becomes *burying*
> *enjoy* becomes *enjoying*

Note these exceptions to the rules:

pay becomes *paid*   day becomes *daily*
say becomes *said*   lay becomes *laid*

PRACTICE 4

Add ed *endings to these words.*

1. cry _____   3. occupy _____

2. study _____   4. stay _____

Add ing *endings to these words.*

5. buy _____   7. try _____

6. portray _____   8. fortify _____

FORMING PLURALS

Some general rules can help us avoid common spelling errors that can occur in forming plurals. First, add *s* to singular nouns in most cases. If the word ends with *sh, ch, ss, x,* or *z,* add *es.* Thus:

word becomes *words*
chair becomes *chairs*

but

church becomes *churches*
fox becomes *foxes*

Second, add *es* for most words ending with *o,* but note some common exceptions:

potato becomes *potatoes*
tomato becomes *tomatoes*
hero becomes *heroes*
echo becomes *echoes*

but

radio becomes *radios*
solo becomes *solos*
soprano becomes *sopranos*
piano becomes *pianos*

Third, change *y* to *i* and add *es* if the final *y* is preceded by a consonant. Thus:

> *fly* becomes *flies*
> *baby* becomes *babies*

but

> *day* becomes *days*
> *monkey* becomes *monkeys*
>> (because the final *y* is preceded by a vowel)

There are some exceptions to these general rules. For example, some nouns change form internally. Thus:

> *woman* becomes *women*
> *man* becomes *men*
> *mouse* becomes *mice*
> *person* becomes *people*

Some nouns change a final *f* to a *v* and add *es:*

> *wolf* becomes *wolves*
> *calf* becomes *calves*

A few nouns add *en* to form plurals:

> *ox* becomes *oxen*
> *child* becomes *children*

PRACTICE 5

Write in the plural forms of these words.

1. box   _____   5. city   _____

2. business _____   6. veto   _____

3. leaf   _____   7. Harris _____

4. cemetery _____   8. tax   _____

HANDLING *ie* AND *ei* WITHIN WORDS

General rules can also guide us in avoiding *ie-ei* spelling errors. First, use *i* before *e* except after *c* or when the sound is *a* as in *neighbor:*

> niece   receive   weigh

Second, use *i* before *e* after *c* or when the sound is *shen:*

ancient sufficient conscience

Third, use *i* before *e* when the letters are sounded separately, not as a single unit.

alien fiery audience

PRACTICE 6

Fill in ie *or* ei *in these words.*

1. effic_____nt

2. consc_____ntious

3. sl_____gh

4. th_____r

5. perc_____ve

6. c_____ling

7. ach_____ve

8. gr_____ve

Besides following rules such as those presented above, you can develop memory tricks of your own, ways that help you remember correct spellings. There is no particular rule or pattern for these memory tricks, and they may work for some but not for others. What is important is that you have ways to remember correct spellings. Here are a few examples that may help:

- To spell the word *separate,* think of the letter *r* as separating two *a*'s.
- To distinguish *stationery* and *stationary,* think of the words *paper* or *letter.* We write *letters* on *paper* called *stationery;* these three nouns all end with *er.*
- To remember that *all right* is two words, associate it with *all wrong,* also two words.

PRACTICE 7

Write two words that you have learned to spell through associations or memory tricks. Explain the associations as well.

1. _____

_____

2. _____

_____

Handling Easily Confused Words

A common cause of misspelling is the similarity between the sound and the appearance of certain words. By definition and usage, these easily confused words are often unrelated. To spell such words correctly, the first step may be to understand the meanings of the words. Here the words are explained with their usual meanings; parts of speech are included when that information may help.

affect, effect

Affect is a verb, meaning to influence:

The damp weather affects his arthritis.

Effect, usually a noun, means a result:

Smoking can have deadly effects on the lungs.

When *effect* is used as a verb, it means to bring about results:

The new rules will effect several changes in football next fall.

accept, except

Accept is a verb, meaning to receive or take; *except* is a preposition, meaning other than:

I would accept that offer except for my agreement with another company.
All the letters were prompt except Mike's.

advice, advise

Advice is the noun; *advise* is the verb:

If she advises you, you will get sensible advice.

PRACTICE 8

Underline the correct choices in these sentences.

1. The supervisor (adviced, advised) her to (accept, except) the promotion even though it meant longer hours.

2. The (affect, effect) of longer hours could be less study time.

3. The book was full of good (advice, advise), but it had a negative (affect, effect) on some readers.

choose, chose

Choose and *chose* are both verbs, but *chose* is the past tense, *choose* the present. (Note: *choose* rhymes with *booze; chose* rhymes with *hose.*) Note the usage in this sentence:

> Before you choose a new car, get advice from an owner who chose from this year's models.

complement, compliment

Complement, a noun, comes from the verb *complete; complement* as a verb conveys a sense of completion or fulfillment:

> The subject complement completes the meaning of the sentence.
> That tie complements your shirt and jacket.

Compliment, used as a noun or a verb, means praise:

> His compliment on my work made me happy; he complimented the quality and the promptness.

conscience, conscious

Conscience, a noun, is a sense of right and wrong. *Conscious,* an adjective, means aware.

> Her conscience is clear because she did not take part in the crime.
> The motorcyclist was fully conscious, though injured in the accident.

PRACTICE 9

Underline the correct choices in these sentences.

1. He was (complemented, complimented) on his poise under stress, a trait he was (conscience, conscious) of.

2. The patrolman (choose, chose) to issue a traffic ticket as a (complement, compliment) to his remarks about speeding.

3. He felt the ticket might (affect, effect) the motorist's (conscience, conscious) driving practices, but he also realized that (affecting, effecting) changes in long-standing habits is very difficult.

4. All (accept, except) one of the speeding motorists had to pay a fine, and that one was left with a twinge of guilt in his (conscience, conscious).

past, passed

Passed is a verb, but *past* is a noun, an adjective, an adverb, and occasionally a preposition. *Past* refers to time gone by:

> When the trucker passed me on the highway, I remembered past years when the speed limits were higher.
> Twenty minutes past the hour, we arrived at the airport, where we passed time until Molly's flight arrived.

personal, personnel

Personal is an adjective, meaning private; *personnel* is a noun, meaning staff or employees, or it can be an adjective with the same meaning:

> The personnel records contain some personal information.
> Plant personnel seldom obtain personal data about the executives.

principal, principle

Principal is an adjective, meaning main or chief; it is also a noun, referring to a school administrator or other leading persons or to money. *Principle* is a noun, meaning a basic law or rule:

> Our neighbors are the principals in the lawsuit; they believe they are acting on high moral principles.
> The school principal, trying to save for her retirement, wanted to earn at least 10 percent interest on her invested principal.

PRACTICE 10

Underline the correct choices in these sentences.

1. The (principle, principal) advantage of using word processing is the ease of revising.

2. A central (principle, principal) of writing is that revision is essential for polished work.

3. The (affect, effect) of easy revision is that students can produce better papers than in (past, passed) years.

4. Writing on (personal, personnel) experiences has very little place in business and the professions.

5. Most companies expect competent writing of all (personal, personnel), meaning clear, correct writing, appropriate for its purpose and audience.

6. For this reason, many students are (adviced, advised) to take as many courses in composition as possible.

---

quiet, quite, quit

Quiet, an adverb, means still, not noisy; *quite,* also an adverb, means very or really:

> The weary traveler was glad the hotel was quiet because she was quite tired.

Quit, a verb, means to stop:

> When the church bells quit chiming and the sirens quit sounding, the street was quiet.

than, then

Than is used in statements that make comparisons; *then* refers to a time:

> The play ended more happily than the movie version.
> I had seen the movie last month; then I saw the play. Until then, I knew only one version of the plot.

they're, their, there

The contraction *they're* stands for *they are:*

> They're going to the movies with us.

Their is a possessive pronoun used as an adjective; *there* is an adverb, sometimes referring to a place, other times used as an expletive (a word added to fill out a statement, most commonly used to start a sentence):

> There will be a crowd at both theaters tonight because it is their first showing of this popular movie.

PRACTICE 11

Underline the correct choices in these sentences.

1. The Library of Congress has a larger collection of items (than, then) any other library in the world.

2. Many people believe that (there, their, they're) unable to use the Library of Congress because (there, their, they're) not members of Congress.

3. (Then, Than) they find out, upon inquiry, that (their, there) is no reason

why (there, their, they're) unable to work at the Library of Congress, assuming they are at least eighteen years old.

4. The library was founded in 1835 with (quit, quiet, quite) modest funding, amounting to only $5,000.

5. Since (then, than), the holdings have grown to a present collection of about 83,000,000 items.

6. Those 83,000,000 items fill more (then, than) 535 miles of shelves.

---

thorough, through

Thorough is an adjective, meaning full or complete; *through* is often a preposition, meaning in one side and out the other:

> As soon as I walked through the clinic door, I believed that I would get a thorough exam.

Through can also have other meanings and uses that are clear in context, such as the expression "through street."

two, too, to

The number *2* is spelled *two*. The preposition *to* begins prepositional phrases or infinitives:

> We went to the store to buy groceries to feed the crowd.

The adverb *too* has two meanings, excessive and also:

> We had too many people for too little food.
> We had problems with seating space, too.

weather, whether

The noun *weather* refers to climatic conditions:

> The weather changed quickly from hot and dry to chilly and wet.

Whether introduces dependent clauses and implies a question:

> We wondered whether we should take umbrellas with us.

PRACTICE 12

Underline the correct choices in these sentences.

1. Educators in the early 1800s designed textbooks (to, too, two) use with the American Indians.

2. (Through, Thorough) the years, books offering (through, thorough) training in spelling, geography, and history were published in Cherokee, Sioux, Ojibway, and other languages.

3. A hymnal in the Choctaw language is intriguing, but I cannot determine (weather, whether) there is music to accompany the poetic texts.

4. A Cherokee hymnal printed in 1833 went (through, thorough) many successive editions (to, too, two) at least 1909.

5. (To, Too) researchers, the Indian languages look like English in some respects, but there are (to, too) many dissimilarities to leave any confusion between the languages.

6. The work of educators in (past, passed) times can be instructive today, if the underlying (principals, principles) are understood and applied.

---

who's, whose

The contraction *who's* stands for *who is*; the possessive pronoun *whose* is used as an adjective:

Who's coming to the party tomorrow?
We wondered whose car was being towed.

it's, its

The contraction *it's* stands for *it is*; the possessive pronoun *its* is used as an adjective:

It's going to be a great party.
The car being towed had its fender dented.

you're, your

The contraction *you're* stands for *you are*; the possessive pronoun *your* is used as an adjective:

You're invited to the party.
Is that your car being towed?

PRACTICE 13 ⎯⎯⎯⎯⎯⎯⎯⎯⎯⎯⎯⎯⎯⎯

Underline the correct choices in these sentences.

1. The Library of Congress can provide some of the material for (your, you're) research project.

2. (You're, Your) project will require many hours of work; (it's, its) a valuable project with (it's, its) own special challenges.

3. If you learn (who's, whose) responsible for publishing that rare book, you may find out (who's, whose) music it contains.

4. If (there, their, they're) not too busy, the reference librarians can explain copyright regulations of the 1800s to you.

5. I would (advice, advise) you to be patient because your research may take longer than you expect, a fact you will learn to (accept, except) with experience.

6. You will become (conscience, conscious) of more sources as you work through the project.

Another strategy for improving spelling is studying a list of commonly misspelled words. Some of the words on a standard list may cause no problems for you, and some of the words that do cause you problems may not be on the list.

PRACTICE 14 ———————————————

Read through the list below, slowly and carefully. Mark the words that you find difficult to spell. Add any words that cause problems for you.

Commonly Misspelled Words

accidentally	apologize	certain	consistency
accommodate	argument	chief	continuous
achieve	athlete	choice	controlled
acquaintance	athletic	choose	convenience
acquire	auxiliary	chose	criticize
advice	basically	coming	definitely
advise	believe	committee	dependent
affect	becoming	comparative	describe
effect	behavior	complement	desirable
all right	benefited	compliment	desperate
a lot	business	conceive	develop
already	carrying	condemn	disappoint
among	category	conscience	dissatisfy
analysis	cavalry	conscious	dying

efficiency
eliminate
embarrass
emphasize
endeavor
environment
equipped
etc.
excellence
excellent
except
accept
experience
explanation
extremely
familiar
fascinate
finally
foreign
forty
fourth
fulfill
government
grammar
grievance
grievous
guard
hear
here
height
hoping
humorous
hypocrisy
hypocrite
illegible
imagery
immense
incidentally
incredible

independence
indispensable
ingenious
interest
interfered
interpretation
interrupt
irrelevant
irresistible
its
it's
jealousy
judgment
knowledge
knowledgeable
laboratory
laid
led
leisure
library
lightning
loneliness
loose
lose
maintenance
marital
martial
maybe
meant
moral
morale
mortgage
necessary
ninety
ninth
noticeable
nuclear
occasion
occasionally

occurred
occurrence
opinion
opportunity
optimist
original
paid
pamphlet
parallel
passed
past
performance
permanent
perseverance
personal
personnel
pleasant
possession
possible
practical
precede
proceed
preferred
prejudice
principal
principle
privilege
probable
probably
profession
professor
psychology
pursue
quiet
quite
receive
recommend
referred
relieve
repetition

restaurant
rhyme
rhythm
ridiculous
schedule
sense
separate
sergeant
shepherd
shining
significance
similar
simile
studying
subtle
succeed
success
supersede
surprise
synonym
temperament
than
then
their
there
they're
thorough
through
to
too
two
tragedy
transferred
tried
truly
undoubtedly
unnecessary
vengeance
villain

weather	who's	worrying	your
whether	whose	writing	you're
weird	woman	written	

Points to Use

- Rely on the spelling rules for adding suffixes and creating plurals, though there are exceptions to each rule.
- Study the list of commonly misspelled words as a reference.
- Keep a list of words that you have misspelled, and work on those words.
- Watch the spelling of words as you read, particularly noting words that you have had difficulty spelling and words that are easily confused with other words.
- Turn to dictionaries and spelling books when in doubt about correct spelling. If possible, run spelling checks in your computer system.

Points to Remember

- Spelling correctly requires care and determination. Applying spelling rules helps, and examining commonly confused words helps.
- Adding suffixes, such as *ing, ed, er, est, able, ness, ly,* and *ence,* can lead to misspellings. Although most words follow specific patterns for adding these suffixes, there are exceptions to learn.
- Associations and memory tricks can help us remember correct spellings, but generally the ones that work best for us are the ones we devise on our own.
- Commonly confused words can be understood if we know the part of speech and the definition of each word. Similar spellings and similar pronunciations can cause confusion; distinguishing these words by part of speech and by usage can clear up the confusion.
- Lists of commonly misspelled words, such as the list on pp. 380–382, are useful for reference and study. The lists become more useful as we add to them the words we have difficulty spelling.

EXERCISE 1. Finding Misspelled Words

In each of the following groups of words, underline the misspelled word.
(These words can be found on the spelling list, pp. 380–382.)

1. separate, experience, you're, complement, athelete
2. becomming, category, advise, dying, government
3. condemn, endeavor, fulfill, here, recommend
4. possession, indispensible, hypocrisy, a lot, through
5. written, explanation, embarass, receive, performance
6. leisure, knowledgeable, psychology, perserverence, it's
7. referred, synonym, acquaintance, eliminate, develope
8. disastisfy, desperate, pursue, shepherd, writing
9. permanent, acquaintance, desireable, guard, prejudice
10. lightning, library, significance, similiar, villain
11. repetition, forty, efficiency, occurred, payed
12. opinion, grammer, possession, relieve, hypocrite
13. noticeable, jealousy, simile, rythm, conscience
14. extremely, rhyme, supersede, apolagize, behavior
15. catagory, equipped, original, loneliness, truly
16. practical, professer, judgment, incidentally, tried
17. perseverance, referred, writting, mortgage, all right
18. precede, worrying, sergeant, studying, suprise
19. subtle, accomodate, controlled, coming, privilege
20. necessary, ingenious, familar, pamphlet, synonym
21. temperament, already, busness, certain, proceed
22. convenence, committee, possible, interest, tragedy
23. parallel, restuarant, interfered, auxiliary, etc.
24. efficiency, chief, illegable, laid, transferred
25. schedule, unneccessary, desperate, criticize, judgment

EXERCISE 2. Proofreading for Spelling, Punctuation, Capitalization, Fragments, and Run-ons

Proofread this essay, writing your corrections between the lines.

The Original Mother Goose?

Is Mother Goose a myth? Or was there a real person who's life served to generate a legend? Scholars endeaver to discover the truth, but no one can be certian. Some authorities believe the Mother Goose tales come from abroad, others think they are a mix from British and American sources. Because the cheif sources disagree, the best advise is to be skeptical about all accounts.

One explaination came to light in a Boston newspaper in the late 1800s. They're a minister gave a fasinating account of a lady whose lifelong love of children and skill as a story teller brought her fame. How accurate his writing may be remains in doubt, but here is the gist of what he wrote:

The flesh and blood Mother Goose has been traced by Church records to the Old South Church of Boston. There the famous name of Elizabeth Goose appears on the list of admissions to the Congregation in 1698.

Readers will be pleased to find that, in making a Goose of herself, this lady married into a well to do family. Born Elizabeth Foster, the future Mrs. Goose was born in 1635 in Charlestown (just outside Boston), she lived there until her marriage to Isaac Goose. Then she moved to a spacious home in Boston. (Desireable property, located on what later became Washington street.)

Isaac Goose was a widower, upon her marriage, Elizabeth became step-mother to ten children. Not every woman would except such responsibility. To that number; she and Isaac added six more. 16 children to rear and tend! The burdens could well have inspired Mrs. Goose to write the celebrated lines, Their was an old woman who lived in a shoe, She had so many children she didn't no what to do.

According to reports—she tended the children lovingly, soothing and en-tertaning them with her stories poems, and songs. This basicly happy woman led a quite life. Also a long life. She lived to be 92 years old.

Elizabeths' work was far from finished when those sixteen children be-came independant. One of the Gooses' daughters married a printer who's name was Thomas Fleet. When the Fleets son was born, giving Mrs. Goose a grandson to coodle, she moved into their household. With a flurry of activity and concern, she was said to put the usual busy mother-in-law's totally in the shade. As she helped with the neccessary work, she sang her rimes, apparently from morning to night, "up stairs and down stairs and in my lady's chamber." Finaly her son-in-law became "alarmed at the fertility of her genius" (according to the minister/writer). In other words, worn out with the old woman.

But wait. The man was a printer, and a quick thinking businessman at that. No use trying to control the old woman and her endless singing and story telling, he said to himself, but practicaly speaking, a few dollars might be made by publishing some of her ditties. No, he probly argued with himself, no one would care about this stuff, on the other hand, anythings possable, public opinion being as unpredictable as it is. After all, he reasoned, maybe the good lord sent this old woman and her silly songs my way to make me a rich publisher.

As soon as Thomas Fleet began gathering her songs, he stopped shushing Mother Goose, rather he encouraged her to sit in the rocking chair, entertaine his child, and sing more. Writing down her rhymes, he soon accumulated enough for a first book. These pieces he printed in 1719, bound into a book, and sold under the title Songs for the nursery; or Mother Goose's melodies for children.

The title page of the book bore a large cut of an actual goose, with its mouth wide open. Goes to show that the proverbial irreverance of sons-in-law is not a recent development. As the minister/reporter said bluntly, 'They [sons-in-law] were just as saucy in the days in Mother Goose as now, and just as ready to turn a penny at the expense of their mothers-in-law.'

As for the book. It's sucess was extraordinary, thru edition after edition it's contents proved irresitable to the buying public. Thomas Fleet had discovered talent, right there in his own household. It occured to him that any goose that layed such golden eggs was well worth keeping around. Goes to show that publishers' enthusiasm for golden eggs is no recent development either.

How Elizabeth Goose felt about the opportunistic Thomas Fleet, history does not say. If our judgement is based on what we know about her, we can beleve that she took it just as sweetly as she had taken all the other trials of her life. She was a tolerant, pleasent woman, devoted to caring for the little ones, she was happy if they were happy. Her songs did make them happy.

In the newspaper story, the 19th century Minister of Old South church wrote about Mother Gooses' book as follows:

It is one of the few books which cannot grow stale or be destroyed. Not Homer or Shakespeare is so sure of immortal fame as Mother Goose. Considering the love in which her melodies are everywhere held, their freedom from anything which might corrupt or mislead. . . . . , their practical wisdom, their shrewd mastery of the motives of human conduct, one is. . . . . forced to admit that her name is among the. . . . .jewels which adorn the brow of Old South [Church].

Elizabeth Foster Goose died in 1727. Weather or not she was truely *the* Mother Goose is highly questionable, but her story is delightful, and the words of Mother Goose—whoever she may have been—charm children to this day.

UNIT V PRACTICE TEST
Chapters 13, 14, 15, 16

Part 1 (50 POINTS)

Examine the statements below. Consider the capitalization and punctuation at the points with letters. If the capitalization and punctuation are correct, write the letter C on the line that corresponds to the point; if the capitalization and punctuation are incorrect, write the letter I.

1. The challenge of growing crops, raising animals, and working on their

own land, is one advantage a farm family has.

   A. _____   B. _____   C. _____

2. I swam faster, and faster, but I moved no closer to the West side of the

River.

   A. _____   B. _____   C. _____   D. _____

3. The buyer has to look at the primary uses for a boat, will it be for cruising

or for skiing?

   A. _____

                           A   B
4. We were on our way east to Michigan, to go sailing.

   A. _____   B. _____

            A (underlining)   B
5. The Reader's Digest, which was first published in 1922, provides the

         C   D
   readers' with brief, easily understood material.

   A. _____   B. _____   C. _____   D. _____

               A (quotation marks)   B
6. The magazine "Scientific American" covers many topics, such as:

            C
   psychology, zoology, and climatology.

   A. _____   B. _____   C. _____

       A   B   C
7. The Mayor of our city, and his secretary, looked all over the office for that

       D   E (Its)   F   G   H
   letter, finally he said, "Its no use, it's simply not here, Jean".

   A. _____   B. _____   C. _____   D. _____   E. _____   F. _____   G. _____   H. _____

                       A
8. My professor said, "this magazine calls itself the magazine of human experience."

   A. _____

                     A   B
9. Many magazines report National news, *Time*, *Newsweek*, and *U.S. News*

                  C
   & *World Report*, are three news magazines.

   A. _____   B. _____   C. _____

                     A   B
10. I enjoy my job at the Department store, because I work at my own pace no

                 C
   matter who's on duty as supervisor.

   A. _____   B. _____   C. _____

11. Buildings are being constructed, roads are being repaired; which I'm glad

$\overset{A}{}$ $\overset{B}{}$

to see.

    A. _____   B. _____

12. Buying a rubber plant for Mother five years ago was a mistake. Now she

has plants' and flowers everywhere.

    A. _____   B. _____

13. The Doctors, who met at a convention on the East side of Chicago,

agreed on the new AMA resolution.

    A. _____   B. _____   C. _____   D. _____

14. During his Spring vacation, my Uncle Jack drove West to the Grand

Canyon.

    A. _____   B. _____   C. _____   D. _____

15. She quoted Shakespeare's lines which my Mother had often repeated,

including the passage that reads, "Ignorance is the curse of God,

Knowledge the wing wherewith we fly to heaven."

    A. _____   B. _____   C. _____

16. Most students can master Algebra and English if they do their homework

conscientiously, remembering it's importance.

    A. _____   B. _____   C. _____

Part 2 (50 POINTS)

Write a complete, correct, original sentence illustrating a proper use of the device indicated. Select any ten items.

1. Italics (underlining) to set off a title:

   _____

   _____

2. Quotation marks to set off a title:

   _____

   _____

3. Single quotation marks:

   _____

   _____

4. A compound (hyphenated) adjective:

   _____

   _____

5. Parentheses:

   _____

   _____

6. The colon (not as part of the salutation and not in the time of day):

   _____

   _____

7. Brackets:

   _____

   _____

8. A pair of dashes:

   _____

   _____

9. A semicolon:

_____

_____

10. An apostrophe to show possession, using a plural possessive:

_____

_____

11. Italics (underlining) for some purpose other than setting off a title:

_____

_____

12. A single dash:

_____

_____

PRACTICE FINAL EXAMINATION

(100 POINTS)

Read each question carefully. Mark your answer on the line to the left of each question. Check your answers with those at the back of the book.

A. TRUE/FALSE

_____   1. Modifiers alter or enrich the meaning of the words to which they refer.

_____   2. A dangling modifier is incorrectly placed in that it is too far away from its reference.

_____   3. A complete sentence must have a subject, verb, and direct object.

_____   4. Only action verbs can have direct objects.

_____   5. Linking verbs are also called state-of-being verbs.

_____   6. A subject complement completes the meaning of the sentence, following an action verb and its helper.

_____   7. Typical helping verbs include *can, will, is,* and *was.*

_____   8. Active-voice verbs are the same as action verbs.

_____   9. Passive-voice verbs are the same as subjunctive mood verbs.

_____   10. The parts of *lie,* meaning to rest or recline, are *lie, lay, lain;* parts of *lay* are *lay, laid, laid.*

_____ 11. A comma plus a coordinating conjunction can be used between independent clauses in a compound sentence.

_____ 12. Coordinating conjunctions include these words: _for, and, nor, however, consequently, moreover._

_____ 13. An adverb can modify a verb, an adjective, or an adverb, but an adjective can only modify a noun.

_____ 14. A sentence fragment is a unit that contains only a prospective subject, and no verb.

_____ 15. A cliché is a trite, overworked expression, stale from overuse.

_____ 16. A euphemism is a faddish, contrived word, one that is meant to impress others.

_____ 17. Correct parallelism means that sentences are correctly joined with semicolons or commas plus conjunctions.

_____ 18. An indirect object is only implied, not stated directly.

_____ 19. Only linking verbs can have indirect objects.

_____ 20. An appositive is a noun or pronoun unit used to rename or identify the preceding noun (or pronoun).

B. USAGE

Select the correct word in the following sentences. Mark a for the first choice, b for the second, c for the third. (Note: Many of these sentences have only two choices; in that case, mark either a or b.)

_____ 21. It was (they, them) who arrived at the party first.

_____ 22. They brought potato chips that (turns, turned) out to be stale.

_____ 23. There (was, were) no other snacks at the party.

_____ 24. No one was more disappointed than Joe and (I, me).

_____ 25. What was the reason for (we, us, our) attending the party?

_____ 26. Luckily for us, each of the rooms in the house (was, were) air-conditioned that hot night.

_____ 27. I regretted that I (laid, had laid, had lain) my sweater on the car seat before going to the party.

_____ 28. I feel (bad, badly) that the party ended so early.

_____ 29. Though short, the evening was great for Megan, Paula, Kevin and (he, him).

_____ 30. They thanked the hosts and hostesses of the party, Steve, Sally, Kelly, and (he, him).

_____ 31. Their friends and (they, them) cleaned up the party room afterward.

_____ 32. The student (whose, who's) idea the party had been enjoyed it the most.

_____ 33. That man is (taller, tallest) than his older brother.

_____ 34. The book looks familiar, but I can't remember (it's, its) name.

_____ 35. (Do, Does) any of your friends recognize the book?

_____ 36. That song, including all six of its stanzas, (seem, seems) overly repetitive.

_____ 37. The music sounds (pleasant, pleasantly) despite the repetitive text.

_____ 38. The composer (who, whom) wrote the music was very talented.

_____ 39. Everybody who heard the song had (his, his/her, their) reaction.

_____ 40. The music (lies, lays) on the piano, waiting for the musicians to arrive.

_____ 41. Neither the townspeople nor the major (was, were) happy when the tax revenues from the state dwindled.

_____ 42. It would have been (them, they) who objected most.

_____ 43. The class elected two delegates to the student council, Tracy and (she, her).

_____ 44. Over the past five years, student government (grew, has grown) steadily.

_____ 45. Paula denied that she (ran, had run) for office every year.

C. CORRECT PASSAGES

Select the correct choice in each set of sentences, circling a, b, *or* c. *(If some sets have only two choices, circle either* a *or* b.)

46. a. My High School English and History classes effected my preparation for college.
    b. My High School English and history classes affected my preparation for college.
    c. My high school English and history classes affected my preparation for college.

47. a. Joe's Mother and Dad are driving South for a Fall vacation.
    b. Joe's Mother and Dad are driving south for a fall vacation.
    c. Joe's mother and dad are driving south for a fall vacation.

48. a. My driving the car for Pam, Karen, Linda, and her was fine until I ran through a red light.
    b. Me driving the car for Pam, Karen, Linda, and she was fine until I ran through a red light.
    c. My driving the car for Pam, Karen, Linda, and her was fine, then I ran thorough a red light.

49. a. "What," she asked, "Are you doing Dave?"
    b. "What" she asked "are you doing, Dave"?
    c. "What," she asked, "are you doing, Dave?"

50. a. After I finish this book, "Tom Sawyer," I can watch television with Peter, Sherri, Joan, and he.
    b. After I finish this book, *Tom Sawyer*, I can watch television with Peter, Sherri, Joan, and him.
    c. After I finish this book, 'Tom Sawyer,' I can watch television with Peter, Sherri, Joan, and him.

51. a. Her exact words were as follows: "Class, read Chapter 3, 'Adverbs' in 'Practical English,' for tomorrows' class and do the exercises."
    b. Her exact words were: "Class, read Chapter 3, "Adverbs," in "Practical English" for tomorrow's class, and do the exercises."
    c. Her exact words were as follows: "Class, read Chapter 3, 'Adverbs,' in *Practical English* for tomorrow's class, and do the exercises."

52. a. After finishing six months' work, I realized that the boss would not give me a raise, that the work would get no easier, and that I would have to move.
    b. After finishing six month's work, I realized that the boss would be giving me no raise, the work was getting easier, and moving was likely.
    c. After finishing six months' work, I realized the boss would be giving me a raise, working would be no easier, and to move was a possibility.

53. a. After Ms. Lindman spoke with Ms. Ellison, she was quite discouraged.
    b. After she spoke with Ms. Ellison, Ms. Lindman was quite discouraged.

54. a. After keeping it for many months, the wine tasted especially good.
    b. After keeping it for many months, we thought the wine tasted especially good.

55. a. After all factors are considered, the farmers still have the challenge of growing crops, raising animals, and working their land.
    b. After considering all factors, the farmers, still having the challenge of growing crops, raising animals, and working their land.

56. a. A good book should move quickly, be able to evoke emotional reactions, and stimulate the reader's thought to some extent or other.
    b. A good book should move quickly, evoke emotions, and stimulate thought.

57. a. The speaker spoke about the corrupt political situation on the lecture platform.
    b. The speaker on the lecture platform spoke about the corrupt political situation.

58. a. Don was happy, believing his luck would improve.
    b. Don was happy as a lark, knowing that there would be a rainbow after the rain and a pot of gold, too.

59. a. Running to catch the bus, Patricia snagged her skirt on the lamppost.
    b. Running to catch the bus, her skirt snagged as Patricia dashed past the lamppost.

60. a. Ralph had two goals: to ski in Colorado and working in Los Angeles.
    b. Ralph had two goals: to ski in Colorado and to work in Los Angeles.

D. WORD GROUPS

Identify each of the following word groups as one of the following:

a.	correct sentence	c.	comma splice
b.	sentence fragment	d.	fused sentence

_____ 61. The speaker continued long after the audience had heard enough, won't he ever stop, they wondered?

_____ 62. That's the trouble with political rallies some of them stretch the listeners' patience.

_____ 63. Listening critically and evaluating fairly, two necessary steps in making a wise decision.

_____ 64. The refrigerator was new, but the motor didn't work right, therefore the customer complained.

_____ 65. When the store manager heard about the problem.

_____ 66. He called the factory representative, and the two of them decided how to help the customer.

_____ 67. Disappointing though the situation was when the motor failed and the refrigerator stopped.

_____ 68. Although our team won the first game, they did not win other games that season.

_____ 69. I can never forget the excitement of the opening night; the entire cast was thrilled with that first performance.

_____ 70. Illiteracy, the inability to read and write.

_____ 71. Even though communities all over the nation have schools, illiteracy persists in some areas.

_____ 72. That salesclerk treats all customers courteously, his manager should give him a promotion.

_____ 73. Most managers watch their workers closely to be sure that the work is done properly good work is essential if companies are to compete successfully.

_____ 74. An engine that doesn't run on oil or gas.

_____ 75. The voters waited patiently election night; they were kept in suspense a long time by a close election.

E. IDENTIFICATION

Match the italicized word group with one of the following choices:

    a. adverb clause
    b. adjective clause
    c. noun clause

_____ 76. He said that _if we wanted to attend school there_, we should apply early for admission.

_____ 77. _That we would attend college somehow_ was certain.

_____ 78. The only question was _how we could afford that college._

_____ 79. The street light _that has burned out_ must be replaced.

_____ 80. That man should mow his lawn once more *before winter arrives.*

_____ 81. The kind of auto seat *that clips on over the back of the car seat* is necessary for a small child's safety.

_____ 82. The car *my brother owns* already has a car seat for babies.

F. IDENTIFICATION

Match the italicized word group with one of the following choices:

    a. infinitive phrase   c. participial phrase
    b. gerund phrase   d. appositive

_____ 83. *Growing up on a farm* has many advantages.

_____ 84. *Growing up on a farm,* a child learns about wildlife.

_____ 85. She learns *to conserve the land and the environment.*

_____ 86. The flowers *growing along the sidewalk* are petunias.

_____ 87. The gardener, *an avid reader of seed catalogues,* had all the choice varieties of seeds selected by March.

_____ 88. *Planning ahead* paid off for her in previous years.

_____ 89. She hopes *to produce another big crop this year.*

G. TRUE/FALSE

_____ 90. Introductory participial phrases are set off from the rest of the sentence with a comma.

_____ 91. Subordination means that lesser ideas are placed in less prominent parts of the sentence so that more important ideas can be emphasized.

_____ 92. Capital letters are needed on proper nouns and on adjectives derived from proper nouns.

_____ 93. Object-form pronouns include *we, he, they,* and *them.*

_____ 94. Long quotations are set off by spacing and placement on the page rather than by the use of quotation marks.

_____ 95. Titles of short printed works and parts of volumes are set off in single quotation marks.

_____ 96. A fused sentence is one that has two subjects but only one verb.

_____ 97. Prepositional phrases can be ignored when we look for subjects, verbs, objects, and subject complements.

_____ 98. A gerund is a verbal that ends in *ing* and works as a noun.

_____ 99. The present perfect tense expresses an action that began in the past and continues into the present.

_____ 100. Good writers want their writing to be smooth, rhythmic, clear, and concise.

Principal Parts of Common Irregular Verbs

Present	Past	Past Participle
am	was	been
begin	began	begun
bite	bit	bitten
blow	blew	blown
bring	brought	brought
build	built	built
burst	burst	burst
buy	bought	bought
catch	caught	caught
choose	chose	chosen
come	came	come
draw	drew	drawn
drink	drank	drunk
drive	drove	driven
eat	ate	eaten
fall	fell	fallen
find	found	found
fly	flew	flown
forget	forgot	forgotten
forgive	forgave	forgiven
forsake	forsook	forsaken
freeze	froze	frozen
get	got	gotten
give	gave	given
go	went	gone
grow	grew	grown
have	had	had
hear	heard	heard
hide	hid	hidden
hold	held	held

Present	Past	Past Participle
hurt	hurt	hurt
is	was	been
keep	kept	kept
know	knew	known
lay	laid	laid
lead	led	led
leave	left	left
let	let	let
lie	lay	lain
lose	lost	lost
make	made	made
meet	met	met
pay	paid	paid
quit	quit	quit
raise	rose	risen
read	read	read
ride	rode	ridden
ring	rang	rung
rise	rose	risen
run	ran	run
see	saw	seen
sell	sold	sold
send	sent	sent
show	showed	shown
shrink	shrank	shrunk
sink	sank	sunk
sit	sat	sat
sleep	slept	slept
speak	spoke	spoken
spend	spent	spent
spring	sprang	sprung
stand	stood	stood
steal	stole	stolen
strike	struck	struck
swim	swam	swum
take	took	taken
teach	taught	taught
tear	tore	torn
tell	told	told
think	thought	thought
throw	threw	thrown
understand	understood	understood
wake	woke (or waked)	woken (or waked)
wear	wore	worn
win	won	won
write	wrote	written

Guidelines for Writing
in Manuscript Form

1. Type or word-process your papers, using good quality paper. Avoid the easily erasable paper because the typing smudges easily.
2. As a second choice, write with black ink on lined tablet paper, preferably wide-lined paper.
3. Use only one side of the paper.
4. Allow at least one-inch margins on all sides of the paper.
5. Double-space your writing. If you must make last-minute changes, write neatly between the lines or in the margins.
6. Indent the first line of each paragraph five spaces.
7. At the upper right corner of the first page, write your name and the date. If your professor so directs, identify your class and the assignment.
8. On subsequent pages, put your name and the page number at the upper right corner.
9. Staple your pages. Fold your papers only as directed.
10. If you have a title, center it at the top of the first page or use a separate title page. Capitalize the first and last words and the main words of the title. Do not underline the title; do not enclose it in quotation marks.
11. For other specific directions, ask your professor.

Correction Symbols

Symbol	Explanation	Example
◯	Capital letter needed	ⓔnglish
/	No capital letter	my /High /School
◯ *sp*	Spelling	(grammer) *sp grammar*
⌐	Two words	alot (correct: a lot)
‿	One word	week⌢end
frag	Sentence fragment	When that happened.
CS	Comma splice	I read the chapter, then I understood.
fused	Fused sentence	I read the chapter then I understood.
num	Spell out	*eleven* N days *forty-two* 42 years
◯ " ◯ "	Use proper order	He said, "Hello." "Hello," he said.
◯ ›	Add comma (often with FANBOYS between clauses)	Joe was late⸲but he came in quietly.

Symbol	Explanation	Example
⌿	No comma (one sentence, compound verb)	Joe was late⌿ but came in quietly.
⟨⸴⟩	Set off introductory elements	After a long delay⸴the plane left.
shift	Shift (often with *you*) or inappropriate use of second person	Accounting is a hard job, demanding a lot from ~~you~~. *accountants*
pron	Incorrect pronoun choice	Between Jim and ⱯΙ *me* . . .
order	Incorrect order	Between me and him . . .
agr	Subject/verb agreement	A crew of three men ~~were~~ *was* needed.
¶, ¶s ¶ing	Paragraph, paragraphs, paragraphing	

Answers to Exercises

Chapter 1

EXERCISE 1 (pp. 16–17)

1. noun 2. adjective 3. adjective 4. verb 5. noun 6. adjective 7. conjunction 8. preposition 9. noun 10. adjective 11. noun 12. noun 13. adverb 14. adjective 15. noun 16. verb 17. adverb 18. noun 19. verb 20. preposition 21. adjective 22. adverb 23. adjective 24. preposition 25. pronoun 26. adjective 27. noun 28. noun 29. noun 30. verb 31. verb or interjection 32. verb 33. noun 34. adjective 35. adverb 36. adjective

EXERCISE 3 (pp. 18–20)

1. 2	4. 3	7. 3	10. 2	13. 3
2. 3	5. 3	8. 4	11. 2	14. 2
3. 3	6. 5	9. 4	12. 2	15. 3

Chapter 2

EXERCISE 1 (pp. 36–37)

1. Students can make ~~immediate~~ improvements ~~in their writing.~~

2. You can improve ~~your~~ writing ~~with practice and care.~~

3. You should underline titles ~~of books, magazines, newspapers, and movies.~~

4. ~~Careful~~ writers underline or italicize ~~those~~ titles.

5. You can ~~also~~ improve ~~your~~ spelling ~~with attention to troublesome expressions like a lot.~~

6. ~~Careful~~ writers ~~always~~ use ~~two~~ words ~~for a lot.~~

7. ~~Every~~ sentence must contain ~~at least a~~ subject and a verb.

8. ~~Separate~~ parts ~~of a two-part compound subject usually~~ are not separated ~~with a comma.~~

9. ~~English~~ students struggle ~~over erratic spelling.~~

10. ~~Root~~ words give (us) [clues] ~~about meanings~~.

11. ~~The~~ connection ~~between the words *sign* and *signature*~~ gives (us) a [clue] ~~about spelling~~.

12. ~~Silent~~ letters ~~in words~~ can be ~~important~~ parts ~~of root words~~, ~~like the silent *g* in *sign*~~.

13. ~~The silent~~ ending *b* ~~in *bomb*~~ is important ~~in the derivative words *bombardier* and *bombard-ment*~~.

14. ~~The typical college~~ student has ~~reading~~ [assignments] ~~of a million words for each term~~.

15. ~~To the surprise of very few people~~, ~~good~~ readers earn ~~higher~~ [grades] ~~in most of their classes~~.

16. ~~The human~~ brain can process ~~about 500 words per minute~~.

17. ~~Some~~ people read ~~only about 200 words per minute~~.

18. ~~A slow reading~~ pace allows ~~too much lag or empty~~ [time] ~~for the brain~~.

19. ~~During the lag time~~, ~~the~~ brain runs ~~ahead of the printed page~~, or ~~the~~ brain works ~~on other ideas~~.

20. ~~Good~~ readers develop ~~good reading~~ [habits] and avoid ~~bad~~ [habits], ~~such as pausing on big words, moving the lips, pronouncing words mentally, and looking back frequently~~.

21. ~~Speed~~ reading is ~~sometimes~~ called ~~"free-fall"~~ [reading].

22. ~~In free-fall reading, the reader's~~ eyes glance ~~down the page quickly~~ and catch ~~only the main~~ [points].

23. Newspapers are ~~ideal~~ material ~~for the free-fall style of reading~~.

24. ~~A steady~~ pace ~~of about 500 words per minute~~ is excellent ~~for most college textbook material~~.

25. ~~Reading~~ experts use ~~the~~ [term *rhythmic perusal*] ~~for a steady pace of about 500 words per minute~~.

26. Students ~~often~~ talk ~~about vocabulary development~~.

27. ~~Vocabulary~~ drills bore ~~most~~ [people] and they do ~~little~~ good.

28. ~~For building vocabulary~~, experts recommend [reading] ~~more~~.

EXERCISE 2 (pp. 37–39)

_____ 1. ~~Long~~ words need ~~not~~ intimidate [readers]

_____ 2. ~~A big~~ word ~~like *hippopotamus*~~ often has ~~just one~~ [meaning]

_____ 3. ~~By contrast, a small~~ word ~~like *run*~~ can have ~~many different~~ [meanings]

_____ 4. You can bank on the bank by the river bank.

_____ 5. In sentence 4, the word *bank* has two different roles and three different meanings.

_____ 6. A typical person may know 200,000 words.

_____ 7. In spite of his or her acquaintance with 200,000 words, that person may read only at the tenth-grade level.

_____ 8. Modern daily newspapers provide today's readers much valuable current information.

_____ 9. Representatives of England and the United States signed a treaty on Christmas Eve, 1814.

_____ 10. That treaty ended the War of 1812.

_____ 11. Today, international news arrives in our homes within seconds through the media.

_____ 12. In 1814, news of the peace treaty arrived in the United States after days of delay.

unpopular 13. The war had been very unpopular in New England.

advocates 14. Some leaders in New England were advocates of secession from the federal union.

_____ 15. Congress debated the treaty and ratified it by unanimous approval on February 16, 1815.

_____ 16. Secessionist talk ceased in a moment with the arrival of peace.

_____ 17. In Boston, musicians and orators hastily staged festive public celebrations.

_____ 18. Out of the momentum and public enthusiasm for those musical performances came a new music organization.

Boston Handel and Haydn Society 19. That organization was the Boston Handel and Haydn Society.

_____ 20. The name of the group reflects the popularity of two eighteenth-century composers.

topic 21. The long and distinguished history of that organization is the topic of several good books.

_____ 22. ~~The~~ publication ~~of successful music books~~ gave ~~the~~ (society) ~~a solid financial~~ base.

Lowell Mason 23. ~~One~~ editor ~~of money-making books for the society~~ was ~~the Boston musician~~ Lowell Mason.

_____ 24. You can think ~~of sentences with objects and complements.~~

_____ 25. ~~For example,~~ the governor offered ~~the~~ (prisoner) ~~a~~ pardon.

_____ 26. ~~The~~ prisoner did~~n't~~ hesitate ~~for long.~~

_____ 27. He sent ~~the~~ (governor) ~~a~~ note ~~of thanks.~~

memorable 28. ~~Your own~~ examples are ~~more~~ memorable ~~than examples in a textbook.~~

EXERCISE 3 (pp. 39–40)

1. ~~The tallest~~ flowers were gladiolas and zinnias.

2. Judges ~~at the flower show~~ praised ~~the~~ gladiolas.

3. ~~Floral~~ arrangements must include greenery ~~with the flowers.~~

4. ~~Good~~ arrangements look attractive ~~in any setting.~~

5. ~~All the~~ moisture has been removed ~~from pressed flowers.~~

6. ~~Pressed~~ flowers are thin and fragile ~~to the touch.~~

7. ~~The~~ lilies appear ~~in mid-June after long dormancy.~~

8. Lilies seem miraculous ~~in their sudden appearance.~~

9. Daffodils and tulips delight gardeners ~~with a burst of color early in the spring.~~

10. ~~Spring~~ flowers stay fresh ~~for days in a vase of water.~~

11. Lilacs ~~in a long hedge~~ separate ~~our~~ houses.

12. They smell fragrant ~~during May and early June.~~

13. ~~The prize~~ winners ~~in this year's flower show~~ will be ~~Marie's~~ roses and ~~Karen's~~ mums.

14. ~~At the fair, leading floral~~ designers display ~~their most beautiful~~ arrangements.

15. ~~Those~~ arrangements look beautiful ~~all week.~~

EXERCISE 4 (pp. 40–41)

d 1. ~~Many~~ joggers are serious^(SC) ~~about their running.~~

c 2. ~~Strenuous~~ running can give beginners^(IO) ~~some unexpected~~ aches^(DO) and pains^(DO).

410   Answers to Exercises

d 3. Running looks easy ~~to a bystander.~~ [SC over "easy"]

a 4. ~~Trained~~ runners dream ~~of marathon running.~~

b 5. A magazine ~~for joggers and runners~~ provides ~~detailed~~ information ~~about the Boston marathon.~~ [DO over "information"]

a 6. Runners travel ~~from all parts of the country to the famous Boston marathon.~~

d 7. ~~The~~ marathon is ~~a~~ race ~~of 26 miles, 385 yards.~~ [SC over "race"]

b 8. ~~The~~ marathon commemorates the feat ~~of a Greek runner in the fifth century B.C.~~ [DO over "feat"]

b 9. ~~That~~ runner carried news ~~of victory from Marathon to Athens, Greece.~~ [DO over "news"]

b 10. ~~At Marathon,~~ the Greeks defeated ~~the~~ Persians. [DO over "Persians"]

a 11. ~~Modern~~ runners participate ~~in marathons for other reasons.~~

d 12. ~~The record~~ time ~~for a Boston marathon~~ is approximately ~~two~~ hours, ~~eight~~ minutes. [SC over "hours" and SC over "minutes"]

c 13. Running gives athletes and amateurs ~~much~~ pleasure. [IO over "athletes", IO over "amateurs", DO over "pleasure"]

a 14. Beginners should start ~~with gentle warm-ups and short distances.~~

b 15. ~~Experienced~~ joggers ~~gladly~~ help beginners and answer ~~their~~ questions. [DO over "beginners", DO over "questions"]

Chapter 3

EXERCISE 1 (pp. 56–57)

1. wise, old, his
2. man
3. advised, gave
4. action
5. never
6. S + AV + IO + DO
7. over the ridge
8. with the banners and bugles
9. cavalry
10. rode
11. S + AV
12. interjection
13. pronoun
14. adverb
15. you
16. can be
17. S + LV + SC
18. they
19. do know
20. S + AV + DO
21. object of prep *of*
22. adjective (modifying truth)
23. in the middle
24. of the . . . garden
25. adverb
26. birdhouse/stands
27. adjective (modifying garden)

EXERCISE 2 (pp. 57–59)

The complete sentences are 4, 6, 8, and 14.

EXERCISE 4 (pp. 60–61)

Use + for numbers 1, 2, 5, 7, 8, 9, and 11.

Chapter 4

EXERCISE 1 (p. 92)

Choose *a* for numbers 1, 2, 4, 7, 8, 12, 13.

EXERCISE 2 (pp. 92–94)

1. who 2. he 3. he 4. he 5. We 6. he 7. We 8. who 9. she 10. she, I 11. we
12. her life 13. they 14. she, she 15. she who 16. they who 17. who 18. he 19. he, I
20. she 21. he 22. he 23. This assistance 24. We or Students 25. we, This effort
26. they 27. he 28. they 29. they 30. we

Chapter 5

EXERCISE 1 (p. 110)

1. me 2. me 3. whom 4. us 5. them 6. he 7. him 8. he 9. We 10. she 11. Who
12. whom 13. her 14. them 15. those 16. they 17. he whom 18. we 19. me 20. him

EXERCISE 2 (pp. 110–111)

Errors appear in sentences 1, 2, 3, 6, 7, 9, 10, 11, 14, 15, and 16.

EXERCISE 3 (pp. 111–112)

1. e	5. d	9. b	13. a	17. a
2. b	6. c	10. b (You) let	14. e	18. a
3. c	7. a	11. f	15. d	
4. f	8. a	12. c	16. e	

EXERCISE 4 (p. 113)

Circle *a* for 3, 4, 5, 7, 8, 9, and 13.

Chapter 6

EXERCISE 1 (pp. 135–136)

1. lies 2. lay 3. Lay 4. had gone 5. has directed 6. had finished, concluded 7. acts
8. are 9. were 10. have been 11. laid 12. has played 13. has laid 14. earns 15. lain
16. lain 17. had finished, lay 18. had studied 19. will have finished 20. writes

EXERCISE 2 (pp. 136–137)

The active voice is used in sentences 1, 3, 5, 6, 10, 11, 13, 15, 17, 18, and 20.

Chapter 7

EXERCISE 1 (pp. 156–158)

1. Each/has
2. Half/are
3. restaurant/stands
4. restaurant/gets

5. food nor service/needs
6. cooks and waitresses/are
7. Lisa Williams/works
8. Lisa nor waitresses/take
9. Everyone/works . . . his/her shift
10. specialty/is
11. pie/tops
12. Jim and I/Do
13. Someone/likes
14. Four dollars/is
15. glasses/were . . . them
16. Mathematics/is
17. Classes/run
18. Half/is
19. Half/look
20. Neither/tells
21. menu/takes
22. Three-fourths/are
23. waitress or one/serves
24. Everyone/appreciates
25. bowl or sandwiches/make
26. restaurants/are
27. Thirty dollars/seems, everyone/pays
28. food or service/attracts
29. waitresses nor atmosphere/compensates
30. family/is

31. family/dines
32. Most/enjoy
33. Most/arrives
34. guest/dislikes
35. it/was
36. reasons/are
37. car, cars/were
38. cars, car/were
39. Everyone/enjoys, likes
40. time/comes
41. waiter, waitress/brings
42. food, service, and atmosphere/were
43. answers/change
44. staff/listen . . . their
45. Jim/is
46. Mr. and Mrs. Smith/are
47. table/stands
48. team/is
49. committee/holds
50. Half/goes
51. Half/go
52. Two hours/makes
53. copy/lies
54. None/takes
55. Most/is

Chapter 8

EXERCISE 1 (pp. 185–186)

1. a	5. a	9. f	13. c	17. c
2. d	6. d	10. b	14. a	
3. b	7. c	11. e	15. e	
4. c	8. e	12. d	16. b	

EXERCISE 3 (pp. 187–188)

Choose *a* for numbers 2, 4, 7, 8, 9, and 10.

Chapter 9

EXERCISE 2 (pp. 211–212)

Choose *a* for 1, 2, 5, 10, 11, 13, 15, 17, 18, and 19. Choose *c* for numbers 3, 7, 12, 14, and 20.

EXERCISE 3 (pp. 212–214)

noun   1. Historians suggest that animal skins were used as early as 200 B.C.

adv   2. Although papyrus was a common writing material for the ancient Romans, skins became more important in the early years A.D.

adj   3. Examples that date from about A.D. 100 are still extant.

adv   4. Skins of sheep, goats, and calves came into more use until eventually they superseded papyrus.

adv   5. The word *parchment* means the skin of sheep or goats, though other skins were sometimes used.

adj   6. Vellum, which is made from the skins of younger animals, is of finer quality.

noun   7. Authorities believe that the skins of younger animals were considerably better in quality.

adv   8. In the Middle Ages, animals were sometimes taken prenatally so that their skins could be used for superb vellum.

adv   9. Processing skins became a big industry since there was much demand for writing material.

adv   10. Because vellum and parchment were expensive, medieval scribes wrote with tiny letters squeezed together.

adv   11. Their page layout was designed so that every bit of the surface was used.

adj   12. By the late Middle Ages, the lettering style was Gothic, which uses narrow letters with little space between them.

noun   13. You may wonder what the ancient scribes used for pens.

adj   14. The Egyptians used a plant stem that could be sharpened to a point.

adj   15. The Greeks used a stone, metal, or ivory stylus which made marks on wax-covered tablets.

adj   16. Hollow reeds, which grew in many countries, also made good pens.

noun, adj   17. How the quill pen became popular is not known, but in the Middle Ages, quill pens that were made of goose, crow, or swan feathers were common.

adj   18. The word *pen* comes from a Latin word, *penna*, which means feather.

adv   19. Because quill pens worked so well with parchment, they remained popular for many centuries.

adv   20. Quill pens were superseded when metal pens were introduced in the 1700s.

Chapter 10

EXERCISE 1 (pp. 249–250)

1. bad 2. happier 3. best 4. good, restful 5. quickly 6. more handsome 7. eagerly 8. reluctantly 9. calm, suddenly 10. quickly, wildly 11. loud 12. anxious, pitifully 13. deeply 14. less excited, sleepily 15. sadly 16. suddenly, rashly, abruptly 17. badly 18. reluctantly 19. saddest, good 20. sadly 21. brave, worst 22. heavy, thoughtlessly 23. real, actively 24. proudly, small 25. richer

Chapter 11

EXERCISE 1 (pp. 273–274)

1. b	5. a	9. a	13. d	17. c
2. c	6. b	10. b	14. c	18. c
3. c	7. a	11. b	15. a	19. b
4. d	8. d	12. c	16. b	20. b

Chapter 12

EXERCISE 1 (pp. 295–296)

1. b,c	5. g	9. a	13. h	17. a
2. g	6. h	10. c	14. a	18. h
3. a	7. e	11. f	15. c	19. d
4. c	8. a,c	12. a,g	16. f	20. h

EXERCISE 3 (pp. 296–298)

Answers will vary. These are possible answers:

1. The writing assignments given on Monday are due Friday.
2. Students must finish their assignments on time.
3. Lisa, who wants to be an underwriter for an insurance agency, should take more time to proofread her job application letter.
4. Because Monica wanted to be a claims adjuster for that insurance company, she wrote her letter and included her résumé.
5. Secretaries for that company must learn a standard letter format.
6. That company uses semiblock format.
7. The largest room in the White House is the East Room.
8. The East Room has been used for receptions, weddings, concerts, funerals, and press conferences.
9. The White House contains many valuable art objects, antiques, paintings, and valuable pieces of china and silver donated by individuals or organizations.
10. The funerals of three presidents, Harrison, Lincoln, and Harding, were held in the East Room of the White House.

EXERCISE 4 (pp. 298–300)

Possible replacements for the given expressions:

1. truth	11. first
2. ask	12. necessary
3. now	13. if
4. truth	14. while
5. enclosed	15. for
6. open	16. fair (just)
7. refer to	17. because
8. surrounded	18. reason is that *or* reason is
9. unique	19. with
10. opinion	20. by

1. payment	6. end
2. many	7. use
3. give	8. put into effect *or* make
4. enable *or* make easy	9. means
5. best *or* greatest	10. aware

1. busy	6. move slowly
2. method	7. late
3. wiser	8. slow
4. stop	9, 10. Can there be a paraphrase when there is
5. final, last	no content to paraphrase?

Chapter 13

___4___ 1. One clear, starry evening, Mary, my younger sister, and I were walking in our neighborhood when we came upon a frightening scene.

___4___ 2. When the old house on the corner of First Street and Alden Avenue was torn down last spring, a big hole remained where the basement had been, and a tree, having been struck by lightning, fell into the hole.

___3___ 3. Set against the night sky, the tree roots, torn branches, and twisted trunk made a grotesque form.

___3___ 4. The owner of the property lives at 8397 North Street, Detroit, Michigan, having left our city after the scare with the lightning.

___1___ 5. He owns houses and office buildings and parking lots in this city, and he manages all of them.

___2___ 6. Once you have lived in the country, you will be reluctant to go back to the noisy, congested city.

___6___ 7. When you are in the city, you can see many things of interest, such as skyscrapers, museums, airports, ethnic restaurants, and shopping malls.

___4___ 8. Randy's trip to the city began December 28, 1989, and ended January 9, 1990, when he returned home.

___2___ 9. When he saw his friend Chris, he said, "You should have been with us because we had a great time."

___2___ 10. "Time was too short," he added, "for all we had to see and do while we were in the city."

___4___ 11. To write a book, one needs time, experience, training, and determination.

___0___ 12. A book that sells well can make an author famous.

___3___ 13. That new novel, which is already a best seller, has made its author a lot of money, hasn't it?

___0___ 14. The main difference between high school and college is that in college a student has more free time and more responsibility for efficient use of his or her time.

___2___ 15. Dan, you do agree with that statement, don't you?

___1___ 16. The important thing is wise use of one's time, not the abundance of time a college schedule allows.

___1___ 17. Looking forward to the next vacation, Jim smiled happily.

___2___ 18. Looking forward to the next vacation is a popular mental pastime when class is boring, difficult, or overly repetitive.

___3___ 19. The third Monday in February will be Presidents' Day, a welcome holiday for college students, staff, and faculty.

___5___ 20. Faculty members, on the other hand, might welcome three, four, five, or more holidays per term.

Chapter 14

EXERCISE 1 (pp. 347–348)

1. The president's office
2. The moment's frustration
3. The trees' leaves
4. The tree's leaves
5. The Harrises' porch
6. Mr. Thomas' suit or Mr. Thomas's suit
7. No one's business
8. Their skates' blades
9. The babies' mothers
10. A month's vacation
11. Its fiscal year's end
12. Her parents' consent
13. Doris' scarf or Doris's scarf
14. The Willises' house
15. The Millers' son
16. Mr. Ross' tie or Mr. Ross's tie
17. The men's jackets
18. His boss' secretary or his boss's secretary
19. My bosses' secretaries
20. The children's pencils
21. Five dollars' purchasing power
22. The reindeer's antlers
23. Professor Thomas' suit or Professor Thomas's suit
24. Everyone's right

EXERCISE 3 (pp. 349–350)

Choose "true" for items 2, 3, 5, 8, 11, 13, 16, 17, 19, 21, 22, 23, and 25.

Chapter 15

EXERCISE 1 (pp. 363–364)

Choose *a* for 2, 6, 7, 8, 10, 14, 17, 19, 21, and 22.

Answers to Practice Tests (Unit Tests I–V and the Final Examination)

Unit I

1. T	15. T	29. d	43. a	57. d
2. T	16. F	30. e	44. b	58. c
3. F	17. F	31. b	45. d	59. a
4. T	18. T	32. a	46. d	60. c
5. F	19. F	33. e	47. a	61. d
6. T	20. T	34. e	48. c	62. b
7. F	21. T	35. e	49. a	63. d
8. F	22. F	36. a	50. d	64. d
9. F	23. a	37. c	51. b	65. b
10. F	24. d	38. b	52. c	66. c
11. T	25. e	39. a	53. b	67. d
12. T	26. c	40. b	54. a	68. d
13. T	27. b	41. b	55. c	69. a
14. F	28. a	42. c	56. b	70. a

Unit II

1. a	11. a	21. a	31. b	41. b
2. a	12. a	22. b	32. a	42. a
3. a	13. b	23. b	33. b	43. a
4. b	14. a	24. b	34. b	44. a
5. a	15. a	25. a	35. b	45. a
6. b	16. b	26. b	36. a	46. b
7. b	17. b	27. a	37. a	47. a
8. a	18. a	28. a	38. b	48. a
9. c	19. a	29. a	39. b	49. b
10. b	20. b	30. a	40. a	50. b

Unit III

1. e	4. d	7. c	10. b	13. d
2. c	5. c	8. b	11. c	14. c
3. b	6. a	9. e	12. a	15. d

16. e	23. b	30. a	37. b	44. b
17. a	24. a	31. a	38. a	45. b
18. c	25. c	32. b	39. b	46. a
19. b	26. c	33. c	40. b	47. b
20. c	27. a	34. a	41. a	48. b
21. a	28. b	35. c	42. b	49. a
22. c	29. c	36. c	43. a	50. a

Unit IV

1. b	11. c	21. b	31. b	41. a
2. a	12. c	22. a	32. b	42. b
3. a	13. b	23. b	33. a	43. b
4. c	14. c	24. a	34. b	44. a
5. c	15. b	25. a	35. a	45. a
6. c	16. c	26. d	36. a	46. b
7. b	17. c	27. c	37. a	47. b
8. d	18. a	28. d	38. b	48. a
9. a	19. c	29. a	39. b	49. b
10. d	20. b	30. b	40. b	50. b

Unit V

1. A. C	5. A. C	D. I	B. I	14. A. I
B. C	B. C	E. I	C. C	B. C
C. I	C. I	F. I	11. A. I	C. I
2. A. I	D. C	G. C	B. I	D. C
B. C	6. A. I	H. I	12. A. C	15. A. C
C. I	B. I	8. A. I	B. I	B. I
D. I	C. C	9. A. I	13. A. I	C. C
3. A. I	7. A. I	B. I	B. C	16. A. I
4. A. C	B. I	C. I	C. I	B. C
B. I	C. I	10. A. I	D. C	C. I

Final Examination

1. T	21. a	41. a	61. c	81. b
2. F	22. b	42. b	62. d	82. b
3. F	23. b	43. b	63. b	83. b
4. T	24. a	44. b	64. c	84. c
5. T	25. c	45. b	65. b	85. a
6. F	26. a	46. c	66. a	86. c
7. T	27. b	47. c	67. b	87. d
8. F	28. a	48. a	68. a	88. b
9. F	29. b	49. c	69. a	89. a
10. T	30. b	50. b	70. b	90. a
11. T	31. a	51. c	71. a	91. a
12. F	32. a	52. a	72. c	92. a
13. F	33. a	53. b	73. d	93. b
14. F	34. b	54. b	74. b	94. a
15. T	35. a	55. a	75. a	95. a
16. F	36. b	56. b	76. a	96. b
17. F	37. a	57. b	77. c	97. a
18. F	38. a	58. a	78. c	98. a
19. F	39. b	59. a	79. b	99. a
20. T	40. a	60. b	80. a	100. a

Index

Salutation, 342, 360
self or *selves* endings, 86
Semicolon
  joining independent clauses with,
    49–50, 52–53, 263, 322–323
  used as a "super comma," 323
  used with transitional words, 50,
    263, 323
Sentence combining, for subordina-
    tion, 190–192, 204, 214–221,
    277–279
Sentence fragments. *See* Fragments
Sentence interrupters, 144, 317
Sentence patterns
  using action verbs, 26–28
  using linking verbs, 31–33
Sentences
  balance within, 268
  combining, using clauses and
    phrases, 188–192, 214–220
  comma splice (fault), 52–53, 261–
    264
  complex, 206, 267
  compound, 206, 267
  compound/complex, 207, 267
  fragments, 51–52, 257–261
  fused, 53, 264–265
  introductory elements in, 197, 266
  necessary elements in, 24
  parallelism within, 267–271
  patterns of, 26–33
  run-on, 52–53, 261–265
  simple, 205, 267
  types of, 204–207, 267
  variety in, 204, 266
Series, handling of, 319–320
Sexism, avoidance of, 83
Shift, pronoun, 82, 84–85
Simple sentence, 205, 267
Single quotation marks, 344
Singular possessive, 338
Slang, 290
Spelling
  commonly confused words, 374–
    379
  commonly misspelled words, 380–
    382
  practice in revising, 383–386
  rules, 368–373
  suggestions for improving, 368,
    373–374, 380, 382
Split infinitive, 183
Squinting modifier, 242
Subject complements, 32
  adjectives as, 32, 237–238

distinguished from direct objects, 33
  pronouns as, 90
  quotes as, 321
  subject/verb agreement with, 150
Subject-form pronouns, 87–90
  as subject complements, 90
  as subjects, 88–90
Subjects, 24
  agreement with present-tense
    third-person verbs, 146
  finding of, 26, 45–46, 143–145
  See also Subject/verb agreement
Subject/verb agreement
  with amounts, 147–148
  with collective nouns, 147
  with compound subjects, 148–149
  concept of, 143
  with indefinite pronouns, 149
Subjunctive mood, 130
Subordinate clauses. *See* Dependent
    clauses
Subordination
  concept of, 203–204
  practice in, 190–192, 204, 214–
    221, 277–279
Superlative degree, 239–240

Tense, verb, 7, 121–127, 401–402
  consistency of, 130, 138–139
  future, 123
  past, 122
  perfect, 123–126
  present, 121–122
Titles of published works, 343–344
Topic sentence, 152, 269
  analyzing, in context, 43–44, 152
  practice in forming, 141–142, 221
Transitions
  pronouns to connect ideas, 79
  words and phrases as, 50, 263,
    317, 323
Transitive, intransitive, 129

Underlining (italics), 344–345
Unity, in paragraphs, 151–153

Verbals, verbal phrases
  defined, with examples, 174–178
  subordinating with, 188–192,
    214–221
  See also Gerund phrases; Infini-
    tive phrases; Participial phrases
Verb endings
  ing endings, 15, 51–52
  irregular verbs, examples of, 128,
    401–402